Black
Eagle
Child

Singular Lives

The Iowa Series in

North American

Autobiography

Albert E. Stone,

Series Editor

Black
Eagle
Child

The Facepaint Narratives

By Ray A. Young Bear

Foreword by Albert E. Stone

University of Iowa Press □ Iowa City

University of Iowa Press,

Iowa City 52242

Copyright © 1992 by the

University of Iowa

All rights reserved

Printed in the United States

of America

First edition, 1992

Design by Richard Hendel

Printed on acid-free paper

Quoted text on page 163 is from

William Jones, "The Culture-Hero

Myths of the Sauks and Foxes,"

Journal of American Folklore 14, no. 55

(October–December 1901).

Library of Congress Cataloging-in-

Publication Data

Young Bear, Ray A.

   Black eagle child: the facepaint

narratives/by Ray A. Young Bear;

foreword by Albert E. Stone.—

1st ed.

   p.   cm.—(Singular lives)

ISBN 0-87745-356-X

   1. Young Bear, Ray A.   2. Fox

Indians—Biography.   3. Authors,

Indian—Iowa—Biography.

4. Artists—Iowa—Biography.

5. Fox Indians—Social life and

customs.   I. Title.   II. Series.

E99.F7Y688   1992

811'.54—dc20   91-29081

     [B]   CIP

For my beloved grandmother,

Ada K. Old Bear, whose

mystical cloak

protects me

from the icy rain.

It was her words

of encouragement

that led me

to Well-Off Man —

and back.

Will heaven wait—

all heavenly over

the next horizon?

—Paddy McAloon

  of Prefab Sprout,

  Kitchenware Records,

  England

Contents

Foreword

Albert E. Stone

"Throughout America, north and south," Eduardo Galeano recently declared, "the dominant culture acknowledges Indians as objects of study, but denies them as subjects of history. The Indians
have folklore, not culture; they practice superstitions, not religions;
they speak dialects, not languages; they make crafts, not art." Indeed, other Native Americans insist, whites in the United States
even at this late date often go further. In many minds, Native
Americans still are not really individuals possessed of (in the thera-
peutic lingo of the dominant ethos) ego and social and gender
identities. Instead, in Euro-American imaginations, they remain
fixed within the Civilization-Barbarism-Savagery myth fabricated
in the European Renaissance, half animals, half humans. Present-
day stories, jokes, movies, even presidential remarks in the Rose
Garden continue to attach wildly stereotyped qualities to the oldest
Americans: Indians are wooden-faced, drunken, noble, apathetic,
spiritually gifted, humorless, etc.

Contemporary Native American literature, like the writings of
other oppressed and marginalized groups, exists in part to counter
such destructive myopia. As a literature of fierce resistance as well as
cultural and individual assertion, the novels, poems, essays, and autobiographies of writers like Leslie Marmon Silko, N. Scott Momaday, Paula Gunn Allen, James Welch, and Louise Erdrich are creat-

ing a rich record of narratives and images. Their stories and lyrics dramatically and definitively enact Native Americans as subjects of history, possessors of culture, artificers of arts, and devotees of religions. To this burgeoning body of writings Ray A. Young Bear, already a published poet of recognized standing, contributes this moving and artfully experimental autobiography.

Within the formal resources of Native American literature, the range of models of Euro-American autobiography has but relatively recently been used for Native American expressive needs. Unlike the slave narratives for African Americans, nineteenth- and early twentieth-century autobiographies of Indians were produced without the liberation of the subject very much in mind. Even before the Civil War, as William L. Andrews has shown, ex-slaves were able to seize control of their personal histories and, often over the objections of abolitionist collaborators and editors, "tell a free story." But Native American narratives were, from the outset, collaborative acts in which the white literate partner wielded far more power than the Indian subject. "There simply were no Native American texts until whites decided to collaborate with Indians and make them," Arnold Krupat declares in *For Those Who Come After: A Study of Native American Autobiography*. This process, out of which came J. B. Patterson's *Life of Ma-Ka-Tai-me-she-kia-Kiah* or *Black Hawk* in 1833, was not basically altered in subsequent cross-cultural collaborations, some of which are familiar to readers today: Paul Radin's *Crashing Thunder: The Autobiography of an American Indian* (1926), *Black Elk Speaks: Being the Life Story of a Holy Man of the Oglala Sioux as Told Through John G. Neihardt* (1932), and L. V. McWhorter's *Yellow Wolf: His Own Story* (1940). Despite knowledge about and sympathy for their subjects, these collaborators necessarily shared linguistic, social, artistic, and moral assumptions with their predominately white readers. Patterson was a Galena, Illinois, newspaperman, Radin an anthropologist, McWhorter a free-lance Western writer, and Neihardt a poet and amateur historian of white-Indian conflicts on the Upper Great Plains. Each tried in his own way to realize autobiography's varied, often conflicting aims: historical accuracy, literary artistry, psychological verisimilitude. The fact that *Black Elk Speaks* has been canonized as an American prose classic is clearly due to the writer's often overlooked overlay of language and imagination, as is also the case with the two other acclaimed collaborations of our age—*The Autobiography of Malcolm X* and *All God's Dangers: The Life of Nate Shaw*. Indeed, none of these remarkable texts fully succeeds in articulating the thought, experience, or expression of its subject.

Though in recent decades Native American autobiographers like John Fire Lame Deer and Mary Crow Dog continue to participate in collaborations, newer writers like Scott Momaday have achieved powerfully personal narratives without white partners. (In fact, to imagine that a Momaday, Silko, or Allen needs an amanuensis is absurd.) Yet Native American writers still run risks as autonomous authors of their own experience. Euro-American assumptions about identity, authorship, and the creative process may interfere with full communication, as also may misunderstanding of the Indian author's degree of control over the publication process. Ray A. Young Bear nicely dramatizes this cross-cultural situation. Suddenly showered with $12,000 of Greek gold from the Maecenas Foundation, Edgar Bearchild (admittedly a thinly fictionalized self) and Selene Buffalo Husband set up housekeeping in a geodesic dome lodge on the outskirts of the Settlement. They equip themselves with a German typewriter, a woodstove, and a portable generator for the TV. This archetypal moment in the portrait of the young Indian writer proves short-lived, however. In his life, seen as a "Journey of Words," the sudden gift of money is less permanently significant than the bitterly frank letter of application that won him the fellowship. Of himself and his community he remarks to his foreign benefactors: "For too long we have been misrepresented and culturally maligned by an ungrateful country of Euro-American citizens who have all but burned their own bridges to the past. I will not tolerate such transgressions of my being and character."

Turning the tables on presumably cultured and history-laden white benefactors and readers worked once to win Bearchild the award; a similar honesty will, I predict, win the attentive reader's appreciation for this book. Edgar Bearchild represents the author as a talented young writer who, refusing the temptations of city or academic life, has chosen to remain in the community of his birth. He writes in full recognition of the grim facts of Settlement life and history. Relatives and friends for at least three generations have suffered poverty, discrimination, unemployment, poor education, alcoholism, apathy, internal rivalries, and exploitation. Bearchild does not hide the fact that he himself was once "the youngest member of the Black Eagle Child Settlement ordered by the court to be treated for alcoholism." Such candor could invite condescension or misunderstanding from white or other foreign readers. In that case, the temptation is to side with the NPWs (Nursing Program Workers) in simply condemning Native American community life and family structure as lifeless, abject, dysfunctional. From this perspective, the book's opening scene might easily be misread. The apathetic and ill-attended Thanksgiving pageant at the Weeping Willow Elementary School is, however, only half of the opening statement. Young Bear's message has two barrels: the meaningless official Christian ritual is to be contrasted with the scene that immediately follows—the sacred rite of the drums and tea ceremony. "The Star-Medicine transgressed the Real-Name structures," he explains later.

Autobiography is one way to combine dreams and the brutalizing details of contemporary Native American existence. One source of personal and community knowledge is learning from the elders, even from an alcoholic root-healer like Rose Grassleggings, herself a fictionalized figure. This becomes a central activity in this personal history of a Native American writer's roots and growth. Separating himself in a new lodge raises a "paper wall" between him and his society. So, too, do educational experiences amid white middle-class youths at Luther and Pomona colleges. Breaking through such barriers involves a double action: dwelling within but also moving beyond the local world of the Iowa River valley. As an insider with outside experience, Edgar Bearchild learns to balance the terrible polarities and contradictions of Indian life in this Settlement. Dreary everyday existence can give way to vitalizing moments of ecstatic religious and poetic transport. Meaningless and destructive drinking and drug-taking can ruin self, friendships, college; yet hallucinogens may also open avenues to spiritual enlightenment and literary power. Traveling abroad can prove almost deadening in the case of Pomona, yet Junior Pipestar's quest northward to Pinelodge Lake, Canada, confirms Young Bear's identity as a spiritual seeker.

One instance of life as contradictory yet interpenetrating realms is Edgar and Selene's encounter with the strobe light. Confronting the mysterious nighttime force which looks suspiciously like a UFO, Edgar bravely but piteously asks, "What is it you want when we live in poverty?" The starry shape in astral motion is reinforced by sounds of the equally eerie owls and the lights in the apple tree. The writer's rifle can do nothing to repel the invaders or explain their presence. The event refuses to surrender a clear meaning, except to underline another ironic feature of Young Bear's life story. Often, in this American childhood and youth, natural history and supernatural events come wrapped in the guise and language of mass-culture images. Tribal or clan figures and stories are all mixed up with *MAD* magazine and creatures from the Black Lagoon, while Jefferson Airplane and Bonnie and Clyde are also protective guiding spirits of rebellious Indian youth. Thus this strobe light episode might remind readers of other American autobiographers as unlike as Annie Dillard and Maya Angelou. Dillard's *Pilgrim at Tinker Creek* contains several powerful spiritual-natural encounters, like the mysterious lights in the cedar tree which she and the once-blind girl see as transfigurations of the physical world. Angelou's *I Know Why the Caged Bird Sings* also resonates with this text when one recalls that, during her rape by Mr. Freeman, the eight-year-old girl thinks that the Green Hornet of radio fame will miraculously come to her rescue.

Neither autobiographer, however, is as attuned as Young Bear to the family and community elders as sources of vital memories of the past. Stories told and retold can illuminate the young artist and ease his isolation. Carson Two Red Foot, for instance, reassures Edgar that he isn't the first family member to move away from the others and live in a separate lodge. His mother, after her husband left her and the children for a fourteen-year-old beauty, led the family away from the Settlement to spend a bitter winter in a bark and reed lodge near the Amana Colonies. Carson candidly points out that his mother was no revered seer but acted out of mental depression as well as fierce family pride. Nonetheless, Carson recalls his difficult childhood with satisfaction. "Often I think that the only true merriment and religious strength I underwent occurred during my youth and early manhood," he observes to his nephew. "All else has been a long uncomfortable adjustment of being an Indian . . ."

This and other interpolated tales told by and about others remind us of the communal nature of this personal story. "No good thing can be done by any man alone," Black Elk remarks to John G. Neihardt at the beginning of their collaboration at Pine Ridge. This characteristically Native American notion of creative activity applies also to this single-author narrative. So many other voices and presences are invoked, in fact, that the lines between self and society are blurred. In this respect, Euro-American belief in the autonomous self as subject and maker of autobiography is again challenged—as it is nowadays in so many women's and African Americans' autobiographies.

Edgar Bearchild's narrative, then, is both a distinctive and a thoroughly American artifact. Its subject and creator are both united and to some degree separated, just as social and spiritual time overlap yet diverge. An American boyhood and youth is recreated within the fifties, sixties, and seventies circumstances of a common American history of drugs, Vietnam, the Doors, and racism. Young Bear exploits the political and ideological resources of autobiography to dramatize the injustices and brutalities, past and present, of Native American experience. Yet internal divisions are also unsparingly displayed and condemned in the penultimate chapter wherein Edgar Bearchild lends his voice to Claude Youthman and Lorna Bearcap and their accusations of educational betrayal of Settlement youth at the Weeping Willow Elementary School. Young Bear's political critique is all too readily authenticated by other evidence, in newspaper and television, of similar social histories in Pine Ridge, Tonawanda, and elsewhere.

Arnold Krupat concludes *For Those Who Come After* in words which anticipate this autobiographical achievement of Ray A. Young Bear: "To an increasing degree, Native Americans for some time have shown the capacity and will to represent their own lives without the intermediation of the Euramerican—historian, scientist, or poet; [and] any future examples of the genre will appear in a context increasingly dominated—at least so far as the white world's awareness is concerned—by autobiographies by Indians who, while deeply interested in the old ways, have become extremely sophisticated in their manipulation of new—Euramerican, written— ways. In their different fashions all of these life histories, and those of their predecessors, deserve study and inclusion in the canon of American literature."

One function of *Singular Lives: The Iowa Series in North American Autobiography* is to reinforce the truth of this prophecy by bringing Ray A. Young Bear and his imagined alter egos Edgar Bearchild, Ted Facepaint, and the others together in an unmediated narrative. In form and substance, this story speaks to all who will heed its voice and share its vision.

Black
Eagle
Child

The
Well-Off
Man
Church

November 1965

The Thanksgiving party at the Weeping Willow Elementary
School had just concluded with the same lethargic atmosphere
it started with. Poor planning and late hand-delivered
newsletters by the Limelighters contributed
to a disappointing evening for the few families
of the Black Eagle Child Settlement who had arrived
early with lawn chairs, blankets, and children
predressed in ornate dance costumes. The fresh,
striking smell of mimeo ink had once again lured
reclusive people out of their homes to join
the Why Cheer High School Indian girls' club
for refreshments—and a pow-wow. Dolores Fox-King,
club president, encouraged community attendance
"for national holidays are celebrated by Indians, too!"
But tribal members were keenly aware affairs
such as Christmas, Halloween, and Easter
were meaningless. More so when wrapped gifts
and fine grotesque masks were unnecessary expenditures;
hard-boiled eggs, of course, were easy to decorate
and hide. As a child, colored eggs symbolized
the return of baskets filled with resilient

green grass, imitation chicks, and chocolate rabbits.
Although these items were donated by the Presbyterian
Mission, our guardians convinced us it was their doing.
Like the time my mother, Clotelde Principal Bear,
walked out from the frozen creek with a stocking
gift-monkey, I knew it came from the mission
by its old clothes, blankets-used-by-mice smell.
And with year's end came satanic celebration
via carved pumpkins, witches on brooms,
and paper skeletons. There was also the birth
(death and resurrection?) of a sad-looking
bearded white man known as the son of God.
But even *He* was far away from our despair,
like the turkeys, stuffing, and cranberries
that were absent from most tables. This get-
together, I mused, was further indication
of our inability to chronologically set
social plans into motion, another attempt
to duplicate another man's observance.

While we were a "tribe" in every respect,
it was unconscionable to help another
individual, family, or clan achieve
any degree of success in their public
endeavors. Behind the pretense
of cooperation were razor-sharp
anchors that raked and dug into
the visions of our grandfathers.
The girls' club, for example, was aptly
represented by the influential Kingfisher,
Sturgeon, Bearcap, Hummingbird, Fox-King,
and Beaver clans, but what mattered the most
was leadership. Ideally, it had to mirror
politics. But everyone knew otherwise.
Community affairs were unjustly manipulated
by a group of progressive visionaries.
If there was an inkling of sympathy
for reinstating divine leadership,

the atmosphere was readjusted by these
illiterate dreamers. Everything was monitored,
including the girls' club: the Fox-King sisters
were there, as usual, headstrong and obnoxious,
as were the Foxchild cousins and the plain Fox
twins, mixed-bloods. Also present were three
of the Water Runner sisters and their Red Boy
advisers. Standing to the side, where they
should be, were the Critical Ones. And
represented at every event was the clan
cursed to a hundred years of suicides,
the Excluded Ones.

It would never work—existence to the year
2000. Although our foreheads were not
misshapened with cedar slats from childhood
to denote tribal class, our Black Eagle Child
society was based on names. Our ancestors'
bones did not have glittering jewels inlaid
in their teeth to tell us of social structures;
instead, names were carried from one fortunate
or unfortunate generation to the next. The clash
between deities of the land, water, and sky
was imminent for human beings as well.
What our supernatural predecessors
experienced, it was said, we would
relive. It was part of our mythology—
and religion. But this was 1965,
and we were older and more stationary
in time.

The brass-studded octagon hide drum sat
upright at the center of the glossy Bureau
of Indian Affairs gymnasium floor, and the few
old men and women who entertained themselves
for a couple of hours with this instrument
through song and dance now sipped cool coffee
and chatted idly about recent community events.

The booming echo of the traditional percussion
instrument and the high nasal tones of the women-
hummers became forgotten sounds lodged
in the corners of the beamed ceiling.
In its place was gossip. There were, as always,
initial dismay and then gradual acceptance
of local atrocities: *Rose Grassleggings*
had again forgiven her husband for unusual
acts he allegedly committed on her daughters,
three of them. Judith, the oldest, was said
to drift in and out of dreams, night or day,
with her mouth slightly ajar; Christina,
the middle child who once had the loveliest
slanted eyes, was permanently cross-eyed;
and Brook, the youngest, was hidden from
the public. There was outrage, but no one
did anything. Castration was a mere fantasy
"under the influence" among the girls' skinny
uncles. And then there was Claude Youthman,
who terrorized a carload of state dignitaries
in downtown Why Cheer for "laughing too long"
at his wife. When the wife was asked by
the farmer selling produce if she had
"a sack or anything to put it (the cantaloupe)
in," the Indian woman panicked at what she
mistook as an obscene suggestion.
She could only stutter back, "Put it in?"
Before the limousine took direct cantaloupe hits,
the men who had brought promises of twenty
houses with indoor plumbing for the tribe
found this misinterpretation highly amusing.
The Farmers Market standoff might have been
funny, but everyone knew Claude's brother,
a trained sniper, had the white men
in the cross hairs of his telescope
in case the confrontation escalated.
The limousine and its promises drove
away and never returned. And every week

Lorna Bearcap made the news. Yesterday
commodity surplus flour was poured over
her lover and stepchild. With white powdery
faces they could be seen running through
the valley before crying in horror.
This, the people speculated, was a result
of the turmoil in being unenrolled.
There had been knives and deliberate
bloodletting in the past. "What's next?"
the people said. There was a firm belief
in tribalhood, equality, and fairness,
but in truth we were such a burden
to each other, an encumbrance, that
our chances of advancing into a reasonable
state of cultural acquiescence diminished
with each novel prejudice acquired.
There were instances of how we went
to extraordinary measures to impede
understanding, humanity, and the over-
whelming future.

All this internalized agony led us to hurt
or seriously injure one another for no reason
other than sheer disgust in being Indians.
Seasons determined the type of aggression people
would vent on one another. The full moons of summer
were notorious, and falls were utterly depressing.
Religious ceremonies were at their peak,
but the train of death ran parallel with ancient
beliefs, picking up passengers left and right.
"Do me a favor," drunks would say in morbid jest
before passing out, "kill me." But everyone
would wake up nauseated by the fact they
were still alive. This reality aggravated
the weak but dangerous ones who then took
it out on their innocent families. Many here
knowingly broke the law, and the rest became
accessories to crime. (The most famous was

the January 1936 drowning of three conservation
officers by twenty spearfishermen. No one
questioned the "stupid white man on weak ice"
story.) We kept awful secrets but dared not
to expose others for fear we would one day
have relatives in similar trouble. And if
the vicious vortex of a community of accessories
wasn't enough, the law in the nearby twintowns
of Why Cheer and Gladwood didn't care "one
stinkin' skin" if guns were pointed and shot
as long as we were on the other end. Investi-
gations were quick and ineffective. Also taking
part in this condemnation were newspapers which
gave our people nicknames like Cucumber
Man, Muskrat Bob, and Indianapolis Isabel.
Sadly, this trio had the distinction of being
arrested for intoxication fifty times apiece
in three years, and through them was found
the justification to ridicule us in public.
Whenever the promises they made in court—
to pay fines or do community duty—were broken
because of a lull in cucumber harvests, fur trapping,
and amateur stock car races, anyone who could read
knew. We were kept abreast of their trials
through extensive quotes. Instead of the funnies
rural folk turned to the court news for "looking
down at the pits of society" time. It became
normal to hear police make jokes like, "I've seen
and fought with more redskins than Custer."
For campaign publicity mayors would frequently
chase juvenile delinquents over our graveyards,
apprehend them with handcuffs, and pose
for photographs reminiscent of hunters
on an African safari. And it was over these
very graves that I silently wished my friends
and relatives farewell, knowing their harsh
journeys were over with while mine was just
beginning. The suicides, however, had no place

to go; they were stuck as shadows somewhere,
watching and wishing . . .

Near the hallway entrance to the gymnasium,
Ted Facepaint and I stood and watched the Limelighters walk across the length of the basketball
court with their long brooms, picking up dust,
pebbles, crumpled paper cups, and cigarette
butts. Beside us, we could hear plans being
made for a collection to facilitate a party
at Lone Ranger or South Street. Since Ted
and I didn't have money, we were ignored.
Like persistent fools, however, we stood
around nervously hoping for an invitation.
The ten-mile round-trip walk to the small
farming community of Why Cheer had become
a weekend highlight. With the cheapest beer
possible, Grain Belt, we would return over
the Milwaukee tracks, singing off pitch
and talking profanely to block the invisible
pain of midwestern Americana. The fact that alcohol-
related tragedies occurred on the cool rails
never bothered us as much as being penniless.
As the group turned to count their money, Ted
thought for a while before suggesting we
attend his grandfather's annual Thanksgiving
ceremonial gathering. Among the six beliefs
of the tribe, this sect was the least I knew
anything of. Either they were discreet or people
made it a point not to talk about them.
I was aware people called them Those Who Partake.
But boldly stenciled in English on a mailbox
on Whiskey Corners Road was the name they preferred:
the Well-Off Man Church, a name which amused me.
Before I could respond with a "no," Ted began
telling me about the gathering itself—
the church: "We pray and cleanse ourselves
with an imported medicine from distant desert

valleys owned by members of the Well-Off Man
congregation. Further, if this plant,
which is a form of mushroom, is ingested
and the mind is free of bad thoughts,
it produces a pleasant intoxicating effect."

So anxious to do something and feeling
largely abandoned by people who I thought
were friends disappearing into the night
toward Why Cheer, I apprehensively agreed
with his proposal. We started our walk uphill,
the opposite direction. In a hopeless gesture,
I turned around to have a final look. The group
had transformed into shapeless objects
followed by the small red glow of their
cigarettes.

Afflicted with a speech impediment since infancy—
his brothers "baptized" him in a flooded
creek where a "strange germ" lurked—Ted laughed
wholesomely whenever my younger brother, Al,
called him Three-Speed after the Schwinn
English bike we all marveled in comic books.
Whenever Ted's verbalization slowed down,
Al would remind Ted to "change gears like
a three-speed." Ted would raise his eyebrows
and inhale deeply and accelerate, walking faster,
talking more rapidly. Since the bike was a luxury
we would never possess (no one ever sold enough
salve or garden seeds to own one), Facepaint
treasured the dream. It represented self-improvement
in school and society. I pondered about this as we
were walking, for our paces were different and more
apparent in motion. (But that was how our later lives
were to be: his impediments would one day cease while
mine would fester.) Before we reached the turnoff
on the community's main gravel road, a squawking

pheasant broke into flight from a utility pole,
startling us. Sensing it was perhaps an omen,
we stopped to take deep, long breaths.

Above us in the central Iowa sky,
the stars shone immaculately, and the pine
valley road was well lit. As soon as Ted spotted
the dim porch light through the trees, he began
to brief me on what to expect, what to do
and not do, that except for a child or two
we would probably be the youngest people
in attendance. "If it was summer,"
Ted said excitedly, "we would descend
into the salamander effigy which overlooks
the lowlands and rivers. The medicine's
effect is spectacular under the earth.
Tonight's gathering, however, will be held
inside Circles-Back's house. Just remember,
Edgar, should it come to you as an emetic,
there are empty coffee cans for that specific
purpose. Try not to think of throwing up,
no matter how terrible the taste."
As we approached the house I thought it
was odd to see eight to ten cars parked near
a house at night. All being sober family types.
Once we stepped inside the warm kitchen
a familiar herbal odor filled my nose
and fogged my thick, black-framed glasses,
giving both of us a chance to relax and blend
into the solemn but tense activity. We unzipped
our coats and wiped our glasses on our shirt-
tails. Plump women wearing floral-print aprons
were exchanging news and busying themselves
with pots, pans, and firewood; men in western
shirts and ironed dress-slacks were puffing
cigarettes in the adjoining room. We were each
accorded a second of attention. Ted secretly

signaled his aunt Louise Stabs Back.
She politely excused herself from the table
where she directed the meticulous cutting,
cleaning, and sorting of both fresh and dry plants
Ted called *A na qwa mi ke tti i o ni*, Star-Medicine.

"Aunt Louise, this is Edgar Bearchild, Ka ka to.
Do you think Grandfather would give approval
for a visitor?" His short, cherubic aunt looked
up at us with warm eyes and calmly replied,
"Ted, I *know* who he is. His grandmother,
Ada Principal Bear, sometimes helps with
the cooking for the feast. Perhaps she may
even be here tomorrow."
Without realizing it, I nodded in agreement.
Upon careful reflection I thought this must be
the place where my grandmother often walked,
even on the coldest winter day, to help out
with the feast—like she did with every
religious group on the Settlement.

From across the room I noticed Ted's war-hero
uncle, Clayton Carlson Facepaint, coming toward
us in a low boxing stance. In the forties
Clayton became well known in the service
for his pugilistic ability. I had read
old newsclippings of his unheralded boxing
exploits. One headline read: "Champion
Joe Louis Spars with Indian Fighter
for War Bonds." Later, Clayton was perhaps
the only Indian in the county—or state—
invited to join and fly bombing missions
with the RAF. He eventually became a prisoner
of war but escaped from Hitler's forces
by cartwheeling down a mountainside
and joined the French underground
where he waged successful strikes against

ammunition and fuel depots. Nowadays,
he was feared by all for his skills
in hand-to-hand combat; with one abrupt pinch
or swift chop to the delicate shoulders
or necks of abusive people, red or white,
he could literally put anyone's lights out.
When he rotated his stocky body toward me,
I cautiously stepped back and nearly fell over
the woodpile. In blinding speed he hooked Ted hard
in the ribs several times, and Ted took it
without flinching. Clayton straightened up
to chuckle and congratulate Ted. He then stared
at me with squinty, knowing eyes.
"You remember?" he asked in a near whisper.
I knew what he was referring to right away;
I remembered the lewd, drunken comment
he made one night about his Caucasian
wife as he forced me to drive him home
from town. Doogie was what he called
her—an Indian reference for a person's
frame spread apart. Out of nervousness
I must have been humored by this,
for he repeated it slowly again in my ear.
I quit breathing, not wanting to inhale
the pungent smell of chewing tobacco.
"The red-headed woman I love is so chubby
she's got balls." Detecting a hint of seriousness
this time, I pretended to be stricken with wonder.
"I have another one for you, Child Edgar Bear,"
he said while raking his butch with a metal comb.
"Listen to this: big rabbits, big white ones
with red 'Thumper' eyes." I shrugged my shoulders,
indicating I didn't know the joke, but images
from *Bambi* flashed in my mind in technicolor.
By Walt Disney. After Walter Cronkite.
Mutual of Omaha. And Walt Hill, Nebraska,
near Winnebago on the ridge where this portly

Mongolian warrior held up the caravan
of horses and wagons with a bullwhip.

Like a dazzling savior, Ted's grandfather,
who was dressed in a dark blue suit and pants
with gray pinstripes, came out from the living room
and nodded his white-haired head. His attire
reminded me of someone from the notorious
Al Capone era; it was magnificent.
"Come on!" Ted said with a grin,
breaking my thoughts from "The Untouchables"
and the piercing, authoritative voice of its
narrator, Walter Winchell.
"Let's go in before he changes his mind."
We entered an unfurnished living room, which looked
and smelled newly constructed. The floorboards
creaked, and the pine lumber scent was overpowering.
Worn pillows and Pendleton blankets were lined up
neatly at the base of the drywalls.
To the south I closely examined
a framed painting of Jesus Christ,
who was descending from the billowy clouds
with a lamb cradled in his arms.
The yellow halo was the brightest object
in the glazed oil painting. "My brother,
Christian, did that," remarked Ted proudly.
The artwork itself was the best I had ever
seen on the Settlement, but I failed to see
its significance. Christianity was the white
man's belief. What the hell is it doing here?
I quietly asked myself.

Soon, people from the other rooms began
to filter in and choose their respective places.
The elder Facepaint sat on the north side,
and he was arranging what appeared to be altar-
pieces. But they were set on top of a crumpled
reed mat imprinted with English letters.

After a difficult time trying to read
the words upside down, I vocalized further
disbelief: "THE LORD LOVES AND WATCHES OVER
THIS HOUSE." Ted tugged my arm and told me
to sit down; we sat below the painting
of Christ. From a small battered briefcase
the elder Facepaint took out a tin "salt-
shaker" rattle with a sparkling beaded
handle and topped with a stiff tassel of deer
hair. Next came four salamander figurines
in black, yellow, red, and light-blue earth
dyes. They protruded lifelike halfway out
of their own separate leather pouches,
positioned to the four cardinal points
around a cast-iron kettle. The elder
Facepaint began inhaling deeply, and I
could see this clearly for he had no teeth.
The loose, aged skin below his cheekbones
outlined this fact. Almost statuesque
in his white shirt and black bow tie
fastened by a German silver star,
the old man sat straight up in
preparation for a prayer. From
the sputter of air on skin, the words
gradually became audible. "For this very reason,
Holy Grandfather, we have gathered here tonight—
to essentially be together, to pray. A multitude
of reasons binds us. You know me as no stranger,
You, Holy Grandfather, the giver of eternal
medicine . . ."

Ted's cousins, Norman and Asa Green Thunder,
knelt beside their praying grandfather.
At some given point in the sermon, they began
measuring and stretching the drum hide over
the small kettle's brim. Speckled and striped
marbles were individually placed beneath
the hide. A white cord was then looped

around each marble over the hide. The kettle's
stumpy tripod legs held the white cord
to the marble-posts in an intricate star
pattern. Before the last marble-post
was secured, steaming *A na qwa o ni* tea
was poured into the kettle, including fresh
pieces. Next a deer tine was used to tighten
the cord, stretching the drum hide even tighter.
Ted's grandfather scrutinized each movement
in the course of his Thanksgiving prayer,
and if there was a slight error or time
lapse committed by his jittery grandsons,
he stopped the proceedings and apologized
to the small water drum which was being
handled and dressed like a small person.
When that was done, he gently shook
the drum and sprinkled the hide with water.
"*Ki tti tta ki tti ta bi wa ki ko ye a ki?*
Has everyone sat down?" he queried
into the kitchen. "Very well. I will begin
by commenting on our two grandchildren,
ko tti se me na na ki, who have chosen wisely
to sit with us on this occasion. It is indeed
a good thing, but they must be told this
congregation and its divine purposes aren't
for fun. There are serious considerations
to make, and they will no doubt come into
contact with our very words, feelings—
and thoughts tonight. They must tell
themselves repeatedly not to feel unkindly
toward our sacrament, which is after all
our sole means of spiritual communion.
Other people within the community
have callously equated *A na qwa o ni*
to eye matter of a negative deity,
but for us, the Well-Off Man Church,
all the good we know in this world lies

within the medicinal qualities of our
Star-Medicine . . ."

Ted and I listened with our heads bowed down;
we were slightly embarrassed for causing concern
and attention. Both of our heads jumped when
the old man pounded out the four introductory
notes on the drum. The Green Thunder cousins
quickly repositioned themselves on each side
of their stout grandfather. In a low voice
Ted told me his grandfather and two cousins
represented the Three Stars-in-a-Row,
the Orion constellation. "Stars symbolize
our religious beginnings." Norman Green Thunder
looked very attentive as he gripped a maple
sapling "struck by lightning" and wrapped
with stringy vine: the staff. The younger
brother, Asa, was securing a pin above
the salt-shaker rattle.
"Following my grandfather's songs,
one will sing while the other drums."
It was hard to envision these two brothers
as nocturnal musicians. For the old man,
their grandfather, it wasn't.
Mesmerized by his eloquent words
and physical gestures—for the drum—
I was unaware all eyes were on me.
In particular, there was an Alexis Bearcap,
whose bulging gray eyes resembled the marbles
under the drum hide, mixed-blood eyes too huge
for their sockets. He was overly intrusive,
and I tried to stare back. He's exactly
like Lorna, his crazy sister, I fumed.
I soon realized my hostility was unwarranted
for *I* was the outsider. Everyone—acquaintances
and visiting Indians—would ostensibly view
my presence as an intrusion. I became acutely

self-conscious and trembled. There were about
twenty-five people in the room, more men
than women. Some of the women who assisted
earlier in the kitchen now sat across
from me, bundled up in Pendleton blankets
and perspiring heavily. My anxiety
subsided somewhat when each person,
except Alexis, caught my eye
and acknowledged me with an almost
undetectable nod or wink.

Among them I recognized "Mr. Jim Matcheena"
(the way we were taught to address him in school),
a short, comical, and loquacious sort of fellow
who made a point of being at all gatherings,
ceremonial or social. Although he was retired
as a government maintenance man from Weeping
Willow Elementary, he had a habit of wearing
his dark green khaki work clothes every day.
He grinned perpetually at everyone and anything.
He ambled about in a tottering manner,
and his short height brought him down
to the level of children who would flock
around him, myself included, to wait
for clownish tricks and Juicy Fruit gum.
However, long before he first noticed
signs of my manhood during mandatory group
showers at school in fifth and sixth grade,
Mr. Matcheena stood out in my earliest memories:
on the morning of my grandfather's funeral
feast in 1954, I woke up and found him
holding a bucket of dishes and cups above me.
But he wasn't looking at me. He was instead
totally enthralled with a young teenaged girl,
Elizabeth Marie, who slept beside me. Her lace-
trimmed dress had rolled up past her navel,
exposing her soft, lithe body.
"Touch her," he said as he saw me wide awake.

"Touch her right here." Before he could say
anything else or act on his absurd suggestion,
one of the woman cooks, outside, perhaps
Elizabeth's mother, yelled out,
"Jim! *Bye to no be na a na ka na nai!*
Bring the dishes (promptly)!"
The trance broken, he grunted
in disdain and walked out the door.

Afterward, whenever I saw him, he would joke
around: a mime reenacting that particular morning
years ago. He knew I remembered. Amid the loss
of my grandfather curiosity for the female
anatomy was firmly established. I never saw
the pretty Elizabeth Marie again. I later
learned she had asked social authorities
in town to send her away or she would
"die like her three sisters and mother."
They obliged the precocious Indian girl
without question. Her father had jeopardized
her future at Black Eagle Child by selling
sacred items, information, and songs
to museums in Washington, D.C., and Germany.
All the daughters except Elizabeth perished
under mysterious circumstances.

Next to Mr. Jim Matcheena sat John Louis,
who frequently called himself "just another
demented soul." I never knew its exact meaning,
but it always sounded impressive. With a redtail
hawk fan in front of half his face, John
peered at me capriciously. He would flick
the fan to the left and then right,
showing his scarred face. At twenty,
he was a lover of alcohol like his father.
While his face was slightly deformed from
automobile accidents, John had a pleasant,
outgoing demeanor. In fact, he had lots

of friends; most were attracted by the adult
characteristics he exuded. We called each other
Chicken Soup after a diagram he once drew
in school of the male reproductive system.
John Louis blocked his eyes with the hawk fan
and silently mouthed the words. I looked away
to keep what little composure I had.

The elder Facepaint's opening prayer touched
all aspects of tribal life. He mentioned the need
for people of all faiths to cooperate, and he asked
God to care for the ill whether they were present
or elsewhere. He also asked for the safe return
of sons in the armed forces overseas. He concluded
Indians basically had little to be thankful for
on this national holiday, but what was crucial
was continuation of our culture. "We make use
of this special time because we are home
and together." Following this, he requested
the First Fire Keeper, X. J. Louis, to bring in
ashes for the incense purification of the altar
and the four "watching salamanders."
The First Fire Keeper came in with a metal toy
shovel and placed it in front of his father,
who then sprinkled cedar incense over
the red ashes. The smoking shovel was circulated
to each of the members, and when it came to me,
I copied their movements: I liberally fanned
myself with smoke and rubbed my arms with it.
Everyone had their own unique way
of purifying themselves. Some used fans
decorated with serrated feathers of pheasants
or exotic birds, while others, especially
the older ones, appeared to be washing themselves
with the liquid and fragrant blue smoke.
Several applied it on their throats
and over their hearts with fans made
from the wings of eagles.

Gift
of the
Star-
Medicine

》《》 《》 《》 《》 《》 《》 《》 《》 《》 《》 《》 《》 《》 《》 《》

After this ritual cleansing was done by everyone,
I was quickly overcome by a sense of giddiness
at my lack of form. I was never a good imitator.
There was a moment when I almost broke into
a foolish grin. I most certainly would have,
but the elder Facepaint took everyone's
attention by gently shaking and nudging
the "child" drum as if from its nap.
Norman Green Thunder, with his oily Elvis Presley
hairdo and Hawaiian floral-print shirt,
drew the drum between his knees and tilted it
at a forty-five-degree angle toward the white
female oak drumstick clutched firmly
in his right hand. Norman's wide, light-
complexioned face was taut and extra-smooth:
a visage which reminded me of a strong
and defiant channel catfish,
right down to the Fu Manchu mustache.
Norman cleared his throat in nervousness.
As he began to drum he held and bent his left
arm and hand down to the drum's brim and tuned
the wet resonating hide with his roving thumb.

When the tone faltered, like an engine starter
on a below-zero morning, Norman slowed the beat
and retilted the drum to slosh the water inside.
Once the tuner-thumb was in the right place
and the drum at a perfect angle, I noticed
the rich tonality of the humming water
trapped inside the cavity of the kettle.
Its intensity and rhythm reminded me
of my heart growing excited in midhunt
at the sight of deer blood marking a precious
fiery-orange path over the frozen snow.
From the drum a fine spray of water arced
outward and landed on the clear pine-board floor,
creating a circular shape like that of an eclipse.

Almost inaudible at first, the elder Facepaint
began a slow wailing song from deep inside
his chest:

> Spirit of Fire, Spirit of Fire,
> Spirit of This. This is the reason
> your medicine will work for us,
> our divine Firefather.

Ted meekly leaned over and in a breath
of apprehension whispered that after the opening
song, his grandfather would recite the brief
but important creation story of their religion.
Four verses later, as advised, the elder Facepaint
began to talk:

"There exists a past which is holy and more
close to us than ourselves. In gatherings
such as we have tonight, we would be remiss
in not remembering it, acknowledging it
as something new for the young minds here.
For us, the aged, we must never let it grow
old, for it is as much a religious history

as it is tribal. We believe it is in part
why our families reside here: Long before
the establishment of Black Eagle Child,
there was a hunter, *ke me tto e na na*,
our grandfather, Te te ba me qwe,
Dark Circling Cloud. He was chosen
one winter by the night sky to receive
the Star-Medicine, *A na qwa mi ke tti i o ni*.
The gift came to him when he was returning
from a long, unsuccessful hunt, going home
from west to east. That time we resided near
the Mississippi River valley. It was common
knowledge that somewhere in the prairie interiors
toward the west a river called the Swanroot
possessed a bottomless bend from which powers
emanated to anyone at any time. The only
trouble was, no one knew whether the tumultuous
upsurge of an underwater river healed or destroyed.
Many people became convinced it served as an abode
for evil entities when not traveling about.
For us, today, it is the exact opposite.
From somewhere below the depths of earth,
the underwater river flowed up and never froze
in winter. To this day, this is true. Many
of our early hunters took drastic precautions
when passing through this area. It was said
people who slept near here never woke.
Te te ba me qwe, because of his fasting
strength, was not in fear when he chose
to bed down over the warm sand of this
mysterious riverbend. The fact is, because
of his hunger, exhaustion, and coldness,
he had little choice. He lay down on the white,
comfortable sand and closed his eyes; he boldly
planned to drink the warm water and to bathe
in it upon waking. That night, he was awakened
by what sounded like a hundred arrows whizzing
overhead simultaneously. The evil spirits must

be setting out, was the thought in his heart.
As he dared to open his eyes to the sky,
he detected four small lights in movement.
Among all the stars these four wavered
slightly. The more he looked, the more
he realized the lights were growing in size.
He concluded they were in descent. Before long,
suspended above him were four luminescent bubbles.
At treetop level the open water began to boil
and mist. Te te ba me qwe said to himself,
'*Me me tti ki me ko me nwi ke no to ki
mani ne ta ma ni*. Perhaps what I am now
seeing has to be good.' Directly in front of him,
the four bubbles of light soon aligned themselves
west to east over the boiling river and began
emitting sparks. From the smoke created by
the sparks, a thundercloud lifted
and traveled upriver. It came to a stop
and sent silent bolts of lightning
to the ground below. In the lightning's flash,
Te te ba me qwe saw the shape of a canoe
drifting listlessly downriver with four
motionless men aboard. When they were directly
in front, the men reached for their paddles.
As soon as the paddles plunged into the river,
fierce thunder shook the land. The four deer-
masked men rowed to where the four lights
had hovered. Then they guided the canoe
to the sand with the thundercloud following
closely above. Wearing tall deer antlers
they each stood in front of what was now four
smoldering black rocks. The four men struggled
to breathe in their tight masks, but they stood
erect. Their antlers became the mirror image
of the lightning bolts and reached back up
to the night sky. When the star-boulder closest
to Te te ba me qwe began to talk, the deer-masked
men vanished as did the thundercloud, and the water

stopped boiling. This was the boulder which foretold
our religion. Te te ba me qwe knew right away
what his role was; he had been selected
to be the principal intermediary.
The second boulder gave us the first
four opening songs. Te te ba me qwe
subsequently learned twenty more sets
of songs. These songs are rearranged
meticulously throughout the night ceremony.
The third boulder gave us rules by which to pray.
Te te ba me qwe memorized the intricate and complex
orations. The fourth boulder, the Fourth Star,
gave us *A na qwa mi ke tti i o ni*, Star-Medicine.
And it is this Fourth Star who stayed to remind
us perpetually of what is true. The Fourth
Star now resides underneath the ridge near here.
The effigy is therefore a reassuring place where
we can go whenever we falter from the weight
of worry. We hereby honor our grandfather,
Dark Circling Cloud, through the medicine
which was once a falling star . . ."

There were tears in the old man's bloodshot
eyes. Even Al Capone must have cried once
or twice at the Lexington Hotel. A lump grew
in my throat, knowing all too well the sorrow
of seeing my own grandmother weep. Being young
I could never pinpoint what caused her despair.
But the suffering came in unpredictable surges
of human emotion. Without warning the waves
crashed on her endlessly. She would be at
the table, peeling potatoes for supper,
or doing ribbon appliqué on dress panels
by daylight near the window or kerosene lamp
when the reality of our poverty would hit her.
The distant oceans I only read about came over
the top of the wooded hill, and the waves raced
down, toppling what was otherwise a semblance

of a strong household. There was my grandmother,
my mother, and my younger brother, Al. When not
at work, school, or the military, my two uncles,
Winston and Severt, would be there. Even with
the family present there was no sight more
devastating than Grandmother crying.
It was as if someone had suddenly died.
I often wept along behind the door or outside
in the shadow of the house, never knowing why.
There was no evidence of physical pain except
the one in my immature heart. The excitement
of the evening came down in the form of rain
from the elder Facepaint's weary eyes.
He lowered his white-haired head
and covered the German silver star
on his chest with his double chin.
Soon, a large brown grocery bag was passed
around the room. We each took four plants
and began eating them. The fresh outer part
of a single *A na qwa o ni* didn't have any taste,
but the inside portion tasted like the chalky vomit-
tasting vitamins my mother used to give me.
Vitamins I could never swallow.
There were violent arguments for health,
One-A-Day brand events which so traumatized me
that I often slept with a pitcher of water
beside the bed, for my throat would clog
in sleep. I turned to Ted and grimaced.
"I really don't think I can eat all of these.
If I take another bite I am bound to get sick."
I could feel the thick, poisonous saliva
coating my tongue from the back to the front.
"Damn, Ted, I'm not kidding," I said, hoping
for a way out. Sensing my timing and reach
for the empty coffee can would be insufficient,
I was drenched with perspiration. Ted raised
his arm at the appropriate moment and got
his grandfather's attention.

"Grandfather, could you appoint
someone to chew Bearchild's medicine?"

The elder Facepaint chuckled before addressing
me. "*Ka tti ya bi ke te tti so? Ka ka to?*
What is your name? Ka ka to?" I affirmed
with an overdone nod. "Yes, I thought so," he said
while searching for additional commentary.
He reflected for a second and offered,
"Your Indian name is an archaic Bear clan
name; it is so old no one remembers its
precise meaning. But I do know this:
the one person you are named after used
to ride horses a lot. He was a superb horseman.
I will therefore call you Randolph Scott,
after the motion picture cowboy actor.
With a name like that, Randolph Scott,
you should have no problems eating the rest
of the medicine." Everyone broke into
a much-needed laugh. Myself included.

The elder Facepaint appointed a short,
well-dressed gentleman by the name of Percy Jim
to chew the remaining pieces. A white folded
handkerchief was relayed to me. I carefully placed
the three pieces in the handkerchief and returned it
the same way to the appointed chewer. In no time
at all, the chewer went through the antics
of a voracious squirrel stuffing the three
large pieces into his mouth. While everyone
observed, he spat the masticated *A na qwa o ni*
into his stumpy hands and deftly rolled it into
a green ball. The green golf ball came back to me
in the white soaked handkerchief.
"Now, Randolph," chided the elder Facepaint,
"swallow the medicine whole and you will be
all right." I knew the task was impossible;
even with my mother I could never down two

small vitamin tablets. Things unimaginable
were done for newcomers here.
"Do I have to do as he says?" I sighed
to Ted. "Yeah, Edgar, you have to,"
he replied sternly. "He gave you permission
to sit with us, and the medicine was chewed
for you. What the hell you want? For someone
to hunt a spoon and feed you? Your task
was lessened by half. It is the least
you can do." Just when the star-boulder
songs resumed, I secretly broke the green
golf ball in half and swallowed it reluctantly.
I hid the other half under my knee and closed
my eyes in repulsion. I thought immediately
of a photograph of the person whom I was named
after: wearing a crumpled straw hat and a ribbon
shirt, he sat slouched-backed on his mount
and Alfred Pretty-Boy-in-the-Woods sat
across from him atop another. The title
read: "Men on horses with summer sun shade
and reed-covered dwellings in the background,
ca. 1904." The knowledge he was a true horseman
was little consolation for the rock hardening
in my stomach. It seemed to demand its own space
and kicked from side to side, making my being
hollow. I forced myself to conjure a mental image
of Randolph Scott. He was getting up from
an arroyo after a lengthy fistfight.
His hair was messed up and dust clung
to his chaps.

With part of a meteorite fermenting under
my navel, I sat back and listened to the eloquent
word-songs. The words in Black Eagle Child language
were ingeniously arranged. They almost sounded all
the same, but upon careful listening, one added
or excluded word or syllable made for an entirely
different song.

THE BLACK STONE SONGS

This black stone has brought us
songs that we must use when
we call down the stars.

This stone named Black Stone
has brought us songs to use
to bring down the star groupings.

Black Stone is the one responsible
for bringing us songs to call down
the bright stars.

Black Stone comes down from above
with songs for us to use to greet Him.

In between the songs, a bucket
of steaming *A na qwa o ni* was passed around.
Ted and I took two dippers apiece. I began
to take note that in spite of the commotion
I could hear the steady whirring of the clock
on the wall, next to Christ. I looked at my
pocketwatch. We had "gone in" at eight o'clock.
It was now ten o'clock. My stomach was warm
and mildly upset, yet my thoughts felt placated.
At Ted's warning, for fear I would gag, I refused
the powdered substance. For some reason we both
looked up and saw John Louis smirk. With his scarred
but puckered lips and cheeks he was hoping
to annoy us. We pretended to be undaunted.
The dramatics with the redtail hawk fan became
more emphatic and womanlike. He now fluttered
his drowsy eyelids like a shy southern belle.
All was well and entertaining until he leaned
forward and mistakenly spit into the coffee can
containing the powdered *A na qwa o ni*.
A fine cloud of dust shot up from the container

and covered his stunned face. For once
the "demented soul" looked hilarious.
John Louis froze immediately, his eyes
blinking and the potent dust falling off
in clumps. Ted and I looked at each other
with raised eyebrows and open mouths and muffled
our laughs in our sleeves. All of a sudden,
in the midst of this, Mr. Matcheena,
the retired clown, crawled outward from
his space on the wall with his rump
protruding high in the air and stared
hypnotically at the damp eclipses on the floor
made by the water drum. He was still there
when Ted and I drank four more dippers
of medicine apiece. Finally, a lady
in a black ruffled dress was requested
by someone to tap the soles of Matcheena's
moccasins. The government clown turned
around as expected, but he digressed
further in disconcertion. He began bowing
to the wall like someone from the Middle East.
In time Ted chanted, "Salami, salami,
baloney," but I wasn't amused.
"Geez, what's wrong with him?" I asked
out of concern. Having no answers, Ted
asked the same of his war-hero uncle.
It was a mistake. Clayton hypothesized that
Matcheena was suffering a horrendous cramp
of the buttock. A sense of fear set in after
I feigned a weak smile at both Ted and Clayton.
Would I be doing the same foolish things
later on? My eyes and finger muscles began
to twitch involuntarily. All around the room
the facial expressions varied. There were far-
off looks, near-smiles at space, or explicit
sadness. I attributed my twitching to the corn
husk and Prince Albert tobacco smoke.
To accompany a prayer, cigarettes were hand-

rolled hastily and lit with the toy shovel.
The smoke hung heavy in the small ventless
room. The water collecting at the edge
of my eyes gave false motion to people
sitting beside me.

Later, when I ascertained Ali Baba
had partially recouped his senses, I bravely
drank more tea. The beautiful word-songs
switched to English, invoking Jesus Christ;
and prayers from individuals who were normally
quiet in public became vocal—and personal.
The physical gestures of the singers
and drummers could be seen in minute,
mechaniclike increments. From the sinewy
muscles my grandmother, the butcher,
pulled over the joint bones of fowl
for the amusement of the cook's children
I could discern all the pulling and tugging
of human muscle in the height of nocturnal music.
Near dawn, I thought to myself, I will propose
to Ted we visit the effigy of the salamander.

At midnight, there was an abrupt lull
and the water drum was put away. The strings
were tightened to cover the wooden salamanders.
The people began to move and question one another.
"Edgar, how do you feel?" Ted inquired sheepishly.
"Like I have to piss," I returned. We were thus
granted approval to step outside, but we first
had to follow a specific pattern on the altar-floor.
Was it the symbol of Israel? Almost immediately,
as we passed the kitchen, I noticed the spherical
dimensions of the linoleum floor. The frosted
ground was the same once we stepped onto the porch.
We briefly stood, exhaling smokes of our breath.
In the cold air I saw swirls of small human figures
with unopened miniature fingers. Like breakaway

pieces of clouds they dissipated behind Ted's
hair as I followed him off the crude porch.
I was beginning to enjoy myself before
my left foot fell through the bloated earth.
I attempted to jerk my body back up but lost
control and fell down with flailing arms.
I landed on an incline and rolled down,
knocking Ted off-balance in the process.
Ted stumbled to the side in surprise.
"Jeeessusss!" he gasped. When I stood up,
the incline transformed into a steep mountain-
side. I lay back down cautiously and dug
my fingers into the crystal blades of grass.
Ted stood as if he was standing sideways
on the wall of the house. "How come?" I asked.
"Experience, my son," he muttered. "Experience."
He lifted me up in one swoop, but the sensation
remained. We staggered to the outhouse. So this
is what he meant earlier this evening—yesterday,
I thought. He could have explained further.
But how—which word describes reality gone mad?
"This is some mountain!" I shouted to Ted
as we neared the peak. In a sardonic laugh
he answered, "There's no mountains in Iowa,
you asshole!" Deeply offended, I climbed
the cliff on hands and knees, half-expecting
giant crab pinchers to reach out from
the crevices. They scuttled about, tested
the elasticity of my knee skin, and debated.
I lunged for the porch rail and dangled until
the earth came right. Ted was nowhere in sight!
But I could hear him talking nearby. I walked
trustingly toward the sound of his echoing voice.
"Ka ka to, isn't this better than Lone Ranger?"
Ted's voice vibrations led me to what appeared
to be the shape of Spiderman stuck to the negative
moon side of the wall. All I could see was what
the porch light allowed me to see: the yard,

porch, and parked cars. The electric light
sliced the rural darkness from the corner
of the house to these objects. From
the divided darkness came Ted's face,
floating eerily in the black ocean.
I reached in to grab the dead swimmer's
shirt, but he grabbed back and took me down.
"Son of a bitch!" I yelled as I fell,
knowing I was not a strong swimmer.
The next thing I knew, I was standing in
the shadow of the house, holding Ted's shirt.
"Cool it, man," he demanded. There was no ocean
to speak of. No mountain. No giant crabs.
And Ted was no Spiderman. The medicine's
effect was unbelievable but thoroughly
convincing. To experience more, we chose
to stay outside.

In his father's station wagon we quietly sat
and witnessed a birch tree give intimate birth
to snowflakes. Up through the birch tree's crystal
veins, we followed the snowflakes before they shot
out from the branch-tips like fireworks.
Rockets telling us the vitality of this
Woman-Tree. Children fell from her branches
in tiny slivers of light. Icicles splintering into
a thousand pieces on gravel. We were enthralled
as they massed together at the tree's base
and started over. Each waited politely
to ride and flourish on one of the veins.
Life renewing life. Oxygen. The spell
was broken by the windshield wipers
Ted had turned on. "The scene can be
changed by simple adjustments." He then
rolled down the car window for fresh air.

Far off in the distance, we heard the group
we wanted to go with, singing and drumming

round dance songs on someone's car hood.
Their drunken enjoyment seemed trite compared
to ours. What we both thought was an illusion
of a large man blocking the window started
talking to us. "You boys have to go back in,"
a husky voice commanded. We were paralyzed.
"Ted, you know about these things," spoke
the illusion. "You must finish out the Star
Journey with the rest of us. This goes
for your friend and guest. Any diversion
from fear or disrespect will keep
the Three-Stars-in-a-Row from visiting us."
Jason Writing Stick, a Sokapaita Indian
from Colton, Kansas, had been asked to look
for us. Ted was sent on in by himself.
"OK, Randolph Scott," said the fat
Sokapaita in a snorting kind of laugh,
"let's go after some Blessing Water
from the riverbend." Out of intrigue
I followed. I simply could have gone back in.
If viewing the Fourth Star was not to be—
had I even asked Ted about going into
the effigy? I couldn't remember—
I should at least see this sacred place.
In a strong, even pace, we skirted
the hillside ancient hunters dreaded,
headed south, and crossed the two railroad
tracks. We trudged along the forest and soon
sunk our heels into the sand. Thick cocklebur
stands blocked our path. I often fished here,
but never in winter—or night. In fact,
I was specifically told to keep away.
Stories of fishermen being spun around
in their boat or strange lights hitching
rides on zipping trains was enough to make me leery.
Except now I marveled at the rich mosaic
shapes of the trees outlined by the horizon
of farming communities miles away.

"We are almost there," said the Sokapaita
as he strained to catch his breath. It seemed
I could hear each nosehair flicker and respond
from the nasal passage to the tune of his lungs.
He was obviously tired. He gave me the empty
bucket and blew a single piercing note
from the *ne ne qwa,* flute:
"Tooooooooooooooo-wiiiiiitiii!"
The shrill nearly popped my sensitive ears,
making the silence of the riverbottom more
intensive. "We'll let the spirits know we are
coming. We must not surprise them."
I was terribly afraid at the prospect
of disturbing some lumbering deities,
screaming back at us like a thousand frogs
in supernatural wattage. I vividly pictured
one monstrous eye opening, some kind of life-form
highly agitated by humans. Then, like a summer
wind that makes clothes whip about and dry,
an unbelievably warm breeze caressed my cold face.
We reached our destination. Dark Circling Cloud
slept on this beach. The stars came down
and gave me the "gift" I was feeling en masse.
The Sokapaita plunged the bucket and captured
the warm water. He then dipped the tip
of the flute into the river and blew four
times to the cardinal points. He played
enchanting notes to the Three-Stars-in-a-Row
until he wept and stumbled to his knees.
I felt sorry for him, an outsider married
to the tribe, but lost all compassion when
he made me carry the bucket back
to Circles-Back's house.

The strenuous exercise brought back
a hint of normalcy. To keep the precious
water from spilling left me expended.
However, upon entering the house and coming

face to face with the sneering war hero
Clayton Carlson, the river walk was erased.
The odd question about white rabbits
was posed again. "Yes," I replied
in a firm obnoxious tone. "The red-eyed
cocksucking albinos are out there."
It didn't make sense. Point was, rudeness
now for rudeness past. Clayton would have killed
me that one night had I refused to drive him home
in the shark-finned automobile. If I was disrespectful,
I wasn't sorry. I contemplated clapping my hands
near his ears repeatedly and watching him squirm
in remembrance of artillery fire. "Capeesh?"
I said, disappearing with the bucket
around the corner.

The people were glad to see the Devil Child.
They even pointed and directed the way back
to my original sitting place via the unseen
symbol of Israel. In the voice of a munchkin,
Ted sang out, "Follow the yellow brick road."
Everyone smiled except the elder Facepaint.
He ordered Ted to be still. At the precise
second I sat down, I perceived the whole episode
of stepping outside as a dream. It felt as if
I never left! I shook my head, hoping to dislodge
the error. Ted sensed my hysteria and calmed me down.
The clock whirred and my watch read two o'clock.
We must have indeed gone outside. How long?
I slumped against the wall. A pitcher of water
was passed around. I took a long, brain-refreshing
drink and remembered the flute, its shrill echoing
in the wooded valley. Yes, it was me, I thought,
in fear of the life-form whose cry of a thousand
frogs drove back the stars. It was me who brought
this water. But where is Writing Stick,
the Sokapaita?

In the summer of 1960 *rumor circulated*
throughout the Black Eagle Child Settlement
that "tiny unknown beings" were seen on the dirt
ridges overlooking the confluence of the Swanroot
and Iowa rivers. Ironically, the first people
to observe these little people were children
who were out for a walk. Of course,
there were skeptics, like the Presbyterian-convinced
tribal members who discredited these sightings as fantasy
induced by European mythology. But the other five beliefs
of the tribe merged as one—the first time—and their
respective leaders made a pilgrimage to the site
and gave blessings of tobacco and food, urging
the spirits not to frighten the very young.
There were no further manifestations afterward
of the finely clothed little people, but another
pilgrimage to the hillside for precautionary
reasons led to the strange discovery of a large
silver craft embedded in the brownish red sand.
No panic telephone calls were made to the police
or national guard. Instead, the five spiritual
leaders repeated the ritual and the craft
was never seen again.—from Severt Principal
Bear's diary, Parsons College, Fairfield, Iowa

"E ni ke e ka ta wi bya tti.
He is almost here," uttered the First Fire
Keeper from the kitchen. Who? I indicated with
raised eyebrows to Ted, forgetting quickly
whether these strange people were associated
with flying saucers. Ted motioned to the ceiling.
I jumped and nearly choked on my own spit when
the deer-masked entity entered the room.
His hooves made a hard clacking noise.
The nonchalant Deer Man stood ominously
with his varnished antlers glistening
in the dull electric light.

It had to be Writing Stick, shirtless
and outfitted in a spectacular costume.
I could not distinguish where the deer mask
was joined to the skin on his neck; it blended
perfectly. He looked like a stag standing up
on hind feet with the middle body of a human
in a woolen breechcloth. How he could maintain
his balance on deer hooves was incomprehensible.
Yet he did it. For a fat man he possessed
the controlled balance of a ballerina.
There had to be pain in the way the feet
were bound with toes pointed to the ground.
But the one item the medicine could not
disguise was the loose bridge of the deer's
long, hollow nose. Breathing still came hard
to the Sokapaita Indian. Using his bronze
shoulders he threw a tied gunnysack
to the floor in a loud thud. Remarkably,
the sack moved and began taking the shape
of a long-legged, calflike animal,
struggling to get up. The Idaho Potatoes
sack bucked and kicked. The mesh netting
parted, revealing the spotted markings
of a fawn. The floor surfaced and expanded
like a little earth when the skittish fawn
poked its head from the sack. It looked around
the room and stared at us. We found ourselves
flat on our backs against the drywall.
There were last-minute checks of the breathing
and heating apparatus attached to the space
suits. Before the rocket fired its engine
we nodded to each other with shaded helmets.

Our collective perspectives became concentric.
The Deer Man hopped on the floor with the agility
of a mountain goat and placed the fawn's sack
into another leather sack and filled it
with white sand, which was passed to him

by bucketloads. Once the fawn was smothered
in the grains of its origin, the executioner
slid down on his hooves like a skier and crashed
loudly into the kitchen. The First Fire Keeper
closed the door. I dared to look around, but
the globelike floor hid the others from view.
The ones I did see had their glazed pupils
transfixed on the lifeless sack near the ceiling.
On command the Green Thunder musicians floated
like dragonflies and merged where they first
sang and drummed. The songs were repeated,
and the sacks undid themselves; the strings
whirled out in furious motion, knocking out
the lightbulb. I heard the fine, shattered
glass slide down. Losing sense of direction
my thoughts transformed into a solitary
and powerless speck of dust. I was acutely
unaware of where I was, whether I was standing,
sitting, or upside down, until sparks shot out
sparingly in the darkness, enticing me to steer
my being toward it.

*"A tta i yo e a ski bya ya ni ne na ta ba ma
ne ko ti me to se ne ni wa.* When I first arrived
long ago I searched for a single human being.
*Ne ke ke ne ta tta i ne na Te te ba me qwe
a mi na ko na ka ma ni A na qwa ma ma to mo we ni.*
I knew then that Dark Circling Cloud
would readily accept the Star-praying ceremony.
*Sa na ka twi ba ki ni me ka wo tti ni a nwa tti ta
ko wi ye a.* It is very difficult to find
someone willing. *Tta na Te te ba me qwe
agwi tta qwa ne mo tti ni ke ko
ki be na me ko ki tti te a tti.
Ne ke ke ne ta ni.* But Dark Circling Cloud
was never reluctant in his endeavors,
especially when he made up his mind.

I know that for a fact. *E ni tta wa tti*
bya no ta wa ki ne ko te nwi a be ko te ki.
That is why I chose to approach him one night.

"*Ke nwe tti me ko tti ke bi ya ki ne to wi*
ki be na. For a long time we resided by
the riverside. *Ba ba me ke wa ki ma ni*
ne no te wa ki. Tta na ne be tti se ki a be na
me tti ki e bya ya ki. Many Indians walked by.
But we accidentally frightened them
in our descent. *Ki nwa tta a ta tti ye qwi*
i no ki a yo e tti na a me qwi Te te ba ma qwe
ta qwi ma a ki a ski ki a ki ke me nwi i ba
e me qwe ne mi ya ki e bi ko tti ya ki.
You, however, the number that you presently
are, as Dark Circling Cloud's kin, including
these young people, are kind for remembering us.
Ne ki me ko ma ni ta tti i tta i ya ko
ki ke te bi no ne be na ke no we tti . . .
For as long as you continue to do this,
you will receive our blessing . . ."

The shooting sparks had taken me above
to the human-sounding voice of the Fourth Star,
the one who remained to teach us the praying
ceremony: *A na qwa ma ne to wa,* the Star
that is God. He had lit the way for me;
He illuminated fully the philosophical
concepts found through the *na ta wi no ni,*
medicine. The asphyxiated fawn was you,
He said, fumbling in our own misguided
beliefs. We first had to be clear in
our thoughts before He could descend.
It did not matter if He was seen as Jesus
Christ—or anything else. The meteorite
was first and foremost a precious messenger.
Sitting on top of two empty sacks, the black
smoldering rock sat now in the center

of the warped floorboards, emitting its own
gentle light. A light which could easily
be looked at without discomfort or pain.
There was no one else present except me.
We were there alone, alone in the whole
universe. Me, a powerless speck of dust;
He, a powerful giver of medicine . . .

In the silence I began to hear confessions,
which were followed by intense and unabated
cries of anguish and grief. A desire to weep
with each confessor encompassed me. When I
gasped to catch my emotional outpouring,
the members reappeared one by one
in the order of their confessions.
At a young age, an eighth grader, I had never
felt so much guilt, so much burden. We
were truly a people in the middle of nowhere
encumbered with poverty and alcoholism.
Babies were hungry, and the old people
lived and died in their ragged but
cherished homes. One minute we were happy,
and the next we were hopelessly wedged
in an abyss of discontent. I saw Ted's
aunt, Louise, sitting on her knees next
to the Fourth Star and the blessing water.
Under her was a red woolen blanket
from the Amana Colonies. A prized but
costly item among ladies of the Settlement.
She sat extremely still and didn't blink
at the fiery sparks.

The medicine-chewer's wife, Mrs. Percy Jim,
began relating her vision: "I was transported
to a lush green valley full of apple orchards.
It was springtime, for the yellowjacket bees
were occupying themselves with the pink and white
blossoms. To smell the blossoms was pleasant.

But the *presence* I felt was even greater.
It was Him, strolling toward me in his
sandals and white robe. Our grandfather,
the one who counteracts evil, stroked my hair
with a silver comb and said that whatever ails
me would vanish." The vision didn't surprise me,
for it had been revealed to me that the Star God
was essentially the same as any other belief.
All Grandfathers were the same. Suddenly
a visiting Indian man from Wisconsin spoke:
"Your star came through the ceiling and hovered
over the young man in the jungle-designed shirt.
I don't know his name. Anyway, the song
he used made my contact possible." As a token
of his appreciation, the man from Wisconsin
took a large turquoise ring from his finger
and gave it to Norman Green Thunder,
the nocturnal singer.

The visions and confessions abruptly ceased;
only the sounds of people catching their
emotional breath and the exhaling of corn-husk
smoke remained. The sparks from the meteorite
soon died down, and once again we were in its realm
of nothingness. I wandered in my immature mind
and witnessed all before me that had to be done.
I said, "Yes," when a landless horizon formed
on my inner eyelids. At first it was like being
at the Why Cheer Theater; I was waiting for
the movie to start. Little did I know that *I* was
the theater. I allowed the vision to materialize.
Bright yellow dots gathered to create the sun.
Next, a clear blue sky appeared and large,
fluffy clouds covered the ocean surface
with shade. I found myself sitting
on a bone-white beach. Sprawled before me
was a chain of tropical islands. Above,
seagulls were flying along the perimeter

of the beach in search of food. Although
the foam-tipped waves rolled in from
a considerable distance, they nearly reached me.
The water enveloped my bare feet and the backs
of my legs. Behind me, the fronds of palm trees
were swishing in the warm draft. I was aghast
when desperate pleas in Indian rang out from
the tranquil ocean scenery. "*A se mi i ta ki!*
Help us!" I counted the bobbing heads
and arms of ten people swimming frantically.
A killer whale's giant tail rose and splashed behind
them as it dove into position for a strike. My eyes
became the lenses of binoculars and focused closely
on the helpless people. This was the selfish group
who had excluded Ted and me from the party plans.
"You're not a bastard, Edgar! Childish Bear!"
someone blurted out. Another pleaded,
"And Ted is no different than you—or us!"
It came to me right there and then that
we had been left out not because
of lack of money but through prejudice.
There were occasions Ted and I chipped in
for others. We were owed.

Buried in the sand beside me was a strawberry
soda. I pried the cap with my teeth and allowed
the icy foam to run down my chest.
"Edgar!" Ted exclaimed. "You're spilling
water on your shirt!" He wrestled the dipper
from my hand and put it back. As I had feared,
I had given myself in a version no one knew.
The congregation looked back down at the floor
when I straightened up. A woman, Mrs. Writing Stick,
asked me what happened. "I dreamed my school friends
were being chased by a whale in the ocean."
"You mean the boys who are asking to come
into the house for protection?"
From the kitchen I could hear several

representatives from the drinking party group
tell her husband they were being pursued
by a large *ma ka te ne ni wa,* black man.
Evidently, after hearing another party,
they had sunk his boat after using it
to ford the Iowa River.

But the black man saw them, swam across
the cold rapids, and chased them on foot
for four miles along the river.
"I can't believe that story,"
replied Mr. Writing Stick.
"I think you stole somebody's beer
and they are now after you. That is not
our doing. Now, you boys go on home
and leave us alone. We are praying.
No Negroes would be out tonight
fishing for walleye. Eh-eh!"
The boys persisted, but the First Fire Keeper
and the Deer Man were adamant they leave.
I could tell by their stuttering voices
they were telling the truth. Each one
peered mournfully into the living room
before leaving to face the killer whale.
"You spilled a lot of water on yourself,
Edgar," said Mrs. Writing Stick assuredly.
"But you're prophetic. And it is only
the beginning. The Fourth Star's medicine
has been good to you. He said so.
Didn't you hear Him?"

Throughout my ordeal I had been horrified.
But now, things were getting back to normal.
It was dawn outside: a beautiful day
was forthcoming. The day after Thanksgiving.
As the morning songs were being sung,
I kept reminding myself I was well.
Rationality came in increments, in fractions.

The process of my disembodiment reversed.
It had been twelve hours and one century.
The members yawned lazily and stretched their legs.
In the other rooms people—the appointed cooks
and their children—began to wake. The aroma
of coffee and frying eggs never smelled better.
Roused from his sleep, a little boy
still wrapped in a blanket was brought
into the room by his mother. Faithfully,
his older sister stood by with a birthday cake.
He was agitated at first when the six
candles were lit but smiled when we began
singing "Happy Birthday"—in English.
Although I felt a bit ridiculous I sang
along with enthusiasm.

Afterward, the elder Facepaint asked that
the blankets over the windows
be removed and the shades drawn.
I felt drained as the slow-motion daylight
entered the room in sheets of brilliance.
One source of light was replacing another
one which had been extraordinary and sacred.
Suddenly, the daylight hit us with such intensity
we ducked our heads. The harsh sunlight
revealed Ted's frazzled tennis shoes on
the edge of the altar. He had fallen
asleep, and he was lying down,
snoring away in oblivion.
Norman and Asa dismantled the drum
as fast as they could. With the last cord
and marble loosened, I felt immense gratitude
for the songs it had given me, to travel with,
to "see" with, and to laugh with. The brothers
each took out a piece of *A na qwa o ni* from
the kettle's iron cavity and swallowed it.
I grimaced in sympathy.
"We have made it," said the old man.

He was talking in a hoarse voice.
"Everyone take care of yourselves today.
Remember to stay for the two meals we will have."

During the course of his grandfather's final
prayer, Ted lazily rolled over on his belly
and released gas from his quivering behind.
The old man scowled but continued the prayer.
Everywhere were hand waves of people,
urging me to shake Ted. But Ted protested
and pushed my hand away. "Tell him what
happened," someone said. "That's the only
way he'll know." He gave way again.
I lowered my face to Ted's snoring face
and said, "Ted, do you realize
you have farted?" The war hero busted out
laughing, as did John Louis.

The congregation fought hard against
the urge of being humored by the antics
of their beloved grandson and nephew.
But the beautiful day had already begun.
It couldn't be helped; they joined in.
Ted warily looked up at me with one eye
and gave me a wink . . .

Alfred E.
Neuman
Was an
Arsonist

The hot and dry season came rolling in
that summer like a ghostly whirlwind upon
my return from college prep classes
for academically deprived minorities
in northeastern Iowa. Although
the uncomfortable Greyhound bus ride
still clung to my nostrils in the lingering
form of fuel exhaust, cigarettes, and the body
odor of long-distance travelers, my thoughts
were still entranced by the beauty of a farm
girl of German immigrant descent. I could still
feel the firm body of Mary Flewge—only three
hours earlier—pressing against me with her
hands hooked and still imprinted on my shoulders
when the rolling mass of particles engulfed me.
(This is where the story actually starts.)
I stood in the dust swirl kicked up
by a faded red-and-white 1956 Ford
after it landed on the gravel road.
It had literally flown across

the highway from Milkman Ridge.
Before being blinded I was able
to see a logo on its door of a plump,
smiling pig on skates and a checkered banner
in its front feet for Arbie's Pig Feeds.
In a state of shock, I stood at the northern
entrance, near Highway 30, of Black Eagle Child
with a taped-up suitcase and held my breath.
"Fucking assholes!" I cussed once the gravel
road came into view. As the car gained speed,
the passengers gave short war whoops; I thought
I almost recognized one voice but dismissed it,
for the person was away for Job Corps carpentry
training.

I picked up the suitcase and started
the long, winding walk up the western slope
of Ridge Road. I looked far up, making sure
the dangerous car hadn't turned around.
This was the last hill of our homeland.
Near the top I took a breather and gazed
southward and below to the vast desolate
stretch of corn and soybean fields.
Synchronous flocks of crows rose up
from their feeding and visiting to scout.
The incessant barking of distant neighborhood
dogs became clearer the higher I climbed.
Geographically, I preferred the rocky terrain
that surrounded Luther College and the community
of Decorah, Iowa. The air was surprisingly cooler,
the people more friendly, and the perspective
of land behind land was exemplary. The place,
I was told, where monolithic glaciers stopped
thousands of years ago, carving out the buttes
and deeply recessed valleys. How I wished
the theory had included Black Eagle Child.
Why didn't the Boy-Chief, who initiated

the historic purchase of our land, choose
to go further north? What made him stop here?

In Grandmother's voice I heard the answer:
"When the three goddesses manifested themselves
at Cutfoot Hill, it was a sign we were to reside here.
It is often related when an ancient hunter named
Dances Lead, Ni ka ne ka ta, was paddling along
a river with a deer carcass in his canoe,
his extraordinarily handsome features caught
the attention of two beautiful, long-haired
goddesses who lived deep in the heart
of the hills overlooking what is today
Rolling Head valley. They descended the hills
promptly and stood on the shore of the river
and called out. 'Come here,' they implored.
'Only for a moment.' Startled at first,
Dances Lead could only ponder the situation,
but he eventually went to them. He followed
the goddesses to a nearby valley where springs
served as the mystical doors of their underworld
abode. He had been chosen to visit and see where
the divinities lived. Here, in the underworld,
the spring weather was eternal, and everywhere
was the captivating reverberation of drums,
a sign of constant celebration and happiness.
When he informed the women of his wish to return,
they asked, 'Why can you not stay? There will be
people here one day, living on top.' He persuaded
them he should go. (In the years that followed,
for some reason or other, perhaps through
the cycle of a woman, the mystical spring door
was closed.) But the story of Dances Lead's
revelation lived and was passed on until
Black Eagle Child, the Boy-Chief, chose
the same wooded hills for his people."

I gathered there were many reasons why
the Boy-Chief chose on behalf of the tribe
to reside here in the middle of a state known
for its rich soil, crops, and resistance
to social change. But it wasn't what stretched
endlessly beyond the borders of the sanctuary
that mattered, it was the people themselves
and their cherished woodlands-oriented beliefs.
It was by a great plan that the Boy-Chief
heeded his grandfather's sagacious instructions
to head north. While there were yet pockets
of skeptics who believed the land was purchased
by the tribe collectively, the credit belonged
to the Boy-Chief and his grandfather.
"The day the tribe chose to foolishly abolish
their memory and wishes," Grandmother often
reminded, "was the outset of our piecemeal
demise." The Sacred First-Named Ones went first.
Today the hereditary chieftains were remembered
by the unentitled bureaucracy that held them
by the choke chain. These grandiose doings
were the last veils and reminders of cynicism.
The name systems remained but only for those
with self-serving interests. And the divine
progeny who came from earth's very creation
were cast aside—thanks to the white man's
equal decision-making process: suzerainty.
The beliefs were granted one hundred
more years to flourish and another
one hundred to subside . . .

Behind me, a dark green Volkswagen beeped
its horn from Highway 30 and scurried up
the hill. I made way, walked to the weedy edge
of the ditch, and looked back. From far away
the driver, a female, reached over
to the passenger's side and rolled down

the window in anticipation to talk.
This was the last person I ever expected
to see. "You want a ride home?"
asked the sensuous and sunglassed
Dolores Fox-King, the first and last
club president of the Limelighters.
Shortly after the Star-Medicine episode,
we dated for eighteen long months before
she graduated from Why Cheer with honors
and a scholarship to Morningside College.
She left me without saying good-bye.
As she was an intellectual four years my senior,
her departure was expected, but I was annoyed
by her noncommittal attitude. The chaos we went
through should have counted for something.
Of course, she saw obstacles I couldn't.
Her father was a retired sea merchant
of Italian ancestry, and her mother's
lineage was untraceable. She was, therefore,
considered an unenrolled Black Eagle. For me,
it didn't matter if our mutual fascination
drew the ire of the community. Dolores
was perhaps the only Settlement girl ever
to be captain of the football varsity
cheerleading squad. As long as I warmed
my round face inside her coat and over
her perfumed sweater, I was content.

Once my parents, Tony and Clotelde Bearchild,
decided to live together to respectfully
await my third brother, Dan, I was to be
their first conflict in adolescence.
They objected vehemently to the goings-on
of an eighth grader and a robust twelfth grader.
My incorrigibility didn't help, which was my way
of protesting. Next to the Cucumber Man I landed
on the front pages of the *Why Cheer News-Herald*:

"Bearchild was the youngest member of the BEC Settlement ordered by the court to be treated for alcoholism. On his return, he enrolled in school. Eight weeks later he was arrested for public intoxication and served 30 days in the county jail. He also served a 15-day sentence for malicious mischief in North Tama. Bearchild had loosened the town's symbol— a cast-iron winding staircase made in Czechoslovakia—from the sidewalk concrete . . ." Under the threat of permanent expulsion from the Why Cheer School District, many people rushed to the aid of a minor with accumulated jail and rehabilitation time. The state civil rights commission came to town, including senators, congressmen, and do-good dignitaries from Boston. Sadly, an area BIA director from Minneapolis died in a plane crash north of Gladwood after testifying at my hearing, which jeopardized operations of the tribal elementary school. One ugly thing after another occurred. Through it all was Dolores's consolation. When civic peace was made and filed away "as the rambunctious antics of a disturbed lad," my parents were still apprehensive about Dolores. They forbade me to wear her WCHS letter jacket, the one I wore at the hearings in defiance. Yet there was a lot to be said of our wild, disproportionate relationship. Obviously, "I learned," and I am sure Dolores used me for "experiments," so to speak. But she was also more than that; her obsessive notewriting led to my first awkward interest in the English language. Unfortunately, when my uncle Severt came home on break from Parsons College one day and found them

stuffed chronologically in his dresser,
he advised their incineration to clear space
for his *MAD* magazine collection.
I recalled his exact words when I objected:
"Don't question me, son, just do it.
If you want to read something worthwhile,
you're welcome to the Diary."
Containing more insight than Alfred E. Neuman,
the passages my uncle recorded in the Diary
would inspirit me just as equally as Dolores's
notes. In particular, there was one section
on "Unearthly Manifestations" which
had an inexorable effect on my dreams
and fantasies.

» «

My Supper with the Baileys: The Year of Realization

Ten years ago when I first mentioned the novel's central plot in public, Professor William Bailey laughed so hard he fell backward from the supper table, spilling a bowl of peanuts and a long-neck bottle of Leinenkugel's beer in the process. He was thoroughly amused with the premise of a midwestern colony of extraterrestrials in the guise of Scandinavians.

A second after his exaggerated dramatics, in mechaniclike precision, his wife and daughter, Louise and Rachel Bailey, joined in with their renditions of astonishment. But the laughter ended just as quickly as it began when I brought the microphone closer to my mouth and reluctantly exhaled the words: "I have a hundred-page draft ready for submission."

The Bailey women got up suddenly and hovered like doting hummingbirds, cleaning up the carpeted floor of the Constellations Lounge. Professor Bailey wrinkled his balding forehead grotesquely into folds of loose skin and twitched his mustache and precious sideburns, eyeing his graduate students to his left and right like a frightened gosling. Professor Bailey couldn't believe it; he brought the question-and-answer period for the English faculty to a complete halt.

"Damn, Principal Bear," he remarked sternly in his unusual state, "you're doing quite well with folktales. The noble Indian stuff is ideal for your talents! Why waste time on something so ludicrous? There may not be a market. Think about that, will you?"

The Bailey women vocally agreed as they simultaneously took dainty bites of pickled pork-snouts and blue cheese from the waiters' plates before passing them around.

I sat back on the crudely made antique chair and took a slow, deliberate drink of the popular Wisconsin beer, hoping a vacuumlike sound wouldn't be created by my insatiability. But just exactly as I feared, I sucked the bottle too much, and it wouldn't part from my lips. When the bottle was properly angled for release, a sound similar to that of a pair of healthy, amorous lips unlocking popped amid the bustling catering activity.

"Principal Bear, would you like dressing?" interjected Mrs. Bailey, stopping behind me in a buzz. She attempted to feign a response to the lustful sound by trying hard not to act overly distracted by our conversation, but she lost her focus and lapsed into a soporific condition. Her eyes turned white by rolling backward in their sockets. I could read her muddled mind: how is one supposed to react to bottle-sucking sounds?

Before I could respond to the professor and trying desperately not to gulp the beer or appear impolite to the obsequious attentions of the "Mrs.," their daughter shifted her obesity on the Viking chair and pressed her massive gut to the tabletop.

Hooolllllyyyy shit, Rachel's fat, I thought. She wobbled slightly in her tight-fitting Easter-blue dress. She was barely breathing due to the food that was still stuck in her esophagus from a previous meal. The nostrils of the pork-snouts squealed complainingly as she bit down on them while manually pushing the others back in.

"Yes, dressing will be fine," I said while composing mental notes: *they overfeed and overinflate their make-believe daughter, Rachel; and they are oversensitive to my detection of their mistakes.*

"What exactly do you mean to prove by writing such farfetched realities anyway?" inquired the professor again with refocused energy. "Severt, if the book bombs, think of what it will do to the first two books of tribal folktales: second or third printing may not occur."

"For Christ's sake, William," I returned, unaware I had accidentally addressed him on a first-name basis, "I am approaching my twentieth year in this torrid sojourn toward the twenty-first century. And I am steadily wearing down the gears I need to shift past the tales routine. If anything, the plot of Scandinavian aliens is merely an exercise in creative detachment. After years of flying-saucer sightings at Black Eagle Child, I am bringing them to life. That's all."

"In what capacity?" asked a curious student, who winced in pain from a swift, calculated kick under the table.

"The aliens research the biological and psychological makeup of a young American Indian writer," I replied while looking directly at the Baileys. "But something goes awry. They end up injecting him with life-altering chemicals. He basically becomes discontent with the role he was meant to have as a spiritual leader and discovers he has deep-rooted anxieties about becoming an anarchist. Such feelings, as you may have inferred, are not his."

» «

Every five years the Bailey family of Valhalla Valley, Iowa, invites me for a July evening supper. And the scenario is unchanging: the follow-up, check-up, analysis, and pathetic pretense to be human beings. Socially, they need me as much as I need them.

» «

In spite of the pleasure derived from my uncle's
bizarre diary passages, I still regretted setting
the artistically folded Fox-King notes ablaze,
not because of what they once meant but how
well they were written. They would begin
with the opening lyrics of popular rock-
and-roll songs, and there was always
a connecting theme to our own turmoil.

The most memorable was "Baby Love"
by the Supremes. Listening to Diana Ross
would forever remind me of the room given
and lost in the dresser for Alfred E. Neuman,
the cartoon character whose face was imprinted
in my cells as an arsonist.

"Do you want a ride or what?"
Dolores reminded me with a start. "Or are you
just going to stand in the heat and stare?"
I opened the door in embarrassment, threw
the bulky suitcase in the back among
a pile of disarranged books, and aimed
my sweaty spine to the bucket seat.
We didn't say a word until we turned onto
the main Settlement road and went downhill.
"Well, tell me, Edgar, how've you been?"
she intoned in an extra-soft voice.
"I've been all right," I answered.
"I just now got off the bus from Luther.
Trying to study for college classes."
"That's good," she said with a wide smile.
"Myself, I've got two years left. I tested out
of my sophomore year. Lucky, huh?"
"Yeah," I said as I examined her
in an askance kind of way. (Indians
rarely looked directly at one another,
particularly old paramours.
It was deemed a sign of weakness,
a stupid unwillingness to accept
incredible odds.) She hadn't changed much.
Only her wavy, light brown hair had grown
longer; it blew into the tight corners
of her glossy mouth. The bright maroon
shirt lit up her bronze-colored face,
and her white jeans accented her slender
but graceful hips and thighs. Her oriental-like

visage was stunning as usual, and her small
physique was held in balance by her firm
breasts. Unlike most women on the Settlement,
her eyebrows were thick and pleasantly set
at an angle toward her temples, like her eyes.
Strangely, the glint of an imitation diamond-
studded crucifix dangling from the rearview mirror
dotted her rouged cheeks.

She knowingly downshifted with ease
by the pine trees near my grandmother's
and lifted her fuzzy eyebrows above
the sunglasses. "Where do you want to go?"
I finally relaxed and crooned,
"Home, Dolores, home."
She reached over and lightly touched
my hand. "I'm sorry for all that I've
put you through, Edgar. I hope we can remain
friends. I've been reading your work in
the *Black Eagle Child Quarterly*
and I think it's wonderful. But do you
think people understand your spaceship
poems?" I got out of the car and ignored
the question. There were other things
I wanted to say as I stood looking in
with elbows on the door and car top.
I dearly wanted to tell her my interest
in writing was attributable to her memorable
notes—and my uncle's diary. Trouble was,
having never been taught to express appreciation,
I couldn't bring myself to formulate anything
that would make sense without sounding sick.
When the plump Arbie's pig sped by again
with its horn blaring, a proposal
for an assignation was about to rise
from my dry lips. Perhaps sensing this,
Dolores Fox-King took advantage

of the noisy pig, shifted to first
with aplomb, and graciously bid me
farewell.

»«

It was the bright reflection
of the Greyhound's large front window
which initially attracted the driver's
attention to the brown valley
and busy highway, one-third of a mile
below. The two passengers—a half-
blond, muscular young man about eighteen
and a thin, attractive girl—were engrossed
in conversation about the previous night's
events when the driver noticed the bus slow
down and prepare to stop on the shoulder
of the junction. The driver reached under
the worn wheel and groped drunkenly between
his legs. He found the copper strands near
the paint-chipped column and brought them
together to kick the aged engine to life.
He released the clutch, sending a barrage
of rocks to the curious cows who had lined up
by the fence to watch and listen.
"What's up," voiced the young muscular man.
The driver laughed sardonically and applied
weight on the gas pedal. "Got to see who's
getting off." The sun's glare shot into
the driver's tender vision. With the alcohol
wearing off, a pain throbbed monotonously
in one temple. The two companions, Junior
and Charlotte, sunk into the exposed seat
padding and held on. Due to the noisy,
idling engine of the bus, the unboarding
passenger couldn't hear the rattling Ford.
The bus driver did, however. He quickly shut
the baggage compartment, trotted back

to the air-conditioned safety of the bus,
and sped away. The hungover driver still
couldn't recognize the bus rider.
"Christ! Watch it! There's cars coming!"
screamed Charlotte in the back seat.
The driver acknowledged the dire situation
by slamming the brakes and soon remembered
severing the line on a stump on an early
morning joyride through a farm pasture.
In a split second the driver had to decide
to either ditch the heap and risk injury
to himself and his occupants or accelerate
in hopes of beating the opposing traffic
to the junction. He opted to accelerate
and mumbled a prayer for the bald tires.
And what about the bus rider now running
across the highway? He'd have to be sacrificed
for the lives of three. He arched his back,
straightened his numb leg, and stood on the pedal,
but nothing happened. They barely reached
the stop sign two car paces ahead of oncoming
traffic and leaped over the highway,
landing right next to the unknown subject.
Before the dust exploded and blurred sight
in the rearview mirror, Ted Facepaint
recognized his longtime friend, Ka ka to,
looking at the car door. And Charlotte
turned around and caught a glimpse of the round-
faced, white-shirted Indian with the suitcase.
"Son of a bitch!" yelled Ted, "it's Ka ka to."
"Ka ka who?" echoed the two passengers.
The carburetor unjammed, propelling the Ford
up the slope like a rocket.

The Introduction of Grape Jell-O

》《》《》《》《》《》《》《》《》《》《》《》《》《》《》《》《》《》《

Grandmother or Nokomis,
who was cooking in the shack outside,
was delighted to see me once she recognized me.
She squinted at me from a distance,
she explained, but her eyesight as usual failed her.
"*We ne a ya bi na bye tti bo si wa ni?*
Agwi ka ski ne na wa ki ni.
Who was that you were riding with?
I couldn't recognize them."
"*A i ma-o tti se ma ni,*
Ti ti wa i qwe wa. Blue Jay Woman's granddaughter,"
I answered, hoping the association was correct.
"*Oooooohhhnn, ni ke ke ne ma we na.*
Oh, as if I will readily know who she is."
Turning over the frybread in the boiling
grease of the skillet, she sighed with
resignation of how poor her knowledge
of Settlement residents was.

I deliberately stood in the blue smoke
and savored the aroma of hot food on a hot summer day.

58

The brilliant white clouds were always perfect
from this angle deep in the wooded valley
as they floated lazily to the east from the west.
The clouds hugged the roundness of the landscape
so much that a convex perspective was given
to whoever looked up. Such a sight, I thought,
would make me forget about Dolores—and the passion?
Bullshit. I tore off a piece of golden frybread,
threw it into my mouth, and inhaled desperately
until it cooled off. Considering we didn't have
a refrigerator, all meals on uncomfortable
humid days were prepared outside under
the familiar shade of a thorn tree.
There would be sticky rice with beef, maple
syrup, and green tea made with cool pump
water today. Nokomis spoke of plans
to accompany my parents on their
travel to Pine Ridge, South Dakota,
for an Oglala Sioux Sun Dance and Pow-wow.
This news took me by surprise;
it wouldn't be much of a homecoming.
She was quite anxious about the prospect
of travel and seeing *A tta a ki* pierce
themselves. "You and your uncle will be home
alone, so watch each other carefully. By day's end
the clan ceremonies will be complete,
and then they will resume this fall at the last
sound of thunder, the Kingfisher's tail."
Talk like this about fall seemed ages away.
I knew Sturgeon would be hunted (or purchased
at the Des Moines Fish Market); the Ancient Bearcap
would be placed on a flagpole, looking out
symbolically for traditional enemies; the elusive
but protective Hummingbird would be remembered
by war veterans: the Fox-Kings would listen
to the wild but startling dreams of young men;
the Beaver would greet all those humans and animals

who benefited by its world-making abilities:
and the Excluded Ones would repeat their prayers
for penitence.

The summer ceremonies were a binding reality
to the clans of Black Eagle Child;
they held everyone by their hearts,
and their reenactment assured passage
for another season, provided there
were minor gatherings as spiritual
reinforcement in the interim. But once
they ceased and the weather developed to dark
clouds, bringing icy rain, snow, and general
hardship, the bickering and verbal backstabbing
started. With the gradual acceptance of modern
change, fate dictated we would lose
some aspects of our multifarious religion.
We never accepted it, however.
We led on proudly on the exterior,
never quite knowing the masks
of our fabulous lives were transparent,
revealing to one and all that our insides
were in disarray. Change was unavoidable;
yet we blamed ourselves for creating new mythology
and rituals from the last traces of the old stories,
our grandfathers' ways. There were critics on how
proper ceremonies should be executed. Possessing
various interpretations of the prayers, songs,
and rituals was inevitable. But exactness
was touted as the only form of communion.
Since parts of ourselves perished slowly
with those who "ceased to see the daylight,"
our keepers emulated the customs in
a languishing way. And disagreements
were becoming frequent among our elders.
We each held them in such high esteem that
we could never doubt their memories,

even if they forgot our own names.
We were advised of adaptations of the sacred.
"He or she shouldn't have made such and such
a rule. It is his or her own and not from the past,"
was the most pervasive criticism.
They, the clans, never gave each other
credit for trying; it had to be the exact
way or else it was a dismal failure.
I stood and witnessed all in awe.
When blame was no longer applicable
within the structure, fathers openly wept
during their prayers; they brought news
of insubordinate sons, the next leaders,
to the masses. Being young I could not ascertain
what was wrong or right, whether I as a son
was responsible for fate itself. To me,
the Spirits were ever-present regardless
of ceremony. They and no one else decided.
Could they not forgive? Or was that a Western
concept? It had to be, thanks to Bible school
I attended for three years as a child
under Grandmother's encouragement.
I was told Jesus Christ will always
wait and forgive and forget one's misgivings.
But George Whirlwind Boy said otherwise:
"Our Principal Religion can never wait
until you, yourself, decide the time is appropriate
to believe and pray. That type of attitude
is almost disrespectful. It has to be
a lifetime commitment, not a momentary whim
like that of the white man."
Whirlwind Boy's stinging comment would surface
in my thoughts and hit me like sleet.
Because of my educational interests,
he knew I was remiss in clan obligations.
My rationale was taken from Earl Youthman,
the Cantaloupe Terrorist's younger brother,

who had given up on life after learning
a useless bakery trade from Haskell
Indian College—and Viet Nam:
"*A wi ta i ni i ne ne ta qwa te sa ni ke tti
ma ma to mo ne ni wi ya ni.* Perhaps it was not
predetermined that I be an accomplished man
of religion. My goal in bread and antagonism
has passed." But I could never quote those
very words to Whirlwind Boy, who exemplified
what Earl and I should be. The old arthritic
man with face spasms had a way of humiliating
anyone, reminding them of duty. When exactly
did my apprehension and doubt begin?

In my past I rode a small bus to the mission
on Sundays for "reading lessons."
That was the premise, anyway.
But the book we studied was a musty-smelling
Bible. Not only did my reading and spelling
skills improve, I was also introduced to grape Jell-O
with peaches. My cousin, Mae Lynn Water Runner,
and I were fascinated by the suspended peaches,
and we took pleasure in scooping our way
down to them. Afterward we would wash
the Jell-O and fruit down with chilled milk.
We eagerly looked forward to Sundays
to indulge in this rare delicacy.
The things we would do for it
bordered on the extraordinary.
One Christmas we willingly played the parts
of Joseph and Mary at the Weeping Willow
Elementary School. I wore a fake beard with a towel
as a turban, and Mae Lynn wore a long sheet.
Our child, the baby Christ, was a huge
and grotesque plastic doll with blue
rolling eyes. We walked down the aisle hand
in hand with tribal members on either side

smiling at us in embarrassment. We didn't mind,
though, not when there was the promise of dessert.
We turned around on cue at the free-throw line
and recited our lines without the slightest fear.

Whether it was images of the desert
illuminated by a glowing star that signaled
the birth of Christ or the names
we possessed that had a direct correlation
to stories of how we came to be and how
the Creators determined what roles our clans
would play—to serve or be served in ritual
(or even society)—it ostensibly came from
a time I could only imagine.
Nokomis respected both beliefs, unlike
Whirlwind Boy. She depended on both during
World War II. "To believe in two, three,
or even four is by far a better means to pray.
Combined, the religions brought your uncles
back from the Germans and Japanese."

Grandmother and I sat down on a tablecloth
under the towering thorn tree. I couldn't wait
to dip the golden frybread into the small wooden bowl
containing syrup my parents made that spring.
Later we watched all the cars drive out from
the last doings of summer. Some families
left by foot and talked merrily among themselves.
The totems had been fed and appeased—
for now. "Our beings are essentially theirs,"
Nokomis had instructed. People who represented
different clans scattered to all directions,
taking with them parts of devotion.
It had been a long day for everyone
on the spiritual—or concrete—highway.
I thought of the white girl in northeastern
Iowa, and I then winced in pain for Dolores.

Like mud-smeared creatures from the Black Lagoon,
my brother, Al, and Mateo Water Runner
emerged from the creek in high spirits,
breaking the stillness. They had a glass jar
full of crayfish and frogs being tortured.
The boys lay down in the high grass,
propped their muddy faces on their palms
and elbows, and debated whether they
should use the bait this evening or tomorrow
morning. "Al," I interrupted, "you better go
because you are leaving for South Dakota
tonight." In the distance a car revving
its rattling engine caught my attention,
and I forgot about fishing in midsentence.
By the pine trees I spotted the dangerous car.
The occupants had gotten out with sacks
and were walking doggedly up the hill.
Before entering the pines, the driver stopped
and waved at us to go over; the other two—
one with dust-colored hair and the other
with a cowboy hat—kept going.
"I think Three-Speed's calling you,"
said Al with a weird mud-crusted grin.
"He's been mizzed all week, cruising around
with two Ontarios." To finally learn
the identity of the person who nearly
killed me by the junction surprised me.
"Pisshead Ted, huh?"
"That's him all right. He's been driving like
Indianapolis Isabel. She must've gave him
some pointers. I guess yesterday they were
making doughnuts at the baseball diamond."
I asked for confirmation again.
"Yeah. His companions come from Claer.
They say they know you from the time
you broke the town's famous winding steps.
The girl is kinda pretty, but she dresses like
a boy. Long loose shirt, cowboy hat,

and jeans tucked into her boots."
"Ontarios in Claer?"
"Don't ask me how they got there."

Grandmother had been listening in
on our conversation in English.
Having worked fifteen years at the Why Cheer
Laundry and Dry Cleaners, she had picked
up enough to know the basic topic.
"Probably a breakaway group," she said.
"Some of the northern tribes leave
their homes and move to the cities,
going far away as possible,
following other tributaries,
leaving everything behind them—
their language, their stories,
their religion, and relatives.
We have them, too. But at least ours
return now and again. Either way,
alive or dead, they always come home "

» «

"Hot time, summer in the city,
back of my neck getting dirty and gritty.
Been down, isn't it a pity?
Doesn't seem to be a shadow
in the city," crooned the Lovin' Spoonful
from the Arbie's Pig Feeds car radio.
"All around people looking half-dead
walking on the sidewalk hotter than
a matchhead.
Every night it's a different world
go out and find a girl.
Come on, come on, and dance all night . . ."

Ted took a long unnecessary drink
of warm foamy beer and lay down on

the sharp pine needles. He concurred
wholly that the heat and humidity were awful.
This was no city by any means, but
there were similarities. Even the pines
were not excluded from stale air.
If he could sleep an hour or two
he would be in reasonable shape to visit
Edgar. What would he say? Hey man,
sorry I almost ran you down?
No, he'd explain about the jammed
carburetor and the brakes going out.
Damn, that was close to manslaughter!
Junior and Charlotte sat down and began
questioning where all the cars were coming
from. There was a mass exodus from the last
doings. Thick clouds of dust rose from
the gravel road below and floated into the pines.
Ted didn't answer; he couldn't without lying.
Instead he faked a body twitch and a snore.
He was good at that, as Edgar would easily attest.
Ted lay still, finding solace in the white
scorching light that flashed on the walls
of his parched brain lining. Once the strobe-
light effect settled into a domestic scene,
a place where he should be, a living room
with family members gathered around conversing
pleasantly, his stomach gurgled, bubbles
traveled up and down his intestines.
His last thought was, boy, I hope I don't . . .
"What's the matter now?" asked Aunt Louise.
"Hey, *to ki no*, wake up. Seriously."

» «

Junior smiled at his boyish-looking
sister and wondered if she still wanted
to meet the Stair-Destroyer.

A ko si ya bi-Ne tti wa na tti to ta,
as Ted had comically translated.
Being the second generation of Ontarios
who resided in the state, Junior
could almost understand Facepaint's
language. His grandfather used to say
their Pinelodge Lake dialect was remarkably
identical to Black Eagle Child's. That each
tribe claimed each other as its breakaway
tribe. The stories were similar: a Nation
under siege, sneaking away in the night
right past the enemy only to have the hands
unclasp and forever lose a people.
Junior wished he could learn more, NOW,
instantaneously. Not knowing your people's
language, in the harshest consequence, meant
excommunication from God. "Language is much
like a body limb," his grandfather had said.
"A physical facet that speaks for the soul,
the all-important shadow in its privileged
journey." Any decision made by the incomplete,
nonspeaking person to not learn the first
language was taken as unkindness to Being.
These were the words you were fed to give back
to the world. "Without them," Grandfather warned,
"you hobble and drag yourself about in the manner
of an invalid, propelling yourself on hands
and scraped knuckles, a half-person.
People will mistake you as a fallen log
on the road of linguistics, for your hollow
half-frame will fit perfectly over a tree stump."
You are there for all the speaking people
to see, a symbol of Getting Nowhere.

Junior was indeed a speechless stump
beside a road with no one near to remove him,
no one willing to carry him home. His grandfather

and remaining family members left Pinelodge
Lake of Canada in the spring of 1916 to escape
the enmity of a notorious medicine man.
A love affair started by his grandfather
had gone wrong, sentencing his parents
and him and all the other relatives—
fifteen in total—to exile in the American
heartland. There could be no going back ever,
the story went, for when the band saw
the mysterious deaths of so many of its
gentle people, Pinelodge Lake voted
to dissolve itself and join nearby tribes
to forestall further sorcery. Unfortunately,
the curse was unbending, and it took the shape
of a supernatural beacon, illuminating the night
in search of Grandfather's accomplices.
If the Blue Light failed to find any,
it took the guise of a traveler on foot
or crutch intent on a "find to destroy."
The stories his grandfather told
were incredible. Fleeing from "witchcraft
gone crazy," the family canoed across
"a monstrous lake" with the medicine man's
daughter guiding the way over the tumultuous
waves. And in her last days at Pinelodge
the grandmother Junior would never know
had surprisingly forgiven Grandfather
for falling in love with the medicine man's
only daughter and conceiving a child with her.
But the old man who was knowledgeable
with the dark ways of the forest didn't.
He transformed himself into a Rat who scratched
weird pictures on the door of his tormentor.
Next he became a trespasser in Grandmother's
dream. When she failed to decipher the code,
she stopped breathing. For four successive
nights after her death the Rat pranced around

the house and stood on its hind legs, howling
like a victorious wolf, its small teeth
gleaming in the moonlight.

Later, the old vengeful man conjured
accidents so inexplicable no one questioned them,
including the dumbstruck Readers of Rat Messages.
Trouble was, the accidents began taking life,
anyone's, child or adult, who was related
to Grandfather: trees fell down on windless days,
crushing nieces and nephews out for a walk along
the lake; knives and forks levitated by themselves
and attacked an elderly aunt and uncle,
maiming them savagely; while spearing
for fish through the ice two cousins shot
each other for no apparent reason;
and the disastrous events went on,
taking innocent lives and bystanders.
The Canadian authorities were baffled
"at a village that destroyed itself."
It was as if the earth opened up,
his grandfather would say,
taking those closest to him.
Fifty-two beloved kin and twenty-one
bystanders died by the winter of 1915.
Everything he was told about family history
he believed, never questioning what appeared
in his judgment as subtle differences
and discrepancies. "A part of you belongs
to the medicine man's daughter," Grandfather
once revealed under delirium. "She was your true
grandmother, the one who guided the canoes."
This statement was quickly denied by his mother,
which did little to placate his questions.
Just then, high above, a breeze blew
through the cluttered pines, and the treetops
crashed ominously into each other. Junior

grew afraid of the coming night. He combed
his sweaty hair and looked at his dark-skinned
sister before lying down.

» «

Charlotte adjusted the brim of her straw
hat downward and spit casually onto
the forest floor. She was now more interested
in meeting Ted's friend, the round-faced Stair-
Destroyer. She gazed past the mass of her half-
brother, past the clustered pines,
fixing her sight on people
the Stair-Destroyer was having supper
with in the far clearing under the tree.

There was something intriguing about
a white-shirted Indian unboarding a bus
on a dusty afternoon, even if he
had nearly been squashed by the heap.
She turned to Ted and watched in amusement
at his twitching body. He was overdoing it,
for he kept time with the blaring car radio.
Anytime now, she surmised, he would fall
asleep, and the shiny, oil-colored flies
seeking shelter from the sudden temperature
change could climb into the mop on his head
and along the rims of his extra-large nostrils,
waking him. Ted's grasp on the beer became weak
instead and gave way, spilling the contents
into the needles. Sensing defenses were down,
the flies and mosquitoes congregated
and had their way with Indianapolis Isabel's
eager protégé. Out of initial concern
Charlotte swatted some away,
but when her company of two began snoring,
a sign for the sacrifices to begin, she gave up.
Even in sleep Junior and Ted sang to each other.

The buzzing and whining of excited insects
grew louder as the feast turned into an orgy.
She could only swat away so many. She studied
the mosquitoes bloating themselves and flying away
with heavy loads of red liquid. As the breeze
picked up, the clouds darkened wildly.
She reflected on the past week with a smile,
the characters Ted introduced her to:
Cucumber Man and Muskrat Bob;
Isabel the Speedster (or Spinster
as Ted called her) who hovered over them
like an overprotective mother; and the woman
who could have been Junior's twin sister,
"wicked Lorna." They were friendly people,
Indians like her, but their homes
and the lives they led were run-down.
Except for the few trips she made
with her parents to northern Minnesota,
going back to the first Indian-owned farm
her grandfather managed, she had never met
other Indians. Not even her extended family
of exiles who were split apart throughout
the hinterland.

She wondered if her aunt Celeste
would drive down from Claer again
with money—and clothes that were her own.
The rock band called the Doors began singing
on the radio: "Come on, baby, light my fire.
Try to set the night on fire . . ."
She pulled her boots back on and slid
down the hill to turn the ignition off.
Somewhere not far away she could hear
the approaching vibration of a thunderstorm.
She reached for the steering wheel and banged
the horn frantically. All that came was a weak
gasp and then a sputter. "Just like Facepaint!"
she shouted at the inanimate car, kicking

the chrome bumper. In the distorted
reflection of the bumper Charlotte saw
herself being covered with the first
few drops of rain mixed with fine
yellow dust.

The
Precociousness
of Charlotte

My uncle, Winston Principal Bear, and I said
good-bye to my parents and grandmother
as they got into the station wagon
by the driveway. The travel to South Dakota
would be easy on the radiator and the travelers,
for the night began to sprinkle
with light rain. The smell of dust
began to rise from the earth as raindrops
plopped around us. The low rumbling of thunder
to the west was a good sign for my father
that the Holy Grandfathers were appeased;
he walked out to the potato field
and released an offering of tobacco
with a voice that was raspy and tired
from the day-long singing. Right then
the torrential showers began.
The ropes on the carrier were hastily
fastened once more by overly cautious father,
aggravating my mother and Al. As lightning shot
forth from the clouds behind the pine trees,
the station wagon slowly maneuvered out

of the muddy driveway and became lost
in the downpour.

Before setting out on our own toward Why Cheer,
Winston and I sat in the kerosene-darkened
kitchen and quietly ate the last of the rice.
We listened to the indecisive but welcome
rain. Getting rides to town was relatively easy
on Friday nights. Since there was little else
to do except stay home, people went after
groceries, others dropped their children
at the theater, and some preferred to "cool
off" at Bender's or Weasel's tavern—
two places whose names became synonymous
with establishments that catered to an
undesirable BEC element. Winston left
first around 8 P.M., and I followed
shortly behind the storm's front.

Halfway to town a familiar-sounding car stopped
behind me and proceeded to trail me for about
fifty yards. I knew it was Ted and his companions.
The car peeled out on the slick surface
of the highway and braked beside me.
"*Ta te bi?* Where to?" he shouted over
the intrusive muffler and rattling rings.
"*O te we ne ki me te ne ta qwi.* To town obviously."
"*Ka tti bo si no we tta hay.*
Then why don't you get in."
Ted stuck his hand out the window
and shook my hand vigorously.
"*A tto wi o tti na wi. Ba na tti ke
no wi ma ma ni sqwa te mi.* On the other
side. This door is broken."
In the exhaust of the muffler,
together with rising mist from the highway,
the door with the friendly, roller-skating
pig was swung open by a sleepy-looking

74

pale young man. He greeted me with an overly
strong handshake and leaned forward on his seat.
I crawled past the frazzled seat and situated myself
beside a young, thin-framed girl who was able
to acknowledge me with her gleaming eyes
and a masculine nod of her straw hat
before the interior light went out.
I shuffled my feet on the floor until
I found a spot free of empty Howard's
shoestring potatoes and Leinenkugel's beer.

The city lights of Why Cheer soon came into view
over the hill beside the fashionable Indian Acres
country club. (This was a retreat where upper-
middle-class whites could go to be by themselves,
free from further association with the poor whites
and Indians, for we didn't play golf—at least not
yet.) Even with the windows open and the fresh
scent of a manicured golf course green,
the stale odor of cigarettes and spilled beer
stifled me. Ted and I tried to converse,
but the muffler kept it at a minimum.
Once in town, entrenched between the rows
of fine neighborhood housing, the muffler
roared louder. We stopped three blocks
from the shopping district and picked up
another passenger—by accident:
Greg Grassleggings, *We be si*, the
Mentally Deranged One, as he was
known by all, jumped in the front seat.
Considering he had never been caught
for crimes he supposedly committed
on his daughters, he was in a disarmingly
joyful mood and talked loud about the rain,
its apparent cleansing effect.
Before he got out in front of Bender's,
he inquired if we needed anything.
Ted gave him six dollars for a case

of long necks and two extra dollars
for taking it out to the railroad depot.
After we picked up the case behind
the crossing signals, we headed back out.
We half-expected a pursuit by the Twintown
cops with sirens wailing and red lights
flashing. Ted speculated they might
have been on a coffee break then,
polishing their billy clubs to
a black sheen in anticipation.

We parked at the tribal fairgrounds
beside the bleachers and opened the beer.
When Ted began introducing me formally to Junior
and Charlotte a group of young people approached.
We greeted them without knowing who they were.
They were girls, teenagers, perhaps on their
first night out: "escapees" meant flashlights
and interrogation from parents at some point
in the night. A drizzle started up, which
riled the young people. They stood patiently
until a brave husky-throated girl asked
for a handful of cigarettes. Being a gentleman
Ted obliged. Once the smoke was divided the group
scurried away. I thought I recognized the voices
of the Foxchild, Red Boy, Grassleggings, and Fox
girls but couldn't be 100 percent sure.
"Strange," I said. "That one girl's voice
sounded like a boy's changing to manhood.
Who is she?" Ted let out a long sigh indicating
he didn't know. Later on he said, "*I ni ye to ki
e we bi ba tti to i ya qwi.* The time for us to be
old men must be here." He was right; it seemed
the night crowd was getting younger and younger.
Of course, it began with us as well.
My grandmother's prophecy came to mind.
"*No ko me se ma a tti mo wa be ka bo ti
e no we ya tti a tta wa i ne no te wa ki:*

76

na i na wa bi mi ke ti wa tti a ski ki a ki
a be no a ki i ni bi ni we bi a qwi ka mi ka ki.
My grandmother tells sometimes what our
forefathers used to say: when lovemaking
begins with the young people, children,
the demise of earth will begin."

Ted turned on the single headlight and wipers
and pretended to strain for a look.
"*A sa mi wi na ni.* That's too much."
"I know," I said, breaking into English
for the benefit of the Ontarios.
I was going to translate what I had just said,
but Ted sensed my plans and cut me off.
"*E ye bi me a tti mo wa ni te bi ke me ko*
a ski ki wa sqwe se a wi ta bi ma ta.
Before you say anything, the girl you
are sitting with is quite young."
"*Ohhn, ke te na?* Oh, is that so?"
"*Ke na ta we ne me kwa ke e yi ki.*
And she also desires you."
"*Ke ne tti ma a be be tte tti.*
You are such a liar."
"*A qwi ma. Na i na i me ko*
e ka ta wi ta kwa o ne na ki tte bi
be ki ski na na to ttte wa we ne i
wa ne ni. No. From the time we almost
ran you over this morning, she has been
asking persistently who you are."
"*Ke swi be bo ne ya bi a bi na?*
How old is she, anyway?"
"*Ne swi ne si we tta me qwa. Ke ke bye*
a no ni. Thirteen, I believe. And underline that."
"*Bi bo ki te be wa ne te bwa to na ka*
tte na ke ne tti me tti ki. If you didn't have
a hole in your head I'd believe you, but you are
such a circumcised individual."
Junior and Charlotte who had been silent

since the introductions laughed out loud,
obviously understanding what *me tti ki ta* meant.
The gentle tapping of rain on the car,
our disjointed laughs, and the rounds
continued until cars began circling
the grounds. To avoid angry parents
we drove to the edge of the Iowa River
and risked getting stuck in the mud.

Later, around midnight, we made another run
to town, stopping first at the Twintown Hotel
to meet our companions' aunt. We then pooled
our money and ordered some more from Grassleggings
and cruised the farmlands south of the Settlement.
The deafening muffler isolated Charlotte
and myself from Ted and Junior. They chattered
away in indiscernible talk. There were many
questions I had for Ted regarding his health
and future, but that would have to wait.
Judging by his role as tour guide
and chauffeur, any serious discussions
I had would wash away in the rain,
flowing with the trash to the sidewalk
gutters of the brick hotel. He was enamored
by the Ontarios who were depending on him
for entertainment—BEC style.
We would bullshit another time.
Although we were together as Indians
in the crude automobile and throughout
the country—related in dialects and customs—
we were like the rural farmsteads separated
from each other by infinite miles.
That was a frightening reality.
Being compartmentalized but always
being apart. I began talking to Charlotte
in earnest. In spite of her youth, I became
captivated by her precociousness. It could
have been the day, Ted's complacency,

or even the idea of being displaced.
She had profound thoughts, and she knew
the night was temporary. "Including you,
Stair-Destroyer," she said assuredly.
Her appearance and attitude seemed
more mature after the hotel stop.
Realizing the situation could turn
irresistible we sat face to face.
My initial qualms about Charlotte
disintegrated in the paralyzing odor
of her aunt's perfume and shampoo.
Ted, who had been spying through
the rearview mirror, shouted,
"*Wah! Ni ke ba ko a so wa ni!*
Uh-oh! You will surely be jailed now!"
Junior, not knowing any other word,
joined in. "*Me tti ki ta! Me tti ki ta!*"
We burst out in profane laughter,
and the glimmering lights of the farms
shot past the open windows like
singular frames of a Coronet film.
The car careened from the gravel road back
to old Lincoln Highway 30 and headed toward
the Settlement. Our heads rocked as the direction
of travel abruptly changed. And I had a grin as big
as that of the roller-skating pig . . .

Before Ted excused himself to join
the round dance singing, Junior followed
him everywhere over the rain-drenched fairgrounds. They walked from car to car and shelter
to shelter, meeting and talking briefly
with people whose names he'd never
remember, much less recall their dimly lit
night-crowd faces. They were friendly, though.
He shook many hands. Inside what was once
a remnant of an exhibit hall a group of men
with female accompaniment were singing away on

an overturned trash barrel. The building
amplified the songs that were thrown out
one right after another. As the enticing
music grew louder, tightly huddled packs
of young women strolled by, ghost-town
beauties who had been hiding all week
from the unbearable heat and humidity.
"Take your pick," Ted had advised earlier.
"They're so tired of us around here,
growing up with them and so forth,
that visitors like you are prized
acquisitions—even if they are nearly
blond, Blondie!" Yes, Junior thought,
it would be good to be with someone
other than Isabel and Lorna tonight.
They were good friends, sure, but
the wine made them hang on to his arms
and thighs with their bodies. He secretly
hoped they wouldn't meet up with them,
including Muskrat Bob and the Cucumber Man.
They would spoil his chances permanently.
He crossed his fingers and listened
to the drumming.

Suddenly from behind, the husky-throated girl
asked Junior for more cigarettes. Somewhat
startled, he turned around. She stood
with her jittery friends in the darkness.
Digging for Kools in his wet shirt pocket
Junior asked, "Didn't your parents find you?"
"No, of course not," said the girl,
lurching forward to accept the smoke he
was dolling out one by one. "We wouldn't
be here." Her reply was reinforced by
a throe of giggles. She was strong-willed,
unafraid, and impressive.
"What's your name anyway? *Qwe tte?*

Or could it be Lauren Bacall?"
The question made her friends reel.
"Well, it isn't *little girl*," she countered
while pretending to fumble with the book-matches.
"And Lauren Back-all, who in the hell is she?
Your mom?" Once the cig was lit she turned
around and gave the others a light or a puff.
"If you must know, my name is Brook. Brook
Grassleggings." Junior tried to get a good
look at the daughter of the bootlegger man.
"Lauren Bacall is a famous Hollywood movie
star," he answered, being very careful
of enunciation. "Well, a while back
she was." Brook leaned dramatically
on one hip and with one hand cupped
the elbow of the arm that held the Kool.
She took a drag and lifted up her chin
in a cloud of smoke. "I wouldn't know
any old-timers, silly." Junior admired
the wit of the long-legged and tempestuous
maiden. "The reason I mention her," he said
above the laughter, "is your voice. You sound
just like her."

As if by signal Brook was grabbed by
the shirttail and dragged backward
to the entrance. There the girls whispered,
and the exchange was serious. Junior wished
he had learned B E C terminology for unabashed
courtship. He squinted toward the silhouettes
and noticed Brook was the tallest—and most shapely.
Tonight, mused Junior, I will spend the night
with a sensuous Black Eagle Child girl who
sounds and looks like Lauren Bacall; I will
give her cigarettes to light the way to bliss.
And her friends will trail behind only to be led
elsewhere by fireflies whom I will beckon to my aid.

That's right, Caesar. He soon began to take note
again of the music. Somewhere deep in the chorus,
he heard Grandfather chanting away: *"Wa wa se si,
wa wa se si, be ska tte na ma wi no, be ska tte
na ma wi no.* Firefly, firefly, light my way,
light my way." It was a child's lullaby from
Pinelodge Lake, the only song he knew. Should
he sing it to Brook? Or her people later on?
Nah, forget that shit. In midthought two girls
approached and coaxed him to follow them
"to Brook."

    » «

"Where's Junior?" asked Ted through
the partially open car window, surprising us.
I apologized to Charlotte for Ted's rude behavior
and answered him in an annoying tone.
"He was with you, REMEMBER?"
"Yeah, yeah. I know that. I thought
he might have returned."
Ted opened the door anyway and hopped
aboard, saying something about "escapees"
who came to the car earlier.
"That's where he's at, I bet.
They started talking to him while
I was singing. Geez, when I said,
'your pick,' I didn't mean jailbait!"
(Considering that most tribal marriages
took place among the underaged traditionally,
the "jailbait" term was invoked sheerly
for amusement.)

The clouds lowered at that point and rumbled
over the river valley. The rumbling divided
and traveled to the floodplains and fields.

A bolt of lightning shot down from the sky,
and a fierce thunderclap followed.
We were first blinded and then stunned
by the noise and proximity of the bolt.
It held on longer than usual, illuminating
cars and freezing people in their places.
For a split second we were in the shadow
of a tall walnut tree. In the pandemonium
Ted began speaking in the reserved demeanor
of an elder. "Tomorrow evening, revived
by rain, thunder, and lightning, the new
Red-hatted Grandfather will stand
by the forest's edge." Near the highway
bridge, another bolt landed, sending
a large cottonwood down with a crash;
small balls of lightning reached back out
to the horizon like eerie phosphorescent
fingers and died.

"Red-hatted Grandfather?" I voiced,
hoping Ted would elaborate further
on the mushroom that indeed depended
upon fierce thunderstorms to grow.
"That's a new one. You never told me that one."
"There was never an opportune moment with you,"
he answered. "I'm referring to the original
Star-Medicine here. Besides, Child Edgar Bear—
as Uncle still calls you—you never came
back. You are a waverer. How better can I
say it? You elude compacts with God."
"Listen," interrupted the uneasy Charlotte,
"while you guys talk about stupid mushrooms,
I'm going out to look for Junior. He may
have had one too many." Undaunted by our
concerns, especially mine, of being struck,
Charlotte excused herself. I held her hand,
but she shook it off in one snap and promised

to be back. With a deluge of hail bouncing
all around her, Charlotte ran off
with both hands over her straw hat.

"On stormy nights like these," resumed Ted,
"lightning implores Grandfather *Anaqwaoni*
to rise from the murky underwater depths.
You see, Edgar, he initially surfaced
for Dark Circling Cloud on the Swanroot
through the four bubbles of light, the stars
who produced the thundercloud.
You remember, don't you?"
"Uh-huh," I indicated, giving him
permission to elucidate for the waverer.
"It was this electrical source which made
Grandfather Red Hat appear on the riverbend.
He stood alongside the four boulders
and the deer-masked men. He was the gift,
the first sacrament. Dark Circling Cloud
welcomed this gift, remembering the songs,
messages, and instructions with clarity."

Instead of seeing a red-topped mushroom,
I saw his own pinstripe-suited grandfather
at sundown, the late patriarch of the Facepaint
family, kneeling beside a red derby hat.
"If you go out for a walk tomorrow,"
Ted added, "you will see him.
He visits us. But it is said he's
unpredictable; he may turn against you.
For that reason, and this you'll remember,
Well-Off Man uses Star-Medicine cultivated
from distant deserts. You see, we were told
long ago by a breakaway tribe that a Valley
of Falling Stars exists. As early as 1913
excursions were taken to locate and bring
trunkloads of medicine across the border
of Mexico. We eventually negotiated

with the two countries and were granted
legal rights to own, harvest, and consume
the sacrament."

The juxtaposition of the hailstorm
and Ted's eloquent narration was unnerving.
He truly believed "Grandfather's visit"
was imminent and beneficial. Although
his unique gift was the kind that
could not be ingested lest one risk
losing sanity and health, he nevertheless
rose annually from the cavernous underground
waterways to measure the degree of faith
held by his followers. He uses kilowatt hours,
I noted, measuring piety through glass-encased
meters attached to the temples of our skulls.
As the first deity, he had to keep track
somehow. But to be spawned by inclement weather
and remain untouchable was a contradiction—
like his title: Grandfather. But then what
wasn't in life?

The names we were born with placed us
into cubicles in which we could never leave
or peep out of; to do so meant capsizing
the lifeboats and thrashing about helplessly
in the sea of acidic mud. We were relegated
to either serve or be served. Originally,
the Facepaints were Painters of Magic
and Protective Symbols for the soldier
clans and their subdivisions. They
were known for accurately depicting
visions on faces and armament.
In peacetime they served the village
and made their services available
for family histories, which were either
scratched on bark lodges, painted on robes,
or expertly woven into pictorial designs.

For generations the diligent Facepaints
ground natural dyes and pigments on stone,
but they were never permitted to express
themselves, to draw their own interpretations
of clan protectors and forest-visitors for fear
of losing the village's accumulative powers.
Conversely, the Bearchilds were deemed
opportunistic and unwise. They clung
to the heels of leaders and learned how
to manipulate others on the pretense of being
close to those who were chosen to make decisions.
At the turn of the century the Bearchilds
were appointed translators for the Principal
Bear and Red Boy factions. On their behalf
they negotiated with the federal government
on delicate matters of progress and were often
in the center of embroilment, mediating opinions
between conservatives and progressives.
Unfortunately, the deterioration of a strong
nation began the day white politicians asked
the Bearchild patriarch for his own ideas
on education and community welfare.
It was then that the master plan was unfolded:
he unknowingly accepted education on behalf
of the tribe. This event threw the lower-named
families even lower. When the trick became law,
police drove out in hordes to hunt down
children for school. Community distrust
grew great, proving again there was a specific
reason why names gave order and stability
to the defiant but immiscible clans
of Black Eagle Child.

From then on the Bearchilds were known
to possess two languages and two personalities;
one never knew which was speaking.
"They were articulate," the journals
recorded, "but they could never be trusted again

to represent the tribe in any official capacity."
I would wince, for I was part Bearchild,
part Principal Bear, revolving aimlessly
in a circle within a circle. The heart veins
came from the earth, and I spoke endearingly
about this spacious interrelationship,
but underneath I was gravely distraught
by the ramifications of the past.
I lashed out like a coiled snake.
At least I'm not a descendant of Outsiders,
I reminded myself during these bouts of self-doubt,
the wanderlusts whose caravan stopped for supplies
long ago and decided to stay. As if ridicule
would lessen the torment, I belittled the less
fortunate to compensate for my own inherited
losses.

The Principal Bears had a false mirror faction,
the Rough Red Faces. I practically deified them,
but only when I felt suffocated and empty.
They never know their rightful place,
I would insist, taking the clan names of others
for their own, foolishly placing themselves higher
than the Real-Names. They were scoffed at by those
who took them in. A harsher penalty came
from the woodlands: every other Rough
Red Face had a nervous breakdown at adulthood,
a time when they were most likely to do most harm.
And then there were the New-Bloods, a family
of light-complexioned elders who were given
special songs of acknowledgment every summer,
the only time they were totally visible.
They would walk through the crowds
or come down from the stands to dance
and be seen by the Real-Names. We each
needed to remind one another of place;
we all gave of ourselves for others to see,
to remember. Contrary to what we perceived

as a lopsided set of advantages,
we were all estranged. The barriers
existed. We were in every sense
a "tribe," but we made damn sure
no one would ever prosper and succeed
without first knowing their place.

For that very reason Facepaint
would constantly dream of preparing
to go on a long journey and revisit
a place that didn't exist,
a place he had previously dreamed about.
The Star-Medicine transgressed the Real-Name
structures. Tomorrow Grandfather Red Hat
would gleam by the pine forest's edge.
The Well-Off Man Church found comfort
in that.

Brook
Grassleggings
Episode

Under the cover of the ticket office roof,
the distant silhouette of Brook Grassleggings
against the white-painted building looked
more impressive than before. She leaned
her long neck and head backward
and exhaled smoke. Her profile could have been
on a billboard beside a Canadian highway,
advertising Craven A's with the Great Lakes
in the background dotted with sails and freighters.
Junior dreamily slid his way toward her,
dismissing the cool water seeping into his tennis
shoes and the sucking sounds it made.
Standing beside Brook, almost slouching from
the weight of rain on their shoulders,
were her vigilant companions with quarts
in their hands. One chugged hers and burped
rudely. "She's over there," the girls said
together. God, I wonder who that mannerless
heathen was, Junior thought. It couldn't be . . .
"What does she want now?" he asked loudly.
"More cigs?" The messengers were quiet as they
jumped over the reflections of pools of water

and mud, grabbing each other sometimes for balance,
leading the way for Junior. This is better than
I expected, he thought. I didn't have to pursue,
do a wicked mate-dance, or cajole the long-legged
Brook into schemes of seduction. Or is she
scheming me? Holy shit! Keep laughing your sweetest,
Brook, he thought, secretly hoping she'd receive
his braintalk. Once there, Junior squeezed between
the pack and stood right next to Brook.
"Hello again," she cooed with arms wrapped
around her hunched shoulders.
"Hello, hello," returned Junior.
"I hear you want to talk. Is that right?"
"Easy," she murmured. "Would you like to drink
some beer with us? We bought too much."
She pointed to the ticket office counter
at the row of quarts and laughed heartily.
"Why sure," intoned Junior as he grabbed
a quart and opened it with the church key.
Your pick, Facepaint had instructed.
With the church key in the air still,
he turned around to the messengers.
"Join me?" Each responded by taking a bottle
and running back to the festivity. Brook
coughed and then became mysteriously quiet.
Junior was reminded of a hungry calculating
heron. Lured by the shimmering stillness
Junior swam forward. They stood close together,
nearly touching, and listened passively
to the steadily increasing rain,
the wild laughter, small family arguments,
and songs that became indistinguishable
from the fleeting and dizzying night sounds.
On impulse Junior grabbed Brook's long cold
fingers and directed them to the west where
flashes of lightning were appearing behind
and above the ominous clouds. They were able
to appreciate the language of weather before

thunder arrived in the first gusts of wind.
Car doors began shutting all around,
and the crowd walked hurriedly toward
the remaining burned-out shell
of the exhibition hall. The wind
picked up and cried mournfully.

High above, the treetops began to sway
to the fury of an impending storm;
branches and twigs knocked down by first hail
fell around them harmlessly. But when the larger
rocks of ice found their way through the gnarly
walnut limbs, the ticket office rattled
in abominable chaos. It was enough for Junior
to curl his muscled arm around Brook's thin waist.
She stiffened and breathed deeply, sending a rapid
heartbeat to his fingertips. With his other hand
he discreetly pushed the door behind him,
felt resistance, and then heard the padlock.
The storm rushed over the fairgrounds
carrying the deafening explosion of electricity
and thunder. Junior and Brook stood even closer
together when the display of forked lightning
stood over them in the shape of an old lady
in a shawl, her hideous body supported
by a crutch and outlined in wicked neon.
Here was the reported phantom, the one
who wished proper burial and passage
to the Hereafter, her misery and entrapment
conveyed through violent weather. She openly
defied them to stare—or run. Previous talks
on ghosts and witches compelled Junior
to start running north with Brook in hand
stumbling behind. He was positive
the supernatural beacon from Pinelodge
Lake had located him and was now preparing
to eliminate his grandfather's betrayal
which coursed through his veins.

It would scan the grounds,
detect his vile presence, and fire a bolt
that would boil his brain and guts,
splintering his tissue in all directions
like the felled cottonwood; the ground
beneath would open as if a bomb had exploded.
Brook would grab her beautiful, blood-splattered
face and cringe at the gleeful Rat circling
and howling like a wolf. Junior's chest
tightened up so much that he could no longer
breathe. As the thunderous cries of the beacon
came closer, his grip on Brook's hand locked
like a vise. "Shit, man!" she protested.
"You want to fry?" All around the brilliant
green color of tall grass was made visible
by flashes from the beam; cars and trucks
drove past them recklessly, their horns
adding to Junior's hysteria. "Get the fuck
out of the rain!" the passengers warned.
But directly behind them was the phantom's
whirlwind, snapping whole trees and lifting them
skyward to dance and march after the stumbling pair.
Junior lost his footing as he looked behind and fell
facefirst into a large mud puddle, cutting his lip
on the cinder rocks. Brook pulled him back out
effortlessly, like a heron grabbing a fish.
She took the lead, running with assurance
and agility.

They ran north far away from the grounds
and turned at the first road, continuing until
a log cabin came into view. On the porch Brook
hurriedly searched for her key while Junior
huddled helplessly against the door with
palms over his ears.
"Hurry, come on inside. No one's home."
Once inside the sounds of the storm
were absorbed by the thick walls; the two

stood wobbly-legged and gradually regained
their breath. "Who lives here?" whimpered Junior.
"For tonight we do," said Brook, lighting a single
candle. Grateful that Lauren Bacall had saved him,
Junior reached out and clung tightly. She took
the opportunity to lead him to another room
and laid him on the quilt-covered bed,
taking off his tennis shoes and gently peeling
down the wet clothes. Junior reciprocated.
"Wait," she whispered. She then brought out
a vase of water and a basin, and she began
washing the wound on his lip and the streaks
of mud from his arms. Junior was guided
to stand behind her. They stood naked in
the dim flickering light, and he kissed her
neck. Junior held one breast and caressed
its cold skin. Brook leaned her long frame
backward and rested her neck on his shoulder.
When Junior reached down to touch her womanhood,
he let out a scream so loud he scared himself
silly and nearly lost consciousness.
He was devastated. Double-checking, Junior
looked at the shadow for confirmation.
The fact was undeniable; whether by touch
or sight, the luscious Brook was half male.
In disbelief Junior fell backward and landed
on his bare ass on the coarse wooden floor.

» «

Post-Brook Episode

Charlotte came out of the night
sopping wet and hopped into the car.
"I can't find Junior!" she said excitedly.
"I looked in each car and he's nowhere.
Can you guys help me look for him?"

"I don't think there's much we could do right
now," answered Ted, pretending to take a gander
at the cars. "If he's not in the area,
he must be far gone. I bet he went
with the girls. Remember? I mentioned
it before." Charlotte agreed with
the possibility and calmed down
with the rain. She took off her
hat and boots and sat back down
beside me. Outside, the clouds
opened, revealing the cordial half-
moon. In the weather's aftermath
debris was scattered everywhere.

We began hearing a lone thumping on
the trash barrel, and then the voices merged;
round dance sounds resonated from the shell
again. The cars which left in the maelstrom
returned cautiously; the laughter picked up
as did conversations about the strong winds
being a demonstration of forgetfulness.
And the "Hyena" family who had been arguing
all night—Mathylde Hi-na, along with her three
chronically unemployed sons and her promiscuous
but married daughter—got out of the same car
and started the same boring argument:
why they were all different from one another
and the despicable EBNO classification.
There were deep sighs from annoyed bystanders,
and in anticipation of a fracas cars were parked
far away. It was unfortunate that "going out"
was a way of socializing; more so when there
were a few who abused the process by bringing
their woes to the night, like the disturbed Hyenas.
They instigated fights, ganging up like sharks
on those who didn't want to listen or sympathize
with their constant bitching. Most people assumed
their bitterness stemmed from the fact they

had different fathers. It wasn't anything novel,
of course, but they had a habit of lashing out
indiscriminately at citizens. For the community
as a whole, this only confirmed the atrocities
of a Mathylde Hi-na—better known as Patty Jo:
in the early part of the sixties she deceived
a succession of men into believing she bore
their children. When she gave birth the grandparents of the men were there at the Heijen
hospital to either accept or reject the babies.
Sadly, all were rejected, but the purported
fathers were strung along long enough
for Patty Jo to affix their respective
names to birth certificates. With these
signatures an application was submitted
to the BEC Business Council, requesting
tribal-enrolled status for her children.
Surprisingly, this was approved without question
or review. From this incident and others
that followed, a caustic nickname was coined
for this group: EBNO, Enrolled But
in Name Only. Ted hypothetically questioned
once, "If an EBNO perpetuates the EBNO crime,
like Patty Jo's daughter, what does that make?
An honorable death of the accused by community
clubbing? AHDACC if abbreviated?
Should we levy an AHDACC? Or should we
just 'Ahttack' her?" What crude jokes we made
about the situation, but our voices were echoes
of other voices, the kind taken from the family
supper table.

"Take note, boys," we were forewarned
by circles of old men whittling spoons,
bowls, and courting flutes. "Don't take
example of gullible, stupid men."
But it wasn't just the men. Sometimes
whole families were duped; birthday parties

grew larger and eventually involved the community.
The attendance was sparse, but the fanfare delighted
the EBNOs. Gullible aunts and uncles clucked
about in a ridiculous fashion like chickens
over the suspect brood, spreading their wings
protectively over their true identities.
In the pretense some even forgot about
their sick and elderly grandparents,
the ones who objected early on . . .

"Uh-oh," voiced Ted with some concern,
looking over to the Hyena family.
"The chickenshit hooligans are getting louder.
Gangway for our own Indian version of rednecks!
Pissheads have 'soitinly' ruined a lot of summers,
haven't they? Giving us a bad rep in town
with the whites—and out here. There should
really be some sort of honor code which
would allow us to club them beyond recognition
and dump their remains in the river as turtle food.
Of course, the turtles might be repulsed
by the stink. They'd let them rot, saying
to themselves, home to maggots only.
That is all their sinister lives are worth.
A mercy killing to assuage our own life."
Ted was 100 percent correct—
about the reputation. But the "clubbing" proposal
was raised in morbid jest, for there was a past
when it was the ultimate form of justice.
The fact of the matter was, when the press
pasted in headlines the insane acts of a select
few to account for the differences between
neighbors, we were personified by the whites
as one and the same trespasser. In the enclave
it was different.

"You can spot them easily," the old men said,
"by their sneering faces as they work the crowds

and houses on the pretext of being community do-
gooders." The old men also claimed they never
stood still long enough, were fidgety and high-
strung with voices purposely lowered in hopes
of concealing urges to belittle or maim.
Considered highly indiscreet, they closed in
on potential prey by protruding and extending
their lower jaws like fish, but it was their
rank hyenalike laughter that gave them away;
and when they converged as a mangy pack
to connive, their English and Indian tongues
were so broken no one was neurotic enough
to understand them. From any perspective
it was complicated to be anybody here,
but the EBNOs, unfortunately, did what
was expected of them. Thus, they became
an intrusion, a cancer. As a student
at Luther College for two summers
I learned of racial discrimination,
the plight of the red, black, yellow,
and brown races, and the need to advance
ourselves. The trouble was, I forgot there
would be nights when one quickly unlearned
the rights of others, nights when
white America seemed far removed from
our vicious vortex. But it didn't take
much to regain composure as we turned on
the spiked wheels of suzerainty.
No song of social protest by Janis Ian
or Bob Dylan could ever undo the chains
and reverse the panorama of the Red Man's
destiny.

"If the Hyenas cannot find anyone to pound,"
said Ted while flicking the switchblade
outside the window, "a blunt instrument
is under the seat. Thou shall not allow
an EBNO to humiliate a BEC is one

commandment we will enforce tonight."
The stiletto blade caught a glint of the moon.
I reached underneath the seat and brought a crowbar
to my side. "Look, all we have to do is drive away
if they start on us," advised Charlotte.
"But that's exactly what they want us to do,"
said Ted. "That's their thing—to flex jaw
muscle. We plan to put a stop to that.
At least for tonight." (It wasn't courage we
found by way of drink, you see; mostly it was
disgust in having seen countless nights ruined.)
We sought and expected a grain of civility
in our people regardless of who they were.
And while we recognized the lineage abbreviations
got out of hand, we all resided in the same
hellhole. Provided no one made waves—be it
an EBNO, an EBNAR (Enrolled But Not A Resident),
BRYPU (Blood-Related Yet Paternally Unclaimed),
UBENOB (Unrelated By Either Name Or Blood),
EBMIW (Enrolled But Mother Is White),
and so forth—a sense of decency and harmony
was possible. With all the divisions, however,
it was like asking poor homeless people not
to fight over scraps of leftover food thrown
out from the kitchens of the wealthy. In our case
food was dignity. There was virtually none
to give, and to those who were fortunate
to possess some, it wasn't nearly enough
to share.

Whether we simply happened to be the closest
to the Hyenas or whether it was by way
of a carelessly transmitted silver glint
of the switchblade, the mother and her sons
began walking toward us with hands behind
their backs. "Let me start it, Mom, please?"
the youngest begged in a rather loud whimper.
The mangy pack halted, and the mother grabbed

the one most vocal by the collar, dropping
her bat. "Shut up and just help your brothers.
Stand in the back; I don't want you to be
accidentally hit. You're welcome to kick
'em once we drag them out of the car."
"Who are you going to drag out of the car,
you bitch?" spoke Ted matter-of-factly,
surprising the lynch mob in their tracks
with the one headlight. "Don't talk that way to
my mom, you asshole," returned the youngest,
who was being restrained from running to Ted's
window. Behind them the daughter urgently
asked for instructions on how to open
the trunk. "Hey, Sluggo!" shouted Ted.
"Come here and suck a sharp dick.
And tell the other stooges they can
take turns. Once each is done I'll turn
the knife upward and split your skulls
in half. And tell your sister I'll run her
down before she can load the gun."

With that, the mangy pack bristled their neck
hairs, bared their rotten, chewing tobacco–
stained teeth, and charged. Before they
were within bat's reach, Ted connected
the ignition wires, and the 1956 Ford
spun on the grass until it hit
the cinders. We were catapulted
from the scene, but two Hyenas—
the one whose glasses were always held
together by Scotch tape and the fat one
with short, curly hair—ran alongside
and managed to cling to the open windows.
"Stop and fight!" they commanded with
piranhalike underbites. Ted obliged by
driving into an oak tree, and the dubious
pair rolled off, skimming like flat rocks
over the wet grass, mud, and cinders.

When the mother and the baby brother
arrived to tend to the wounded,
Ted backed up toward them and spun
the snow tires, throwing sheets of black,
pungent mud over the Hyenas. As we were spinning
in ecstasy, a baseball bat got caught under
the wheels, and it shot out like a twirling
baton, glancing off the mother's mouth
and landing square in the belly of her
approaching daughter, who fell to her knees,
throwing up corn and beans on the sawed-off
shotgun she was carrying.

A
Circus
Acrobat
on the
Grass

We sped from the fairgrounds at an extremely
high rate of speed, heading north with the lone
headlight. We turned onto a muddy side road
where Ted thought Junior could be found.
We shut the car's eye and became the night,
closing in on the unsuspecting heron.
Before we reached the old Grassleggings
cabin Ted asked how we'd feel about going
back "to check the extent of Hyena damage."
I may have paused for a second, but the thought
of making things worse than they already were
changed my mind. Hoping Ted would be content
with a report, Charlotte offered Patty Jo
was at last sight mud-covered and bleeding
from the mouth. She stood over her daughter
and could only scream. In the rearview
mirror Ted saw her attempting to shout
but couldn't, for her tongue was a loathsome
stump of meat. We remained in the car next
to the cabin and shook from the gore—
and the promise of retribution somewhere
far ahead. Yet there was exhilaration

that we had finally exacted a toll called
a favor. Close to it, anyway.

"I want to propose a toast," said Ted
with his bottle raised to us in the backseat.
"We did it for the safety and welfare
of the tribe." Imitating our decision makers,
who were expected to not be disagreeable,
independent-minded, fair, and expeditious,
we raised our bottles and returned:
"For the good of the tribe."
"Further," continued councilman Facepaint,
"it has been found in the chambers tonight
that said Hyenai have long taken advantage
of the peaceful inhabitants of Peyton Place.
Do we agree unanimously, council members?"
"Here, here. Hi-ya, Hi-ya. Hi-na, Hi-na,"
we returned. "I therefore curse Patty Jo
with a permanent speech impediment. For
all the lovers she deceived and betrayed,
it is befitting. And for her sons, the 'Three
Stooges,' I pass a sentence of cinder-embedded
scars on their cheeks and bulbous wino noses.
And because the daughter takes after her mother,
I hereby order a psychiatric examination
to determine what causes the child abandonment
syndrome." "Yeah," I said, feeling elated and wicked.
"Send her to the nut ward at Heijen hospital.
That is, if she doesn't die in the ambulance.
You know how they are. They give new meaning to substandard medical care." We clinked the bottles
together and gloated. In the middle of councilman
Facepaint's oration on "Codes of Tribal Conduct,"
the wailing of an ambulance siren could be heard
coming along the highway from Twintown.
There was one initially and then another
followed. Together they grew louder.
Toward the east, through the fog-draped

swamps, the cherry-top lights of police
blinked brightly, reflecting off the water.
Following closely behind were the headlights
of assorted vigilantes and concerned groups.
"Looks and sounds pretty serious,"
said Charlotte. "I think we should go back
and see what's wrong." Ted sat silently
before debating the consequences.
"Bloody hell! There's a chance we'll
get picked up for assault. Maybe drunk-
driving, no driver's license, and a couple
of add-on charges for good measure.
They want to nail our asses!
Especially minors. Meaning *us,* Charlotte.
Me and Edgar. Underline that!"
"Well, simply not being there makes things
worse in my opinion," answered Charlotte
precociously, ignoring Ted's exclusion
of her as a minor. "We'll be fugitives
in a few minutes, and they'll enjoy the hunt.
They've had all night to polish their billy clubs.
Right? To quote you guys. And then where do we go?
The people there are so mizzed, they'll tell
the cops where we are. Everyone saw."
"She does have a point, Ted," I said,
becoming more impressed with the Ontario
girl's logic. "It's just the natural process.
If we go back and tell our side of the story,
that we were fleeing from attack, it will
make sense. If we run, it makes us appear
guilty. Why don't we walk back?"
When the police lights were parallel with us
to the south about a third of a mile, the door
of the log cabin swung open on its squeaky hinges.
We turned our heads and looked toward
the candlelight which illuminated
the antiquated but well-kept interior.
To our dismay a partially clothed person

ran out and cleared the high porch steps
in one bounding leap. It was Junior, clutching
his pants and T-shirt as he flew through the air.
He landed like a circus acrobat on the grass
before losing balance. Trotting behind him
toe-and-heel was a naked person. By all
appearances the pursuer's torso was female,
but a side angle indicated otherwise.
The half-female person delicately ascended
the porch and called out, "Junior, wait.
Don't go!" I immediately recognized
the husky voice as that of a Grassleggings
girl. But it was the silhouette of male
protrusions juxtaposed on a body with a pair
of breasts which totally blew me away.

Charlotte could only issue a faint gasp.
Ted cussed sternly. Junior was on the lawn
doing a Charlie Chaplin routine; he rose
thrice only to slip and fall back down. His naked
pursuer stopped and noticed where we were parked.
She . . . he ran back in, closing the door.
Everyone began calling out. "Junior! Junior!"
Disoriented, the muscular Ontario stood up
and found himself facing a spotlight.
(In the mayhem we had forgotten to keep track
of the police, ambulance, and assorted vigilantes.)
In his white shorts, thinking perhaps we were the ones
with the one headlight, Junior raised his arms.
The second the police siren began, blaring away
in announcement of the "skinjin" discovery,
Junior froze like a jacklit deer.

» «

She has found me, thought Junior as he wavered
on mosquito-bitten knees. Her beacon is trained

on my vocal chords; there's no escaping her paralysis.
"The guise of Brook stole his voice," sang the phantom
in a voice greater than the hymn of a thousand angels,
all amplified by electricity that was in the mist still—
supernatural wattage ricocheting triumphantly
off the trees, water, earth, and sky.
Oh, Grandfather, he cried to himself.
Dear, dear Grandfather, instruct me as to what
I should do—RIGHT NOW! I wish not for my body
to explode into large unidentified chunks
of flesh. There are large-winged carrion eaters
here, for Christ's sake. Daily their shadows
crisscross the land they created eons ago.
The sacrifice they made, exchanging their once-
beauty for hideous heads and a penchant
for decayed meat, is a disappointment when they
meet characters like me, disrespectful of everything
that is living, taking all without prayer
or offering. The inability to remember gifts
that can heal, songs that entice sleep, love,
and mystery is unforgivable. Goddamn, they
will argue over me at daybreak, hopping around
my crusted heart with their open beaks and orange
talons. Death must be better than this.
Grandfather, please.

Blinded, Junior could only picture the phantom.
She was holding a crutch that also served
as an evil, flashlightlike apparatus.
Taking careful aim with pupil-less, fiery-red
eyes, the phantom edged close and inhaled in
a hollow, raspy breath. She redirected
the beacon's power into the deepest part
of Junior's encoded memory and sang louder:
The men of the family lifted their oars
and plunged them into the lake, keeping time
by heart's blissful intonation. Dimly lit

by the starry night, the medicine man's
daughter stood on the lead boat,
giving directions periodically,
indicating treacherous wave height by arm,
and speaking all the while soothing words
to the angry underwater spirits. Remarkably,
Junior found himself in his grandfather's
sinewy body, reliving the escape from Pinelodge
Lake. These were the very boats his relatives
used. He was there in mind in another body.
He looked carefully over his shoulder
at the Northern Lights. Suspended in the middle
of the orange moon was a light, flickering eerily
behind the scraggly wings of something demonic.
The lead boat rocked in the swells created
by these wings, and the occupants held on
to each other.

Lurking far below were gilled emissaries
whose scales were composed of human retinas.
In their horned, snakelike bodies they swam along,
hoping desperately to disrupt the young woman's
trance. They took turns surfacing and showing
their moldy fins, but it was to no avail,
for she was well versed in the supplication
of such deities; the emissaries had no
choice but to accept her gratuities
of meal portions and tobacco. In her voice
they could hear her father, summoning
their aid and repeating a chant
that asked them to capsize the boats.
To prevent this from happening,
she avoided looking directly at their
bodycount eyes. Nor did she look backward
whence she came. Because of her commitment
the emissaries could only escort the exiles
to shore.

Without knowing why, Junior called out
to the young woman. "Nokomis! Grandmother!"
She turned around and spoke:
"When the four-legged being first rings
the doorbell, don't open the door. Stand behind
the curtains and wait. Take a peep and you will
see a spotted fawn pretending a paper sack
is stuck on its head. If the doorbell rings again,
open the door quickly, reach out, and remove
the brown paper over its head. You will
surprise whoever intends to visit you,
and that person will not have a chance
to revert to the dead person's face
it originally wished for. Greet it in
your tongue; by daybreak the visitor will rot.
Before that occurs, though, you will learn
its transportation secrets. The bones
and plumes are rolled in invisible leather
packs tied to its spiny back. Ask for them.
Affixed to limbs, there is metamorphosis.
Whatever you do, don't dress as you are now."
The young woman, his real grandmother, returned
to divine navigation. The moldy tail fins of giant
creatures sliced through the undulating waves.
The sound of oars splashing the lake water
took immediate leave of his ears
when the phantom ordered him to F R E E Z E.
Aborted from the past, Junior awoke
to the sight of his muddy thighs, a good sign
he had struggled in the earth's womb to extricate
himself from guilt—and a reminder of infancy.
Extrication from the invisible. Adolescence.
Invisible leather packs. Maturity.
Charm contents. It did not matter which.
Nothing could. Nothing could change him
into what he most desired. Bone affixed
to limb was bone affixed to limb.

The spotlight guided a group of uniformed
officers and reporters in ponchos over
the impassable driveway. One minute
the partially clad suspect was there
with his arms up, and the next minute
he was being led away by hand by
a young barefooted girl in a straw hat.
The reporters' flashbulbs excited everyone.
Expecting the worst, the vigilantes fired
their shotguns from the road, and pellets
whizzed past the plastic-covered hats
of Sheriff Wiggley and his deputies.
Glass from the windowpanes of the log
cabin shattered at each incoming volley;
roof shingles splintered and some broke free,
indicating heavier lead, possibly buckshot,
was used. A curtain moved and shots rang out
again. There was interminable chaos.
The authorities cussed sons of bitches
before ducking for cover. An unseen car roared
and came into mechanical life. The spotlight
searched and found it spinning violently
around the corner of the old cabin.
The one-eyed Ford straddled a tractor road,
took traction, and headed east toward the swamps
with the suspect's pale legs swinging wildly
from the backseat window. The sheriff and his men
unholstered their sidearms in disbelief and shouted
a warning. The shotguns spoke from the road again.
Including the nearby soybean field and a windbreak
row of birch saplings, the log cabin was repeppered
with pellets. The .38 caliber revolvers blazed.
A cloud of blue smoke parted as the shooters
stepped forward. Did you catch the car's markings?
asked Sheriff Wiggley. Did we even hit it?
Arbie's, sir. What? The markings. North Tama plates.

Possibly Claer. How many occupants? Three or four.
Do you think anybody's in the cabin?
Hard to tell, sir.

With its partially blown-out stoplights,
the one-eyed Ford reappeared on the tractor road
before making a successful dash into the swamps,
catching everyone off-guard. No one, especially not
the police, realized the car was a mere fifty yards
away, hiding in a nettle patch. It had cleverly
stepped to the side and shut itself down:
aware a conversation was taking place
between the predators to determine what
had just occurred, the mechanical animal
hunched its paint-chipped back over
the kindling, fanning the embers with
its abrasive paws. In its sweet, oily
breath a tiny spark took hold and became
a flame on the end of a wooden stick.
The beastly contraption lifted on hindlegs
and analyzed the wind with its nostrils
before ramming the burning stick into
its chrome skull. Falling on all fours,
it made the rumbling sounds of an engine
and drove away.

The Year
of the
Jefferson
Airplane

》《》《》《》《》《》《》《》《》《》《》《》《》《》《》《》《》《》

One pill makes you larger, and one pill
makes you small. And the ones that mother
gives you don't do anything at all.
Go ask Alice when she's ten feet tall . . .
—Jefferson Airplane

Five long years after my last experiences
with the Star-Medicine, at nineteen years
of age, I found myself at Pomona College
in Claremont, California. The transition
from the prehistoric Midwest was shocking,
to say the least. Shortly before I graduated
from high school I decided to try college (life)
rather than take my chances with the Viet Nam
conflict. The fact that my cousin Hector Reveres
Nothing was the sixth in Tama County to die
in that Asian country had a chilling effect.
But his loss, unlike the others, almost went
unnoticed, for I never knew him. Hector came
to me as a faceless body, wearing a military
uniform on a ride he took with us once.

When I thought about the insanity which
surrounded his loss, I recalled the fine
golden braids wrapped around his shoulder.
At that particular moment he was closer than
our families were, and we would have something
in common in the future: we would
share places on O'Ryan Hilltop, a cemetery.
The only difference was, there was no rush
on my part to get there.

As the young soldiers returned home
they were either dead or wounded.
Most never said anything when
the opportunity arose to reflect,
while others had an ability to see
the past as a means to begin. And
with those who safely returned some
were emotionally crippled with a nightmarish montage of handkerchief drownings,
ass grenades, and digits as targets
in exchange for gin, a pass out, and care.
Out of this came the choice for California,
studying instead of being shot at. Thus,
it was an era of war protests—and drugs.
It was no surprise I found solace
in the latter; they took politics
and their terrible reasons away.
But they also caused my downfall.
Of course, I sometimes think any
successful matriculation would have
taken twice as long due to centuries
of cultural malignment. Well, that
was my excuse. This much I know for sure:
my early encounters with natural hallucinogens
were instrumental in insuring my survival.
Perhaps I did indulge a bit more than
the rest, yet I did my best to catch up

with my inadequacies. But the race
to understanding one's place began
ten years earlier—without me.
It was a lonesome, depressing year.

Imitating what was done by young,
naive people and considering I was vastly
out of place in a prominent upper-class
institution, I grew dependent on synthetic
Star-Medicine for shock relief.
I was in need of a cure from
the horrendous absence of relatives,
friends, and the Black Eagle Child landscape.
Bullshitter that I was, I boasted to fellow
classmates that I was "well-traveled"
on the mind-expanding road. I was often
asked to guide others drop. But the courtesy
and notoriety began to take their toll:
the differences between synthetic and organic
were more than I could handle. That
realization didn't surface until later,
when it was too late. Even when I did it
out of need instead of pleasure.

There must be nomadic-prone genes
in Indian blood, mentality, and cellular
composition, for Ted Facepaint and I went
the same way together—out from Tama County
to the eclectic West Coast. This wasn't
the plan. It was sheer coincidence that
Ted somehow got his diploma and promptly
heeded the advice of a teacher to pursue
education instead of house-building.
Ever since the Arbie's Pig Feeds fiasco,
we had lost touch but were able to send
word of our plans through friends. Ted
was enrolled at the College of the Desert

Cactus near Palm Springs, which as I
was apprised was about an hour's drive
due east along the San Gabriel Mountains.
"Somewhere past the smog." Unlike most Indians
who chose Haskell Indian College in Kansas
or the Institute of American Indian Arts
in New Mexico, we went to the western edge
of the North American continent. Going
as far away as possible from "the rest"
seemed the most logical choice.

We were like the fat golden carp
we always saw in Onion Creek,
swimming upstream and away from the rivers.
We would follow the tributary wherever it went—
just to be different. Ironically, the westerly
direction signified the place of Black Eagle Child
Afterlife. On my first meeting with the Pacific Ocean
I offered tobacco . . .

For three months, while we were recovering
from the novelties of geography and academia—
both dry and unpleasant—Ted and I could only
communicate by telephone. We made no further plans
to uproot ourselves. We had already done enough.
Too much, in fact. On the 12th of December,
however, just when radio deejay Wolfman Jack
was insulting callers from Tijuana, someone
knocked an Indian knock on the door of my room
in Smiley dormitory. Stunned, I got up and turned
the radio volume down. "Who is it?" I asked aloud
in English. "*Ba ke na no sqwa ta mi no tti se ma.*
Open this door, grandchild," the voice implored.
"*Ka tti agwi we na ka ska ta wi a ni ni?*
Why did you not hear me?" spoke another voice.
There were two of them; I became excited.
Visitors! When I unlocked the door, a long body

in a ragged army coat and white jeans lunged past
me and landed on the cot. It was Facepaint,
long-legged and miserably drunk—mizzed.
With his face half-buried in the pillow
he started to laugh. He then sat up.
"*Ke se ki e ni?* Did I scare you?"
he asked with a smirk. "*Ke no wa tti*
me ko agwi ba ke na ma ni i skwa te mi.
You didn't open the door for a long time."
I was stricken with disbelief by the voices
that came thousands of miles away—one a wino
and the other an elder. They sounded so real.
I half-expected to be transported to another
dimension when I opened the door. For sure
I thought I'd see the people who possessed
those voices standing on the snow-covered
porch of home. "*Ke to ki, bo ki ti?*
Are you awake, asshole?" Ted dug his red,
warped lips into the pillow and began
kicking the air in a frenzy. "You should
have told me you were coming," I said.
Even under the influence of sloe gin
his tricks of impersonation were phenomenal.
"Oh, like an appointment, Professor Bearchild?"
he whimpered. "Pisshead, you nearly scared me."
"Yeah, I should have called you," he replied
as his glazed eyes examined the posters
on the wall. "Then I wouldn't have gotten off
in El Monte," he said. "Del Monte? Whatever!
And I didn't know I could get another
bus this way. I hitchhiked and two Mexicans
who happened to be maintenance men here
picked me up this morning. What bitching luck!"
"Listen," I said with the hope of finding
out more information. "You say you got here
this morning. Where've you been the remainder?"
From his coat pocket Ted threw out a book

of matches. On the white cover was a drawing
of a rabbit with a pink eye. "That's where
I was—the Pink Rabbit Eye." It was a strip
joint frequented by white clientele who wore
short, tight blue-jeans that were rolled up
at the ankles, revealing the white socks
stuck-in-the-fifties look. With greased-up
hair they wore black clothing with cigarettes
tucked inside the shoulder portion of their
T-shirts. Word circulated on campus to stay
clear of these Neanderthals. "We were only
five miles away when we decided to stop
for beers at the Pink *Me ttwe* Eye,"
related Ted. "Once the naked women filed
in and danced on a stage, I forgot about you.
Everyone was yelling, 'Squat! Squat!'
Me and my amigos joined in the obscene
revelry. By midafternoon I had the sense
to call a taxi. Holy shit! That's all this
place needs, isn't it? Two Tama County skins.
How does the round dance song go now?
'Tama County spells the end of the world—
a place you leave but never really do'?
We should follow Youthman to prison,
get a degree there, and publicity in *LIFE*.
Right?" I didn't reply. Instead,
I faked a laugh, fooling him back.
I could sense then that we'd initiate
more trouble than delight. More pain
than comedy. The summer of wild young
bucks wasn't over. We sensed an overwhelming
change before us; what we couldn't foresee
was our agony. There was a recurring dream
I had of us suspended over the earth:
we hung like caught animals on the same
pole. We were tied to the pole by the veins
of our legs and arms. We could either

watch our blood dry in the sun or we
could eat them away—to fall earthward.
To get it over with.

Shortly after Ted landed, he excused
himself and curled up in a blanket.
At the first detectable snore I gently
removed four Budweiser Malt Liquor cans
from his coat and began sipping them.
Through the open window on the second
floor of Smiley, I sat in the warm,
oily breeze. Its thick haze was stuck
on the mountainside. A dark, stagnant
cloud stayed in the valley. Sometimes
there were afternoons when the tops
of palm trees couldn't be seen.
The disgusting night before sunset.
A season without whiteness and bitter
chill. Behind the smog the mountain peaks
were being covered with thick blankets
of fresh snow. Earlier, back home,
my father had chopped six to ten armloads
of wood for the back-up stove. A winter
routine. Although there'd be a stacked supply
for two to three days of burning, and all
for a blizzard that never came, my brother
would chop the same amount after school.
Chances were, supper was black-eye bean
soup with strips of bacon and dumplings.
The blue smoke of frybread grease
would stick to the ceiling until
the windows were opened for ventilation.
While I grew obese on burritos, stuffed
peppers, and chilled shrimp at the cafeteria,
I longed for BEC delicacies:
the commodity surplus menu of ancient Woodlands
people. And any time now my uncle would enter
the house with a belt of squirrels swinging

from his blood-crusted hip. Boiled squirrel
with dumplings tomorrow. My two sisters
would break through their small skulls
with tablespoons and scoop out "walnut-
flavored thoughts." My mouth watered.
Nostalgia and Budweiser . . . I read Mother's
letters again.

October 6, 1970
Edgar

Thought I'd write. just a few lines to you. Hope this letter find you
in good health. as for us everybody at home is fine. but we'll be having cold weather coming. I hate it. And in a way its alright too.

Got scared hearing they having big fire in Calif. State. Hope it
didn't come your way. And was hoping you won't get in part of
putting it out. (dangerous thing)

We didn't go to a big wedding. We was to tired to go. Her belly
was bigger than a watermelon seed anyway. We pick corn again and
dried it too. Not to much. I guess enough for winter (*āsh*) I got
lots of work to do. I'm still picking bean and got to dried pumpkins
too. I haven't got to that work yet.

Winston and Jack has been going hunting fishing and loaving.
lazy. Once has brought 2 Canadian *gresse* forgot how to spell it.
Anyway 2 big duck. (She-she-buck) understand. And the other day
Winston brought Robins and granny told Winston give it dogs.
Winston said he wanted to tastes Robins. Granny said its to much
work. (I imagine)

I think "Kool Cat" is shagging up with one of Scarmark's daughters. I think thats the smallest one. Her name is Mary Anne Know
her? Nice pick Angel girl (shh) They call Scarmark's son "Little
Scab" I heard. Howard Courting was telling us he went to Norman
Maple's part Friday. And said The drunks were talking about the big
Wedding. And said they are Showing off. And she four months P.G.
and said Lucky couldn't go to sleep with Thomasina. honeymoon.
because she already P.G. drunks! oh-well there tough luck!

I'm putting your things away books and pictures. I wishing. We
moving this weekend. that what Tony is planning. and I hope we

get to move. We're out of gas bottle gas that is. Been chopping wood. Because I don't wanna pay for gas two times when we move. And we don't have hot water. but I'm used to that not having hot water. And I'm using electric skillet to cook. and I'm doing alright. The car is at Ben Gay. He got sick again. twice now. the fuel pump gave out and Ben Gay is fixing it. And I haven't get to town to send alarm clock. the one we got with green stamps. Remember I said I was going to send it. Well, I never got around to it. (over)
2 weeks ago

Edgar

Received your the other day and was glad to hear from you. and I hope you still feeling fine. as for us folks here are fine just slight cold and etc. (shh)

The weather here is been bad. We got rain misty rain. Its been 3 days now. and the Ridge Road is Very muddy.

I only can send 5.00 again. We been tight on money. the Northern Propane Gas come and ask us to pay our gas or they'll take my gas stove and heater. So for 2 weeks now I'm paying them 40.00 a week. So I owe them $52.00 now. I wanna pay that off. So they can fill the tank for the winter. Out here at new home we're out of gas so we don't have hot water but we manage. I hate to order again. Oh well that life.

I'm still trying to make tape and send them to you. I stole send recording from Howard but don't tell him. I got two step song. I was going to borrow Matt's tape recorder but they left for Kansas for drum dance. I'll try again this weekend. I finally send alarm clock.

Why Cheer got pants taken off by Indianola this past Fri. Al said the team cried on way home.

I like your poems and I haven't read yet again. Everytime read kids will be jumping all over me. And they bug me. (shh) Al's word. Oh yeah, Edmond is home. it's been one week now. I guess he got lonesome. And Shirley Squirrely (spelling) is living with man from South Dakota. His name something do with aroow in arm.

Well i better close now so. be good boy. don't smoke too much. Excuse my mistake and writing.

Clotelde

November 22, 1970

Edgar

I'm sorry I didn't get to write to you. I have been very busy. I'm working at Belle Plaine. this is my third 3rd week. I'm working but I don't have dough. But if I have some I'll send it. Ok!

Well, we've got winter here. So early. Its 20 degrees out side. Cold. real cold. you'd have to bundle up when we go outside. How is it here? Nice and warm but cloudy I suppose Its a pleasant season here now.

Paw-kee-wah-key. get it. but they could only get one pheasant a week. they are carry some kind of sickness for eating to much weed killer. Understand me.

About school. that alright with me. as for me just so you stay in school. I know how hard it is when you are savage. I wish I had more schooling than just 8th grade. And granny didn't care if I went to school or not. She should have spank me once in a while. I'm work on weekdays. and I just can't get Why Cheer newspaper. on Saturdays it closes. if granny go to town I'll ask her to buy it for me. about 12 copies. then you have something to read.

Howard C. was saying he planning on going to Calif. to see that one eye man. Oh Barry I forgot his name. He working at Conrad north of Sherifftown. I mean Howard. but he going get layed off soon. So after he quit he'll take off for Calif.

I was talking to Margaret Frank too. She was thinking if her boy could enroll here. he'll finish his schooling in Dec. I guess he's been running around with Jane Francis and they are related. Close. Her boy is planning on going to school in Kansas. And I suppose that girl is planning on going over there too. and Margaret didn't like it.

I'm writing whats come in my mind. I guess I'm all messes up. They had Turkey dinner or supper last at Weeping Willow. The pow-wow. *Comedy*. brought some turkey (gobble gobble) and ham. they suppose had big supper.

I read on newspaper Stanley Fox is going to Missouri for grade school. I suppose after Christmas. He's a robber here. Him and Mr. Afraid rob grocery store on main street.

This will be it for now. hope you can read my writing. Al is writing to you. his letter inside mine.

Clotelde

(Al's letter)
Monday nite
around-10.00
RED POWER . . . (yea)
(Hi)

Again. this is the 2# one i wrote this beganing of the week. so i going to write to you while it's still in my mind. I might not a time this week I mean I might forget it. did you dig that letter you got before this one. Anyway i was feeling like a voodoo child (dig). anyway shit to that. Jesus! its getting cold down here what about there is it still warm (lucky shithead). Hey man when are you coming down there's not action when you young bucks left. nothing but shiting around here (no action) its ok. I think at least its peaceful around here for once HA! HA! anyway there's still some guy around here who still drink maybe just one. got your letter today. you know those things you sent me (COORS things) well I put some of them on my wall anyway they look cool.

I made a new girlfriend in town. A whitey. I couldn't buy meat from her. HA! HA! She said "Lord knows you're a voodoo child" after that she said "the night you was born I swear the moon turned a fire red," no just kidding Hey man! how do you look are you fat HA! Or are you the same size. Sent me a picture of you ok if you have time. I might sent some cool pictures of me. the 2# jimi hendrix, the next, in united states. a red jimi hendrix. HA! HA!

Time to go brother. orders to chop pain wood. say hello to my Mexican girls over there . . . sure, sure, sure.

sing on, Al

(P.S. From Clotelde. I'm just going to tell you not to order those dirty pictures for Al because he still a little young for those. I'll open that letter I was telling you. And oh those picture I hate them. So I'm not going to show them to Al. He might get ideas.)

November 28, 1970
Edgar

Thought I'd write to you. I think I haven't wrote to you yet. A couple days. I don't know. to many things on my mind. work. cook and try to clean the house. with is always messey. Seem like after I clean they just go ahead and throw thing all over the place including your father and Al. big kids.

They had a adoption at Tim P. place last Sunday for Anne Valley Fox's sister from oklahoma. but for here and there were lots of hungry Injun including us. all kinds of Indian and white people too. And this Sunday they have feast at Chesters again. I was going to call but I was afraid you might not be. And anyway I always make wrong number. Remember that jean we lost I found it. I didn't wash it. when I went to wash you clothes. Remember?

Wayman Jr. have a baby sister. lots of babies coming. How about that. Winston and Mateo. just went by this morning each driving tractor. propably combining the fleid. forgot how to spell it. No good head or brain. Anyway I hope you understand.

Samson is home on leave. and look neat with a good hair cut, but I don't know when he leaving. Al talk to him. and said he probaby go and see you. if he remember. He said it only 60 & 30 mile from his base.

Drunks here are getting bad. Shitting in their pants. Gino was telling us, they did it. a months ago at Bender's Place. and W. D. Ear did it at Weasel's. they are getting bad. W. D. and Mary Jean are separated and the Welfare people came a took all kids from them. to bad. S. Bulldog got what he likes. He was parked at Sebastiani place Saturday. And Thundertalk was with Sadie Washington what a pair! Winston just drop by. He broke a disc. and going to get another disc him & Mateo combine some corn yesterday. they are busy pair. the other day they were at ole place.

Monday

My letter to you was a delayed one. Did you get the money I send through a fast way. I had to pay 11.50 for sending it. I've got a trunk Sat. So I'm going to send it today or tomorrow. We're having rain and cold weather. I will write another letter soon. don't take part in those college kids been partying. Okay! School's alright. Maybe you might be hurt or shot off tank in vietnam like Vincent August. He can't walk. Sorry for him.

Clotelde

From the day Black Eagle Child servicemen
began losing their precious lives in South
Viet Nam—Hector Reveres Nothing, James No
Body, and Dick Good Turkey Boy—I did not envy
the thought of being drafted. This was why I
was here. The one knee that everyone said
would ultimately prevent the passing
of my physical was a bad gamble.
The very reason which brought me to Pomona
dissipated in the yellow and brown tint
of a premature night. Loneliness was like
death, the death of myself and all those
around me.

My grandmother was the last person to bid me
farewell before boarding the train in Marion,
Iowa. September 6 was the date. She gave me
a small spike-tip stone to wear in a locket
necklace over my chest. "This past spring,"
she instructed on the platform of the train
depot, "as the swamp buds were on the verge
of poking through dead leaves and weeds,
I found this twin-gift and prayed for it.
Take this with you; it will surely protect you.
In each adversity you encounter—whether or not
you are aware—it will point like an invisible
sharp knife in front of you."
I touched the locket with my perspiring
fingers and wondered if depression would qualify
as adversity. After the last beer and Ted's
irritating snores, I grabbed the closest
books and walked to the library for a session
with Nietzsche.

It was a real night when I returned from
Honnold. With studying complete, it
was refreshing to hear the blues
of John Lee Hooker coming from my room,

along with laughter and conversation.
The Sears portable record player was turned
up to maximum volume, and Ted was weary-looking,
but he had showered and changed into my shirt.
He seemed cheerful, eager to socialize; in fact,
he had already started by inviting my friends
who were merely passing through for drinks.
Three cases of malt liquor were stacked neatly
in the middle of the room. Jasper Iyatoo,
a Zuni Indian and fellow Pomonan, sat in
the dim candlelight with his silver
jewelry shining from his fingers and neck;
Albert and Duane Palacio attired in white shirts
and black slacks had brought their companions,
Elvia and Oleta, with net shawls draped
over their bare shoulders. The talk
was festive, and the sweet air of *mota*
was strong. Handing over a cold beer,
Albert said, "You'll have to catch up,
Bearchild."

Away from view and inside the closet
I unfastened the stone protector
of my heart and apologized with utter
sincerity for what I was about to do.
I sat down on the edge of my bed and accepted
the brass pipe from Ted. The seeds popped
in the red-hot bowl and shot out in the room
as Ted began reciting his tale of being lost
to the two attractive, long-haired girls.
Oleta, the one with slightly reddish
hair, reminded me of Rita Hayworth,
and a line from Marty Robbins's
cowboy-related song came to mind:
"Out in the West Texas town of El Paso
I fell in love with a Mexican girl."
Ever since I first heard the song
at the BEC barbershop and pool hall,

I liked it. Now, I knew why. The more
I peered into the shadows at Rita,
the Señorita, the more she looked like . . .
Dolores Fox-King? Charlotte the Ontario
Maiden? Romantic ghosts nevertheless.
One-sided infatuation with young women
came easy; it was a bad, unhealthy habit.
Cheap, ill-timed affairs nearly ruined me.
My mind imagined a lot of situations I could
never place myself in with females due to fear
of rejection. I assuaged the past with harmless
fantasy. If an innocent girl on campus made
the smallest effort to converse with me out
of courtesy, I blew it totally out of proportion
and embarrassed myself silly in the process.
I trembled as only an obese person could when
my telephone call for a date changed to an
assignment query. There were so many beautiful
girls of all persuasions that I fell in love daily.
But there were few who shared my interests.
An athletic Mexican-American girl named
Colleen was a true goddess, a breast-
measuring contestant during the first
week of orientation. We were friends who
became lovers after much bickering for one
whole month. What a pity! To hold her hands
made me weep; to embrace her made me wish
instantaneous coma. Her long eyelashes resembled
Daisy's, a woman-cow on the cartons of milk
back home, and her skin was smoother than
the palms of a well-kept raccoon. When I first
gave these complimentary associations of Colleen,
Albert and Duane laughed. "What a dude! Don't tell
her that, please. You've gone this far; don't
blow it." I disregarded their advice
and repeated the primitive routine.
Colleen laughed as well—kindly.
She was attracted mostly by my blood,

genetics more than anything bonded us—
the glorious history of Mexico.
It was at best an uneven trade-off:
a glimpse of ancient Woodlands wisdom
for a precious face and body. Physically,
we fit like a puzzle: my gut on her trim,
muscular stomach, her famous breasts
on my flat, bony chest; culturally
we were separated by galaxies. All that
could be seen when we slow-danced were my
chicken legs, leading, shuffling about,
and scratching the floor for support.

One day the pastel sketches of Colombian
deities thumbtacked to my door disappeared.
The mourning phase for the cartwheeling
goddess from West Covina ensued.
A despondent artist once rose from sleep
and penciled in a fat man on the highest
point of the pyramid in the sketch.
He also drew in a woman brandishing a golden
dagger. The blade caught a glint of the sun
before it gouged out Higgledy-Piggledy's heart.
"Beautiful woman of the universe,
daughter of the gods," said
the hieroglyphics at the bottom
of the stone slab, "the fat man
forgives you for feeding his heart
to the eagle and serpent."
Later on, at Jasper's suggestion we drove
out to the foothills in a pickup and parked
in the middle of an orange grove. It was there
three capsules of synthetic *Anaqwaoni*
were opened and offered. Ted and I debated
briefly. Alcohol dominated our better judgments;
we stuck our tongues out like thirsty children
and downed the powder with beer.
"Look, there they are," Ted pointed

to the constellations. A half hour later
he acknowledged them again. No one questioned
the reference to the Three-Stars-in-a-Row,
and I wasn't in the mood to explain.
Everyone shrugged and gazed at the stars.
"My grandfather is sitting in the middle
with his newly pressed suit, and the Green
Thunder nephews are on either side. They
are preparing to bring the stars down,
and in the kitchen the Deer Man has stuffed
the fawn in a gunnysack." Ted nodded to
everyone and said, "Oh, we'll be all-right
people." Right when he said that there
was a growing tightness in my stomach,
and a river of sweat flowed from between
my sensationless fingers. We patiently
waited for the surge of mosaic colors
and fluid motion to take control.
It began in the corner of our peripheral
vision, doing small tricks at first until
the movements merged into one and spewed
rudely into our dilated pupils. We saw
the night sky as Van Gogh painted it a hundred
years ago, circular light around the stars,
light that circled around other light.
Interconnecting stars, implosion and explosion.
The sacred meaning which kept trying to reach us
one second left just as quickly as the next
preparation for explanation began. The silence
of the orange grove was now loud swirls
with vivid currents of rainbow fragments
of landscape. The trees came alive by moving
as if they were submerged under water.

One of the girls became alarmed at the shadows
of animals running playfully between the rows.
They were coyotes who had come down from
the mountains to visit the suburbs.

With Ted's vocal ramblings and the paranoia
instilled by the nearly domesticated coyotes,
it was a struggle to reach a comfortable
plateau. However, once the stomach unraveled
itself, there was serenity. The tires
of the semitrucks within ourselves
splintered on the hot pavement and could
at last rest. In the river I could see
outlines of coyotes standing still under
the trees. They were curious.
"Will they attack—or have they been
known to?" asked Duane, Albert's brother,
in a querulous tone. "Nothing without
a ceremony," spoke the crystal-laden Jasper.
"What's that supposed to mean?"
"I mean they will treat us with respect
until our demise. They wouldn't dare harm us
without a ceremony first." The statement
of considerate death from a pack of coyotes
petrified everyone. Albert jumped up in
anger and started his truck.
"Let's get the fuck out of here!
This place is getting creepy."
Only a week previous Albert had shown me
a macabre memento from Viet Nam; it was
a V C skull inscribed with the numbers
of his infantry. The orange runoff
of a wax candle coated the skull's
rotten teeth. On the fast drive back
to Claremont I told Ted about Albert.
"*Wa ta se i a*. He is a veteran."
"Then he shouldn't be necrophobic,"
whispered Ted. "Not when he keeps
the ultimate symbol in his dresser."
Rita Hayworth adjusted the shawl
over her shoulders and spoke:
"I bet it has to do with Jasper's
comment about death with dignity.

What made you say that, anyway?"
Jasper hung on to the railing with
his glowing fingers and said nothing.
The approaching neon lights reflected
first off our faces before each minute
beam connected everything.

At the gates of the colleges the engine
overheated and stalled, like its driver,
Albert—the keeper of a warrior-skull lamp
from Indochina. The coyotes, too, must have
retreated to the valleys, escaping for no reason.
There is a sense of comedy when running from
the unknown. Sitting like mutes under the traffic lights,
I thought of the recent dawn I mistook an earth
tremor for distant thunder. Had I been a coyote
I would have known the differences on the soles
of my feet. I eventually found myself
on the sidewalk huddling with other dorm
residents. We had nowhere to run. The first
tremor caused a power blackout. I had wished
earlier for Pacific Ocean thunderstorms
to cleanse this arid land. I even planned
to walk out with an offering.
The Spirit's rain would cleanse me. Ted.
Everyone. I would pray for all. When
the second tremor loosened and sent clumps
of creosote down the stovepipe, I rolled in
my star quilt and waited for the roof to sing.
Instead, thunder spoke from the walls.
When the third landwave rattled
the stovepipe inside the brick chimney,
the earth broke open. Far below bubbles
of light were floating up from underground
rivers. High above fiery stars aimed
for the bend on the Swanroot.

I had at last transformed into a shimmering
speck of dust sprung free from a dark,
circling cloud, an atom representing
my anatomical being. I was floating along
with the mute entourage, feeling, seeing,
and hearing the enormity of the Star-Medicine.
Its presence made our calming talk sound
like whimpers of newborn but abandoned babies:
"I sometimes feel as if I have dropped out
of my mother, wet, dazed, and wobbly-legged,
and my umbilical cord is dragging in the fine,
worn-out trail over the dusty plains.
Mother, sensing the danger of falling
behind the group, takes her cool
shadow, and the scorching heat awakens me.
I whimper for assistance but receive none.
When we reach a mud puddle I see my reflection
for the first time. Such forlorn eyes I possess.
The dry ring around my black eyes resembles
the ring around a sad robin's eye."

In each palm tree there were cores of light
ascending and descending from trunk
to frond. Elevators converting
and releasing the air we breathed.
I had seen this exchange before during the first
Well-Off Man experience, and it was shortly before
Jason Writing Stick, the Sokapaita Indian
from Kansas, separated me from Ted, asking me
to accompany him to the mystic riverbend.
A conversation was in progress between
people and I was participating, but my speech
was meaningless in the overall formation
of the Clan Galaxy. Life-giving trees,
the breathing earth. We imparted all sorts
of speeches on craft and wisdom, and we believed
in them without question, getting offended

always at traditional perspectives,
but in everything She was always there,
in the east, rising with the sun
to look at us, giving us plants from
Her own being. That was the most important
concept to keep. Not individuality!
Not the characteristic "I am what I am"
Popeye bullshit. I take all this with me,
I inform Ted. This constant glowing and re-
glowing. I become a meteorite, the star-
boulder who brought the First Songs.
The three mystical men carry my smoldering
and blistered body from the canoe
and gently place me on the sand.
The ancient hunter, the gift-receiver,
knelt on the cobblestone street between
Scripps and Pomona colleges.

Before the entourage crossed the street
the men expanded their chests and let out
a series of war cries and whoops,
trying to outdo one another. The women
covered their ears. "That was some walk!"
gasped Ted. Red spirals of light wobbled
out of Jasper's taut, sneering face.
With a mural of a column of Roman soldiers
on the wall behind him, Jasper assumed
a defensive posture with his invisible shield
and bolt of heat. The Romans in body armor
and lances came to life and conspired.
Suddenly, from somewhere behind our ears,
a loud crackling voice spoke out:
"FREEZE! Or we'll shoot!"
Like jacklit deer we huddled together
and froze in our tracks. We were held
at bay by blinding miniature suns,
coming from the east and west.
The deities screamed through the squealing

tires of the cars rushing toward us.
Another command crackled. Albert shouted
behind us. "Can't you hear? Get your arms up!"
If that is what they wish. A sign of respect.
We raised our arms in submission.
The First-Named Ones showed themselves
by coming into the light of their divine
vehicles with the barrels of their shotguns
and revolvers. Their weapons are simple,
I said, and understandable. I looked around
and saw we were paralyzed. The mosaic tornado
and the rapid shadow in between made us into
lowly zebra-striped souls. "Ah man! What's this?"
protested Jasper as they pushed him behind
the spectacle. Ted was next. He couldn't speak.
"Hey, Three-Speed!" I cried. Above the crackling
din of a council I heard Jasper verify Ted
was from Palm Springs. Why did they need
to know this? The grip of a god's hands
on my wrists was forceful, but I was confident
the contact was part of incredible sharing.
The god's words were like sledgehammers
hitting me in the gut. "I'm from the Pomona
Police Department." Two police officers
and a black plainclothesman stood
in front and questioned me about our evening.
I twitched and spoke without knowing what
I said. To my left were the flashlit faces
of Ted and Jasper: brown, sweaty rabbits
with dilated pupils. They extended their furry
palms. Duane, Albert's brother, began to moan
and tremble uncontrollably. "Albert, I'm not
going to make it. I'm . . . going to tell them . . .
I'm O U T-t-t-t of it!" In a fearless voice
his brother said, "Relax, dude. We haven't done
anything." They shined flashlights on their palms
and smelled them. "No smell of gasoline here
on anyone, sir." The plainclothesman ordered

the guns to be withdrawn; men with shotguns
retreated back to colorful cars. The immaculate
black man in a suit and tie explained there
had been a firebombing at the ROTC building,
and since we were walking away from the area we
were suspects. They instilled such fright
in us that no one complained. Terrorists don't
announce their places with war whoops.
Only Indians. Long after the police and campus
security drove off we were unable to talk.
The Mexican girls who had been courteous
throughout the ordeal squawked like hens
in a chicken coop at the break of day.

Long after I bid everyone farewell
I was still sick. At dawn Ted packed his pockets
with day-old pizza and left. From the window
I watched him melt in the morning fog with his
thumb asking for a ride. He danced an old-time
dance as each car refused him. With arms out
and slightly bent inward, and with the chest
expanded and the neck and head rigid, he firmly
implanted the balls of his toes twice each
in succession in front of him to the pavement.
He had one arm behind the small of his back
with an outstretched hand that simulated
the movements of dangling eagle feathers;
his other arm swung back and forth
with the thumb extended. The Star-
Medicine Boy had at last come down
and was going home. I dragged myself
to the shower stalls and drenched
my cold body with freezing water,
hoping to dislodge the trespasser
who stared at me from the mirror.
It didn't work. From the closet
I took out the Invisible Stone Knife

necklace, the Gift-Twin, and wore it.
I then asked him for forgiveness.

In the weak but warm rays of the sun
I saw how frail and thin my body was.
I hadn't eaten properly in days.
A hideous nakedness hung on a skeletal
frame. My thighs were chapped from the dry
desert air, and my lips were cracked.
Withered and abandoned I wanted to weep
for once-youth. But I couldn't.

The
Human
Parchment
Period

1975

Ted Facepaint:

Following our escapades in California
I started hitchhiking back to Iowa—
without the luxury of companionship.
Since I'd dropped out halfway into spring
semester, the College of the Desert Cactus
wouldn't pay my bus ticket home.
When I last spoke to Edgar his bags
were already packed. Luckily for him,
he had a poetry reading in Minnesota
and a one-way plane ticket the week
after he quit school. I was counting
on the two of us walking across America,
feasting on its grandeur. In thinking back
now, I was somewhat angered to learn
he would leave in class by way of L.A.
International. The last of our feral years.
Interaction afterward was minimal.
Edgar's interest in writing saved him
from hurtling through space alongside me.
He couldn't have withstood the microscopic

dust and debris which were steadily chipping
away at the concrete foundation of our bodies,
exposing the vulnerable wire foundation.

"There has to be another dignified way
to fall to earth," he used to mutter.
He equated us and anybody else unfortunate
enough to be associated with us as sad beasts
tied to poles with our own arteries
near the stars. It was an odd comparison,
one that I never fully understood or appreciated.
Once or twice I even thought he was secretly
poking fun at my Star-Medicine religion.
While he realized there was little to be gained
from his so-called Journey of Words, he soon
created a paper wall from tribal responsibilities—
and our friendship. Having known someone all your life
and having lived with them in the same place,
I was content to dive off the raft that was ready
to break up anyway. My only hope was to not
disintegrate in a fierce sandstorm,
the ugly ocean of sand. The long, tranquil
highways of the desert nauseated me
even when I was in high spirits.
I was headed home, though.

Facing malnutrition, I contemplated the small-
town assassination of a lonely white man
in Wingham, Nevada—to stave off my own death.
That's the event I most recall—and getting lost.
It was an uncomplicated offer: "Murder me tonight."
The haggard, unshaven employer tempted me
with peanut butter and jelly sandwiches
with icy milk. "After you do it,
dig in my left pocket—the small one—
for five hundred-dollar bills. They will be folded
into triangles. Inside one there'll be a phone
number for my ex-wife. Call her up and say,

'Camille, dear. Samson's snore can be heard
all the way to Dreamsville, Ohio.' She'll know
what that means. How about it, son?
We got a deal?" When I told him
I'd consider the offer over another
sandwich, he thanked God for sending me
and crossed himself.

I awoke that night from under the highway
underpass as the desert cooled. I stole into town
in a state of numbness. (Before meeting the person
in question I had resorted to a diet of hardshell
bugs and warm water that I kept mixed in a Pepsi
bottle.) In the savior's living room I took
a deep inhale of fried pork chops before I hammered
his head with the bottle. My sole intention was to render
him unconscious and no more. It worked. The derringer
he had left on the kitchen table under the Cracker Jack
box was not as appealing as I originally thought.
The generous stranger moaned and briefly jerked
on the couch on the third and final hit.
I was still feeling weak and delirious as I
emptied the last drops of bug-water over
his splotchy forehead. It was my way of saying
thanks for the leftover pork chops and the money,
which got me up and going again. Oh, I did call
his ex-wife and recited whatever I remembered
about Ohio: "Camel, dear," I said. "Samson sleeps
tonight and wants you to know he cares still
for Cincinnati . . ."

With a full gut and an aversion
for company, I sat at a rest area bench
two hundred miles north from the Pepsi clubbing.
There, I was approached by a frizzy-haired
wordless woman, who began kissing the length
of my arm from fingertips to shoulder
in sultry abandon. It was a set-up.

In the midst of passion, I was garroted
from behind and dragged to the tumbleweeds
where I was severely trounced. They took
seventy-five dollars from my pockets and stripped me
to my socks and underwear. Although they
deliberated taking those as well, something
changed their minds. Thank goodness, I thought,
as I wiggled my sweaty toes and felt the sharp
triangles of the four bills.

I was spread-eagled for several hours
in the harsh sunlight. As the sand reflected
back, I slowly baked. In those excruciating
hours I began to reminisce:
had I seen something like this once?
The Circus Acrobat, Junior, instantly came
to mind. I saw Charlotte again, running out
into the popping flashbulbs of the reporters'
cameras. She led a reluctant Junior back
to the car under a deadly rain of bullets
and buckshot. It was a risky move.
We could have died were it not
for the protective guiding spirits
of Bonnie and Clyde. Yeah, that's true.

Bearchild's uncle, Carson Two Red Foot,
said afterward Junior and Charlotte
were probably reenacting a Bonnie and Clyde
gangster shoot-out which took place many years
ago in Iowa. "There's spirits in the air,"
Carson told us in a somber tone,
"floating around aimlessly. These belong
to the once-lives of people who for some reason
or other, perhaps through acts which caused
their own demise, have no place to go.
No heaven—the Hereafter in our case—
and no hell. I suspect their spirits sensed
the kind of insane trouble your Ontario

friends were in and decided to help."
We scoffed at the association then,
of course, but later on two "gangster
ghosts," a man and a woman, were reported
roaming the fields and swamps around the old
Grassleggings cabin. They'd open the window
curtains together, reveal themselves,
and close them rapidly.

Carson eventually went on to tell us
of the time he was playing softball
in southern Iowa. "It was my turn up at bat when
the distant chatter of machine-gun fire opened up.
All the white and Indian players around the diamond
knew the criminals had been located. The exploits
of the hunt had been heavy in the newspapers.
We beat the Little Bohemia team by forfeiture;
they left the game because they wanted to see
the shoot-out site. The Indians didn't go;
we knew better. At least we thought
we were safe where we were . . ."

So there I was, buried in the desert,
a half-naked "skinjin," surrendering to the cosmos
with a smirk. I hadn't thought of the Ontarios
in a while. We kept clippings of Junior's
photographs published in the *Why Cheer News-Herald*
and forwarded some to Claer. Clad in his shorts,
Junior stood with his arms and chin lifted to the night
sky. The caption read: "A Buck Buck-Naked. An unknown
assailant who took part in the Hi-Na family beating
asks for forgiveness from someone named 'Beacon.'"
The situation was treated as a comedy. In fact,
the photograph won an award for being the best
among all of Iowa's newspapers serving
a population of "five thousand citizens or less."
As expected, there was absolutely no mention
of the Gladwood and Why Cheer militia and vigilante

groups who shot up the Grassleggings cabin
and "the famous heap." The sad thing about it was,
we never saw Junior again, or Charlotte.

Bearchild could only fantasize about the bewitching
virginal beauty who was, in fact, a full-fledged woman.
I confessed to Edgar that Charlotte made me promise
to tell all admirers she was thirteen years old. Evidently,
it kept most away. Actually, she was twenty-one years old;
she just looked young. Like the Hyena family,
I don't think Edgar ever forgave me for collaborating
with Charlotte, an "unrequited lay." On the other hand,
I could sympathize with Patty Jo Hi-na and her split
tongue. She had good reason to have vengeful thoughts
whenever her unnatural lisp worsened. Whenever
you met her in grocery store aisles, she'd coil
in defense and hiss, flicking her snake tongue
between the Rice Krispies and Shredded Wheat displays.
Her two embarrassed sons chose not to go to the clinic
to have the cinders removed from their cheeks.
The daughter, regrettably, suffered a miscarriage
on the spot from the bat-rocket. The fictitious
sentencing of the BEC tribal council
I pronounced that night for the Hi-na crimes
was *indeed* prophetic.

» «

Edgar Bearchild:

Nineteen seventy-five was the year I was among the 160
grateful recipients of a creative writing
fellowship from the Maecenas Foundation.
In the application I sarcastically wrote:
"Because no other voice should ever/can ever
replace the original voice of the American Indian
poet, especially one who resides at the place

of his birth and not in the city or academia,
I merely seek to compose meaningful narratives
as experienced within the Black Eagle Child Nation.
For too long we have been misrepresented
and culturally maligned by an ungrateful country
of Euro-American citizens who have all but burned
their own bridges to the past. I will not tolerate
such transgressions of my being and character.
If it is a pacifier these people desire,
then I propose they suck on something else . . ."

Surprisingly, the news of the fellowship was sent
by a Republican senator, Dan Frazier. The telegram
shook like a brittle, transparent leaf in my hand;
it seemed to possess a life of its own and was unable
to determine when to continue its descent to earth.
I had seen the green of spring zip by so fast,
and the hot, dry summer left no beads of perspiration
on my hairless chest. Further, the Swanroot and Iowa
rivers rose to their banks and receded in the late fall
rains without a single witness. Nothing, not even
the language of weather, could shake the leaf
from the sturdy branch of the red oak.
At a point in the atmosphere where the rain
changed to harmless clumps of wet snow,
the telegram loosened itself finally
from the branch and landed dead center
between my fingers.

"Dear Bearchild, Edgar.
It is my great pleasure to inform you
you have been awarded a $12,000
fellowship from the Maecenas Foundation
of Athens, Greece. Your poems alone symbolize
the spirit and tenacity of Americanism.
Please write should you ever need help
in the future. P.S. I am an ardent fan
of another BEC celebrity, C. Youthman.

Do you know him? Senator Dan Frazier.
Nov. 12, 1975."

When the red oak was at last bare
of any leaves, I saw behind it a man
deathly afraid of words that were not his.

The snow gathered in drifts around the geodesic
dome lodge that was to be the first
home for Selene Buffalo Husband and myself.
With the fellowship we purchased a German-made
typewriter, reams of high-quality paper, and
a new woodstove and hired carpenters
to install a plywood floor at the lodge.
Later, at Selene's suggestion, we bought
a portable generator that powered the RCA
television and the lamps. Never in my desperate
wishes did I believe a vindictive application
would be accepted for funding. All in all,
it was a short-lived miracle. Our life-style
pretty much stayed the same. We chopped wood
for warmth and hunted for game and fowl
with a pair of new rifles and sidearms.
For supper we would dine on either pheasant
omelettes or grilled walleye and California wine,
setting aside portions for the grandfathers
and grandmothers. We could have bought
a used mobile home and hooked up to utility
poles and the new water line—the one stalled
by the renowned Cantaloupe Terrorist—but decided
against it. After discussing the work we had given
to the design and structure of the lodge,
we chose to remain on the hills overlooking
the rivers.

As the morning snow melted on the skylight
windows, birds like kingfishers, bluejays,
and cardinals would look down into the single room

while pecking for drinks; in multitudes crows, hawks,
and eagles would circle above and threaten us with wing
movements; and the fast-moving clouds gave us pictures
of our love and hope. Along with new poems I began
writing stories as told to me by my great
uncle, Carson Two Red Foot, and my maternal
grandmother, Ada Principal Bear. These stories
were recorded and then translated and revised
back into English. It was a momentous winter.
The fingers would hit the keys all day. By sundown
they would squeeze triggers and down fox squirrels,
or they would tie fishing line to Rapala lures
and Mepp's spinners tipped with a minnow or leech.
The bitterness I had felt for the Central Plains
Arts Agency was expertly decapitated and shoved
into the embers of the woodstove. It ignited
like a mouse's nest doused with lighter fluid
and shot up violently through the tin chimney,
scattering like ashes from an incinerated existence
over the valley. Ever since my return I had deluged
the CPAA with letters asking for program information.
But my correspondence went unanswered for five years,
and when I visited the office in Plains Falls
there was nothing but fake, nervous smiles.
Lines from famous poets, novelists, and artists
were misquoted and bastardized, while I paraphrased
codes of unlawful discrimination. I subsequently
visited six staff offices, but each underling called up
the other on the telephone to purposely disrupt
my questioning. "Please, Mr. Bear Butt,"
the executive secretary said accidentally.
"Whoops! Excuse me. The head administrator
is sick and won't be in until next week."
It was to no avail. The elusive tactics
were familiar. (Administrative bigots tend
to hide behind their defenseless, suckass
employees.) The head administrator,
having county ties, grew up believing

anyone from Black Eagle Child was an
unclean heathen. All those who sat directly
beneath the director were entreated to listen
to ugly lies of how we lived, ate, loved, and
breathed and what we smelled like.
"After so much hate talk at the golf club,
church, and business breakfasts,"
I recorded in *Journal of a Woodland Indian*,
"there has to be a subtle transference
of bigotry in the genes from one Why Cheer
generation to the next . . ."

To forget those who knowingly violated
the laws of freedom, I immersed myself in songs
with a longtime friend, Pat "Dirty" Red Hat.
We'd practice with the other members
of the Young Lions Drum Group from eight
in the evening till two in the morning.
Since Selene and I had some money to travel
the pow-wow circuit, transportation
was not a problem. Pat knew this.
Plus, he had a way of convincing
anyone to treat songs as if they
were people. He had a strong influence
on my poetry; the tribal songs he composed
stemmed from the hearts of our grandfathers.
The complicated rhythms and simplistic messages
incorporated into his songs could not be expressed
or communicated in translated text. For the sake
of remembering, however, I wrote some down:

ENCOURAGEMENT SONG FOR DANCING YOUTH

Ba na tta ni mi ta ki ma mi kwa so
na ka mo to na ni ka ta me ko na ki sa ka ni
ni ka ni (no) na ni mi to no ki ya wi.

To the child who is dancing,
dance hard when I sing for you; don't stop;
lead the way and dance for your life.

》《

SHINING BLACK EAGLE CHILD DANCER

Bye tti wa ba me ko ma tti na e ka ta
bye tti wa ba me ko ma na ma ka te ke ti wa a be no
wa wa se so ta.

Come and look at the best dancer;
come and look at this Black Eagle Child,
the one who shines so.

》《

WE SHALL SING FOR YOU

We wi te bi ma ni na ka mo ni
ki na ka mo to ne be na
wa ba to tti me to se ne ni wa-
e me me ta ya i wa na tta tti ki ka sa no.

For the time being we shall sing
this song for you;
show the people
that you are having fun, lift your feet (in dance).

》《

THESE BELLS

Tte na we a nay
tte na we a nay
me nwe se to wa

ma na ni mi to
be se ta mo (ko)

These bells;
these bells;
this individual makes them sound good;
this dancer;
listen to them.

                    —Pat D. Red Hat

For as young as he was, Pat was gifted
with music composition; he also had a superb voice
capable of producing the highest or lowest voice.
It was incongruous to hear sweet, reverberating notes
come from the mass of meat and fat which was Pat.
Expressing himself with music was his best side.
On the coldest damp evening he threw out songs
without end, making the champion dancers compete
vigorously. No matter how much we tried to keep up,
there were occasions when it felt useless.
If he complained of a sore throat, we learned
to disregard it, for there was no difference
in his pitch and delivery. He only wanted
to make you feel important.

To know, to sit next to, and to sing with one
of the best regional drummers was an honor.
"Singing isn't everything," he'd say
whenever people introduced themselves,
bearing handfuls of money or gifts
in appreciation of his talents. "We each
have our own priorities. Edgar's is poetry;
Selene intends to revive the beaded shoulder bag;
Tom's interest is woodcarving and museum/gallery
exhibits; Peter yearns to become a certified welder;
and Jake . . . once he signs himself into the detox
program, has aspirations to resume dancing.

These aspirations are important. Mine,
as you know, are fast cars
and slender women." We'd laugh, knowing
he was preoccupied with the opposite sex,
his infamous side.

The man with the voice of four different men—
the Quartet—was disarmingly humble; he rarely
glorified his accomplishments. His influences
came from his grandfather, who left wax
cylinder recordings from the early 1900s.
A sense of guarantee that our songs
were historically authentic,
free from the modern intrusions
of classical or rock music,
reinforced our trust in Pat.

The Young Lions proved to be a psychological
crutch; we egged one another to achieve.
If we fell, we rushed over to prop up one another
with attention. We united our voices and sang
for those unattainable items, and we didn't care
one iota if people criticized us as an unlikely group.
The fact Selene sat at the drum with us as a woman
was deemed a taboo by several older musicians
who had no other recourse for venting
their jealousy. We concurred women were somewhat
restricted, but we took Grandmother's advice:
"As long as she doesn't drum on a religious
instrument, then it is a restriction I haven't
heard of." We were enigmatic in that we didn't
seek to become a "good pow-wow drum." Our goals
were different. From the early days when we
banged on the washtub with branches,
our desire was to become professional artists.
We took incentive from the annual Black Hawk
Commemoration in Rock Island, Illinois.

Huge crowds of tourists and their families
flocked to the hillside every Labor Day
to watch the dances. Entertaining
and educating those who wanted
to experience a small but important facet
of the tribal arts while honing our skills
in the process was a definite goal.

» «

Around 1973, at about the time Selene and I
began living together, someone knocked on the door
of my parents' house. The weekend hadn't even
started when Clotelde announced Facepaint wished
to speak to me at the door. She reported he looked
rather disheveled and "slightly miserable."
I hadn't talked to him much since our infamous
return from California. My reasons were simple.
The long arduous task of pasting paper to every
inch of my body had already begun, and all that
remained was the wait for it to set like a cocoon.
I figured a metamorphosis was my only salvation.

Once the sunlight entered the bedroom,
Selene had agreed to spin me as I hung from
the ceiling like a giant piñata.
Otherwise, in her own words, I'd be another
"preserved face on the shelf of depression,
on permanent exhibit at some carnival
sideshow, a wrinkled face with blue lips
for all the world to see." The prospect
of my decapitated head being next
to Ted's own bottled-up head and body
fluids frightened me. Hence, the paper wrap.
Rumor had it Facepaint was spending his days
with the group cursed to "a hundred years
of suicides," commiserating with them.

This I could do without, for anyone
who believed in old labels would live
and plan their lives accordingly.
Facepaint knew this; he was the one
who said so.

As bloated as I was in layers of white parchment
Facepaint could hardly recognize me. He reached
out and lightly jabbed my stomach. "You look like
the Pillsbury Dough Boy!" I covered the spot
he touched and mimicked a chuckle with small black
seal-eyes blinking. "Come on in," I signaled.
I extended my stumpy arms to the sides
questioningly after he sat down at the table.
"I need food, man," he replied, shaking
his head in dejection. In the manner
of an astronaut I waddled to the cupboard
and carefully took out five cans of Campbell's
Alphabet Soup, a can of chili beans, and a jar
of applesauce. "Can I take this loaf of bread, too?"
I nodded an approval. Ted stood at the doorway
with a grocery bag and shook my thick,
fingerless hand. His last words were,
"Watch it, Edgar. Your umbilical cord
might get caught." Looking down,
I did notice the copper ventilation tube
had been dragging throughout. When I looked
back up, he was gone. Outside I could hear
neighborhood dogs give chase to someone
on a fast, leg-cranked bike.

» «

Inside the paper cocoon I was terribly alone.
I could only imagine Selene's blistered hands
turning me gently to dry. In the blindness
the words from my childhood and past alighted

on my sluggish tongue. Limited by space
I could only transpose one or two words to a page
with a short, dull pencil. Memorization was essential,
and when it failed, I started the sentences over again.
One day, having spent countless Big Chief tablets
on "The Bread Factory" poem, I proclaimed myself
the King of Revision. Believing it was a revelation
and a half, I relayed it through the copper tube
like a projectile from an Amazonian blowgun.
Selene returned a note: "Underestimation
of one's abilities *can* be a good thing."
At last I was able to document my feeble
beginning. Childhood was a precious epoch.
How I even ever came to be confounded me.
It was incredible to think back and see faces
of people who were no longer. I saw these
as warm, windy days when families were strong
and united. My survival was more than a miracle.
And I was in a rage for my inability to find
ways to say thank you. Contrary to the beliefs
of many, there was indeed a past.

IN THE FIRST PLACE OF MY LIFE

*It is often said that before the Almighty Creator took the red-colored clay
in his cosmic hands to gently shape and mold the first human beings, he
wanted to be absolutely sure these people would have a knowledgeable
leader who would guide them through the suffering and beauty of
earthly existence.*

This leader, he must have felt, had to be a direct part of himself.

*To insure the best possible guidance for these people, in a manner simi-
lar to the extensive preparation he had done for the anticipated arrival of
these people, the Creator tore out a piece of his own heart and created O
ki ma, the Sacred Chief.*

*Considering the last turbulent and painful days the Creator experi-
enced before the jealous gods sent the Great Fire and Flood after him, it*

seemed appropriate that a progeny of wise decision makers be comprised exclusively of his own sacred flesh and blood. This he did . . .

The beginning of personal memory and history is perhaps the most important connection I have with Ma mwi wa ni ke, the young O ki ma, Sacred Chief, who founded and initiated the purchase of the Tribal Settlement in 1856:

From a distant and vague time, his grandson, Ke twe o se, my maternal grandfather, reached downward from his wooden-frame bed and called me with large outstretched arms and encouraging words. "*Ki sko, bya na yo*, come here."

He sat in the southeastern corner of the small two-room house waiting for me. Like a newborn wobbly-legged fawn taking a trial walk in a meadow of tall grass, I went to him. Attracted initially by his toothless smile and puffy, slanted eyes, I struggled past a beam of harsh sunlight and lost sight of him momentarily.

On the wooden floor beneath me I could feel the worn subtle divisions of boards; in the brightness I could see individual specks of dust float and swirl past me and then disappear in the draft.

From the cool darkness, he lifted me upward gracefully in one swoop into his arms and placed me on his knees. The year was 1952, almost a hundred years after his own grandfather established our five thousand–acre sanctuary in central Iowa.

As soon as the Creator made O ki ma from the flesh of his heart, the other human beings were then sculpted from the red-colored clay, and they named themselves appropriately from their very beginnings.

Akin to a father attending to the well-being of his children, the Creator instructed these people on the tactics and skills of hunting and fishing, and he also showed them when and where to plant seeds for gardens, as well as how to live in peace and to respect one another and the various but essential life-forms around them. He also taught them how to sing, dance, and pray. He shared with them only the good things by which to live. And they venerated him in return.

Yes, the Creator had meticulously prepared this earth for these people. From the claws of the muskrat who dove into the great body of water to retrieve mud, remnants of a previous earth, the Creator shaped the round

earth; from the twigs and bits of grass brought by the bluejay and mourn-
ing dove, the Creator turned these into forests and prairies; and from the
vulture's once-beautiful wings came the gouged-out valleys, hills, and
mountains. Yes, the Creator had done much for these people.

All he desired was for these new people, their children, and their chil-
dren's children to remember him through the four seasons in prayers,
stories, songs, and intricate ceremony. For as long as clan remembrance
to his specific wishes continued, they would survive.

In the first place of my life there is the image of my grandfather
imploring me to walk to him. In the second place of my life there is
my grandfather again, but in this memory he is the one who is attempting to walk:

With the door wide open to the summer night, my grandfather
prepared to stumble out of the small house with the aid of three
young men. It seemed the difficulty I experienced walking to him
afflicted him instead. The little earth on which I once stood was
now under his feet and growing smaller with hardly any room to
stand. I began to feel that something terrible was wrong; he would
subsequently lose balance and fall.

From the kerosene-darkened walls of the corner where he made
his bed, he slowly held out his arms. The young men placed themselves under them, lifting him cautiously to the floor and then
outside.

From the wooded hill above and east of the house, locusts,
crickets, and tree frogs directed the start of the night songs in uni-
son. Soon I could no longer hear the four talking men. Instead there
was a buzzing sound that swiftly came and left, like the flutter of
rapid wings. It brushed my face with its breeze and became still.

I later realized it was only Grandfather's low voice, giving constant instructions. In soft respectful voices the young men were
responding and informing each other what they were doing,
where they were. The metamorphosis of arm to wing and mouth
to beak . . .

In the third place of my life there is a fiery-red sunset. It is being
followed by a thin, horizontal fragment of blue sky, which itself is

being trailed by the ornately speckled lights of the night sky, covering the earth-island like a blanket with deliberate perforations. Starlight coming through clothes of poverty.

Three opposing parts of the day are visible as I waver on a well-trodden path of dirt and sparse grass. For clarity I try to look upward to distinguish the colors around me; I am intrigued by their variations and mysteriousness. Although I am quite a ways from my point of origin—the small unpainted house—I am not afraid or alarmed.

Somewhere on this path once, I think aloud to myself, my sick grandfather was guided to the thickets. I therefore adduce this path leads to a boundary where humans can vanish and reappear as dust-like shapes in the last faint beams of sunset. A whippoorwill, *ko ko we a*, begins to call out on the hillside.

In my plastic imitation chaps, boots, and cowboy straw hat, I am content just to stand, slightly off-balance, watching in astonishment as the three hues of earthlight follow the westward sun. As this light illuminates the forest floor nearby I can see umbrella-shaped plants glisten like vast rippling water.

With the last of the day's warmth on my face and the cool stars coming over my shoulders, I straighten my body and rise upward, flying beyond the branchtops of the forest, and become a witness to an extraordinary renascence:

We tti wa ba ki, from the east, a whizzing star travels across the landscape, lighting the area briefly with a blanket of silver glare. After the fiery star passes the slow fusion of night and day, it explodes in silence and disintegrates, sending multicolored sparks over the horizon, over my inquisitiveness. By some powerful decision I believe the star has been sent for my sole benefit—to enthrall me. I gasp and tumble earthward.

In the fourth place of my life there is an irreplaceable loss. On July 23, 1954, an aged woman—the same one who had opened the door to let my grandfather and the three young men out—led me to the adjoining room of the house where a body was rolled perfectly into red-and-blue-patterned blankets.

She pointed and then began speaking words I had little comprehension of. I was taken aback by the orderly scene of a person who slept without breathing.

"*Ma na ke ke me tto e ma i ni ke e ki tti ne ka ne na qwi be no tti ni e ya. A qwi na na tti ni ne a bi bya tti ni.* This is your grandfather; he has left us and will now go far away. He will never come back."

If he has indeed left, I asked myself, why is he still here in plain view? And where could he go if by chance this person asleep is not him? The thought of my grandfather going somewhere didn't coincide with the utter stillness of the unseen person.

There was no place one could possibly go on this little earth. Could he have gone behind the two hills? Or did he hide in the ravine by the creek?

I could not make sense of the attention his apparent departure brought. All night generous but wordless people came and left, bringing food. I could no longer hear the insects and frogs. Instead, there was a row of sitting and kneeling men with gourd rattles and a wooden barrel drum, chanting melancholic songs that put me to sleep.

The next day and for two days afterward, streams of people kept coming, but still no one knew where my grandfather was. I was sure this was the reason so many came, to assist in the search. The realization that he was the subject of much concern heightened my anxiety. Even when people congregated inside and outside the house to chat and eat, with the air filled with the aroma of corn and chicken, sweets, fruits, and frybread, his absence made me extremely lonely.

On what was perhaps the fourth and final day we sat down on the large grassy yard to eat the cooked food. When I finished I found myself under an apple tree, looking up at a pale, hooknosed man whose reassuring voice finally told me what everything meant. "*A qwi ke na na tti ni ne ya bi bya tti ni ke me tto e ma.* Your grandfather will *never* return," he said.

I was positive these visitors had tried to tell me that but had failed to get through. I had enclosed myself securely from all explanation. What had been so hard to understand was right in front of my face in the form of two grandfathers.

As the feast was drawing to a close—evident by clinking silver-ware and the scolding of impatient children by their parents—the same men who sang several nights previous came out from the pro-tective shade of a maple tree and sat down with the barrel drum propped in front of them.

A carton of Lucky Strike cigarettes was opened, and the packs were distributed to each of the singers by the same male attendants who had set out the tablecloths, dishes, cups, spoons, and kettles over the yard. With lit cigarettes in their mouths the singers quietly joked with one another; a few drank coffee, placed their heads to-gether, and hummed in search of a tune.

The pale, hooknosed man who had enlightened me earlier stood directly in the middle of the festivity. I hadn't noticed before that he was wearing bright, sparkling clothes. He looked elegant with long swaying leaves of corn and the shimmering cottonwood trees behind him. He stood on one end of the yard where the people sat and ate. He did not speak or look around in curiosity as the others. The red fibrous wool of the blanket bound to his waist and lower torso, along with the intricate floral beadwork and yarn ties around his head and arms, reflected the fine weather.

"*Ma na ke i no ki ke me tto e ma. I ni ni a be tti i tti te e wa ni.* Here is your grandfather now. That is what you must always think," said the aged woman who opened the door, taking my hand and lead-ing me to him.

"*Ni ne a bi ska ma ye ke me tto e ma ni.* He will take the place of your grandfather."

Finally coherent, I studied the hooknosed man and came to the conclusion he was already my grandfather; he had espied my loss and consoled me under the apple tree in a familiar voice.

As the relatives began to stand in anticipation of a dance, I lis-tened to the instructions given him by the leader, telling him where to go and how many times this should be done. When the man with the sparkling clothes spoke, he sounded different. But my grandfather and his voice were just within him, I thought.

As soon as the attendants picked up the tablecloths and silver-ware, we stood in a group behind my grandfather-to-be. When the last communal drink of water was drunk and the last chewing gum

154

opened by restless infants, the aged woman drew herself down and began to whisper.

"*Ma ni ke me me tti ne ni ke ski wi te ke ma qwi ke me tto e ma i ni a.* This is the last time we will have to dance with your (previous) grandfather."

I shielded my face with the one free hand for shade and looked upward. The aged woman held a handkerchief to her mouth and took short, sudden breaths as she cried.

Like the fierce crackling sound that precedes thunder, I was startled by the unexpected rumbling of the barrel drum by an elderly gentleman wearing sunglasses on his wide nose and a red Dutch bandana around his neck.

Although he had previously appeared tired and unimpressed by the proceedings, he, too, became someone else. From behind the old singer's sunglasses there emerged another person whose bent body combined the vocal strengths of a dozen men. He called out encouragingly to the other singers, and they joined in as a chorus with the same fervor and intensity.

Like the echo of thunder heard leaving a valley and heading through another in the distance, the song was sung by all until breath's end.

The rumbling slowed down and then stopped altogether.

The elderly man paused briefly to slosh the water inside the barrel before bringing down the wooden loop-end drumstick into a steady resonant beat over the wet cowhide.

The drum's strong vibration passed through the bodies of all those who were clustered around my new grandfather. It was as if our heartbeats were controlled by the deep, thunderous hum.

In exhilaration we huddled together and took several steps forward.

The music lifted above the crowd of dancers and stayed in place before lifting further, flying away, and then coming back to encircle us like an eagle whose powerful black and golden wingtips brushed our faces, waking us, telling us to see this dance through for my grandfather . . .

Many years after the incident with the whizzing star and my grandfather's departure, I stood in a garden which was being cleaned for plowing. I wore an impressive denim coat with short white fringes of plastic on the sleeves and shoulders, and there were tin medallions of standing horses over my chest.

Numerous fires were being set to mounds of dried cornstalks and roots. Together with two other children, I stoked the hot fires with a branch. We were amused and partially mesmerized when the thick black smoke followed us where we stood, as if to protect the fire from our intrusive branches.

Unaware that embers were dangerous, I placed a branch with an invisible flame on my shoulder and quickly caught fire. White scorching smoke shot from my coat, and my nostrils sucked up the heat. I coughed in horror and couldn't breathe. I spun in a circle, tripped, got up, and ran wildly in an effort to extinguish the body-fire.

In the mayhem, with mates chasing me and screaming, a woman grabbed and threw me violently into the clumpy garden. She rolled me like a ball over the dust until the fire went out.

In the calmness I looked up at the white clouds and blue sky, and I distinctly remembered the whizzing star. I personified that very star, tumbling and sizzling with bits of my being spread out over the green foliage.

The woman who doused the fire with garden dust would become my mother, Ne tti ta, and her mother was my grandmother, Ne o ta mo qwe, the aged woman who held my hand as we danced for the last time with my grandfather. She was the earth herself . . .

》《

When I at last became old enough to differentiate the basic rights and wrongs and apply them accordingly within family and social perimeters, my caretakers began to intensify their teachings on how to take care of myself, what to avoid, how to be friendly and re-spectful of others, not to lie or be mean.

To prevent even the earliest form of criticism, I was not allowed to wander anywhere by myself like an unwanted or wayward child, nor was I permitted to visit houses and the like.

This is what I was told whenever I expressed a desire to walk to a neighbor's house and play with friends my age:

"*Ka ta na ta we ne ta ka ni ne ko ta ni a ya ni. A yo ma e o wi ki ya qwi. Wa ni mo tti qwa bo se wa ni ne wo ne ki me te ne ta qwi me ko ko i ya ki ta tti me ko. A yo ki ki wi ta. Ne tti a be tti ki i ka ma wi ki ya bye ni' ni bi i ne ne ki me to se ne ni wa ki. Na no tti ke me ko a wi ta ke ko e ne me ko sa be me ne ko tti,' ki i ne ko be na.* Do not desire to go anywhere. This is where we live. Should you traverse about, if you are seen, somebody will surely say things about you. Stay here. So people will not say, 'He is always preoccupied with houses.' 'His caretakers must not care for him,' is what they will finally say."

The few occasions I objected to or questioned this travel restriction, comparing myself to the children given the freedom to travel the roads by themselves, I was duly reminded of how an elderly woman, a neighbor, nearly drained the life out of my infancy to extend her own. The possibility someone could harm me by touch alone never failed to deter me.

In the mirror I would peruse my round face and see the pockmarks and long fingerlike scars on my tender skin. This was evidence of her ill-intentioned visit.

Stop and listen, I was told, before you get angry with us.

"You were asleep in the hammock the afternoon your nemesis came to welcome you. You were but a month old, a baby. She had never stopped by before for any reason. So when she made much of this visit we became suspicious. We didn't know exactly what she had done until a day or two later. Her visit was a pretext. You became very ill with convulsions accompanied by a high fever that couldn't be brought down. We then reminded one another how she had been ever so delicate with her touches on your chin and jaw. On the places her fingers came in contact, your skin broke out in blisters."

So to that end I listened and never again dared to venture beyond the natural tree, field, brush, road, and hill borders that encompassed our house. By nightfall I would peer out the windows and wonder if the green light would show up and reenact the dance of the battle, my breath or hers.

While there were many houses up and down the community's lone gravel road, I didn't know which one housed the descendants of the old woman responsible for my auspicious beginning.

»«

In spite of all the warnings, however, especially when I became older, I was twice as inquisitive of the different-mannered and different-looking men, women, and children who occupied the neighboring houses.

I was soon aware we were but one small family in a community of families. If I didn't see enough people through school or feasts, I sought inconspicuous ways to go to them. To accomplish this I would request chores such as getting water from the pumps or wells throughout the area, or I would get myself appointed to deliver messages written in syllables to my grandmother's associates.

Directly west of our house, past the creek and over the gravel road, there was a white two-story house with green shingles that reflected a thousand glittery suns in winter. It sat menacingly on top of a large, well-rounded hill. In the summer, the area was completely engulfed by shade from stocky oak trees and well hidden by berry bushes and tall uncut weeds.

An old man, Jim Percy, whose cheeks were in a state of perpetual movement, lived there. Sometimes he would have a family of visitors there who were unusually shy; they would scatter like mice in an opened cupboard if I came up the path with a bucket.

One person, the father, would remain for a moment; he would greet me and then walk away, leaving small wooden carvings of helmeted soldiers or racehorses on the bench for me to look at and handle. They came in varying sizes, but all had the same exquisite pose: the soldier bending low with a rifle slung barrel-down on his shoulder and the riderless horse prancing about victoriously.

Knowing there were no toys as perfect as the carvings on the shelves of the Ben Franklin store in downtown Why Cheer, I entertained plans to swipe them once. I discarded the notion when I realized there would be no suspects except myself. I also felt there was more substance in seeing the mice scurry.

The days old man Jim shuffled down the hillside he would bring us fresh vegetables from his immaculate garden. Like his scarce visitors he wasn't talkative. He stood for the longest periods of time, listening to my grandmother. Like a trained seal he'd grunt an approval or shake his head "no" in disagreement.

I finally figured out his demeanor one day: he was saving his breath for the epic prayers he delivered at Ghost Feeds. His knowledge and gift of communicating to the deities who controlled our destinies kept his schedule busy. Without the slightest flaw or pause, he recited the stories of our origins, detailing the reasons everything was in order, using archaic words whose place was limited to prayers. I understood very little, but I was sure the Controllers received the messages.

Jim Percy's house looked down at the seven houses in the valley. From the northeastern point where the reclusive woodcarver sat, one could scan the length of the gravel road as it hugged the hill before going to the pine trees, crossing a bridge and the creek. With the buckets full and fresh water chilling my senses from arm to thigh, I marveled at the sight from the woodcarver's bench; it was a spectacular bird's-eye view from any angle. Looking into the car interiors without being seen was exciting. Whether the passengers were headed up or downhill, they were visible.

Below the bridge, the shiny wings of dragonflies lent an air of charm to the creek. High above were vultures, birds who had sacrificed their beauty when they sculpted the land for the Creator. On windless days the intimate conversations of people or lovers below out for a walk could be heard. I froze and listened to each word.

As autumn approached, the hill revealed itself and the house suddenly loomed above in the fast clouds. Without the usual cover of leaves and tall grass, the rigid movements of someone's silhouette could be detected. It was the woodcarver engrossed with either the flamboyant posture of a horse or the fingernails of the fearless soldier. If he spotted you, he would stand and take two steps into the horizon, leaving behind the figurines and their grease and shoe-polish stains.

» «

Electricity was fairly new then, and our neighborhood was the last section to be dependent on kerosene lamps. Largely unaware of technological advantages, I found the dull yellow lights pleasant, for they signaled a day had come to its end. The games ended and mothers became vociferous when their children didn't come in. We were reminded that as long as there was darkness, there was the promise of evil.

I remember one particular night when I was transfixed by a strange orange light; it was triangular in shape with a cluster of dark lines, hovering and intersecting close to old man Jim's roof. The bright structure was almost as tall as the house itself.

Before it got too dark I scaled our hill and peered unsuccessfully to the other side; I even walked to the farthest edge of our garden but could only see more trees.

By the time I was getting ready for bed there were red sparks leaping out erratically from the orange light. I could have asked Grandmother what was going on up there, but I was determined to find out for myself. (Actually, I thought Grandmother would side-step my question and offer a simple, rational explanation.) Anyway, from the moment I fell asleep right up to the very moment I opened my eyes, I dreamed a drum was beating rapidly.

"Nokomis, Grandmother," I eagerly announced in the morning over rice, eggs, and frybread. "*Mi ke ne bi na te ka a ka wa ta ma ni.* I could go after water, if you want."

Such an offer to volunteer work rarely went unheeded. More so when waking up early assured one longer life. Grandmother re-kindled the fire in the tan and green-edged woodstove for hot dish-water, and buckets were poured into others to make two empty.

"*E a i,* yes," she said. "*A be ne tti ma ne bi ne na ta we ne ta.* I always have a need for water."

At the precise moment the sun was beginning to filter through the oak-covered slope I walked onto old man Jim's yard with an outstretched neck; I was surprised to see circular rows of parked cars with fogged-up windows, signs that people were asleep in them still. Some of the cars I had never seen.

On the other side of the house I saw a group of people file out from a white canvas tipi. To see such a large contingent emerge from a tall, narrow lodge was unbelievable. It was apparent no one had slept; they yawned and stretched. The older men huddled in groups and smoked cigarettes with their heads bobbing in lively discussion; the women stood in line at the two outhouses and laughed wantonly.

Jim Percy was the last to exit through the blanket door of the tipi; he strolled uncaringly through the wet, frost-covered grass in his moccasins.

What I had seen the previous night was the top cluster of tipi poles and the lodge's orange campfire radiating through the canvas covering and portal. I placed one hand on the cold pump handle and poured water into the top with the other. Once the vacuum caught, I held the handle with two arms and worked steadily until the buckets filled.

Jim Percy had walked far beyond his garden and was about ready to enter the meadow. With the daylight everywhere he resigned himself to the situation; he clasped his large hands behind his back and walked to the forest's edge without once looking back. In less than the moment it took to place the buckets together evenly on the pump's platform, I missed his entrance. The tattered gray sweater he wore blended like animal camouflage against the bare trees.

》《

The first decade of my existence was spent under my grandmother's roof. My immediate relatives consisted of my grandmother, mother, two uncles, and younger brother, Ma qwi ba tti to, Old Bear Man. Without an automobile, it seemed we hardly went any-where. If we did it had to be within walking distance and only for brief visits.

We were related to and well acquainted with the children of our uncles' and mother's half brother. Ba tti to and I were first cousins to the Water Runner sisters and their little brother, Mateo.

From what little information I was able to gather and determine, this was the extent of our world of relatives. I was pleased, though, and I never questioned who I was or where I came from. That issue didn't become important until later.

Much of what I encountered and recollected as a child but didn't fathom for the longest time gradually took on a new meaning. Like my two ever-present uncles, Winston and Severt, who I came to realize were two of the three young men who helped my sick grandfather walk early on in my childhood, the other man being their cousin, Howard Courting. They were part of my second memory. Anyway, my grandmother said something in reference to my deceased grandfather which perplexed me.

"*O swa wa ni ke tti se a ki.* Your uncle's father," she would say. The mere vocalization of the word "father" intrigued me, for I was not informed children like Ba tti to and myself were supposed to possess one. We knew of no such relationships. Sure, the Water Runner cousins had one, but I saw no differences between their father and our uncles. Basically, Winston and Severt were there, perpetually older, wiser, and protective.

Ironically, whether by way of this void or unfamiliarity, I did not harbor a longing or need for such a figure. Like that whizzing star I often pondered, impervious to all else within its speeding surroundings, my sole purpose was to blaze ahead.

》 《

In retrospect it is clear now where my interest in storytelling began. During the winters whenever my grandmother would lean over the table and delicately cup her hand over the lamp to blow out the flame, I knew beforehand I would be taken in mind and spirit to another world.

In a room lit only by the snow's paleness coming through the frosted windows, I would lie still on the floor and patiently wait for awe-inspiring tales of the supernatural past when the forces of good and evil fought a battle which eventually led to the very Creation of our lives:

"Once, long ago, gods dwelt upon this earth. They also dwelt beneath the earth, and far away where the stars are now. They were like people, marrying and rearing children just as people do now, and they were tall, big, and mighty. Over them ruled the Greater God; he was mightiest of them all. He, too, had taken to him a wife, and of the four sons who were born to him two were destined to become Great Gods themselves.

"They were different from all other children before them, for, even when very young and small, they were more powerful than those who were older than they. And the older they grew, the stronger they walked in their might as Gods. Many gods beheld the growing strength of the two boys, and they became jealous . . ."

From this ancient conflict and animosity between our spiritual predecessors, I was told, came the origin of death and impermanence through the younger brother and the creation of the tribe through the older brother. "It recounted his benevolent acts toward men, his teaching the people the way to live, and his preparation of a home after death in the spirit world." This was not only the most sacred story of our past but it was also a long prayer recited at religious gatherings.

Just as sacred were the Winter Stories, *A te so ta ka na ni*, that were told only in the winter season. On the other spectrum were *A tti mo na ni*, Stories, which focused on tragic and humorous lessons learned from personal or vicarious experience. Quite a few related to unexplained events; some pertained to our immediate family, clan, and tribal obligations.

Through my grandmother's narratives on the multifaceted aspects of cosmogony, I developed an early cognizance for the unseen but ubiquitous presence of powers who maintained a permanent control and effect upon our lives. Although we were brought about by way of spiritual turmoil between our ancient predecessors, the rivalry of Light and Dark was a continuing reality. In a sense, it remains a day-to-day encounter, a constant balancing of forces, an uneasy truce. It was a forceful impetus upon the clans to honor the Creator's ancient wishes. Considering the sacrifices made in order that we may be, it was a seemingly small request. The survival of the tribe was contingent on our own adherence to the spectacular Gifts given long ago.

Religion or the Principal Belief, according to Grandmother, was and is the only conceivable means of entry to the Hereafter. To faithfully accept Belief was to remain free of negativity. To be ignorant, uninformed, and oblivious to one's origins was to openly defy "the one who created you" and invite adversity.

It was explained incessantly how insignificant we as mortals were within this expanse. All weather—rain, snow, sleet, hail, and wind—was the Creator's own doing. And two of the annual seasons—spring and fall—were set aside to commemorate his teachings.

We were greatly indebted to the Creator.

"One should never take for granted the air we breathe, the water we drink, and all that we see before us," said Grandmother. "*Ma a ki Me te qwi Ne ni wa ki ne ma so tti ki*, These Wooden Men (Trees) that stand here," she would add with emphasis while pointing to the oaks on the ridge, "are sacred beings themselves capable of thoughts and feelings. Each one that you see, no matter what kind, is alive as you and I are. The same applies to the cooking fire outside where I place portions of our meals. Fire is a transmitter of prayer, including the moss-covered boulders embedded on the bottom slope of the hill. These are his. All water is his whether from a lake, river, spring, or rain. The Thunderers that flash are our Grandfathers, and they, too, are part of his domain. Whether through fire, stone, water, and thunder, one must frequently offer sacred tobacco to these watchful entities."

During the first spring thunderstorms, we were handed tobacco and told to stand outside in the pounding rain and release it for the passing Grandfathers. Sometimes after our meals I would be asked to collect small pieces of bread, meat, and fruit in one saucer which was reserved for the fire or green boulder for our deceased relatives.

In winter we were reminded that the snow-covered ground symbolized his return. His very body covered the earth to replenish the plants—food and medicine—for another season. But mostly it was a visit to see whether we were abiding by his ancient wishes.

Ba tti to, my brother, and I were therefore strictly forbidden to roll and shape snow into a figure resembling a human. As much as we wanted to, we did not make snowmen. The idea of creating something from snow was a nonhuman endeavor. If we dared to lapse into forgetfulness, we were reprimanded and ordered to haul extra sledloads of chopped wood.

At day's end, when large, decorated snowmen stood in the neighboring yards, our yard was desolate.

This acknowledgment of an invisible, life-affecting element, hovering around us, instilled respect and understanding of our tenuous existence.

How We Delighted in Seeing the Fat

By Carson Two Red Foot as Told to Edgar Bearchild

During one particularly harsh winter—an unforgettable season in which our beloved father, John Two Red Foot, deserted the family for a young woman named Ma tti qwe ta tti ta, the One Most Afraid—we were camped along the wooded bluffs of the Iowa River near the Amana Colonies. The year was around 1908. Including our mother, Martha, there were six of us—two girls and three boys. Of the children I was the oldest.

Traditionally, the tribe broke into family groups during winter—to basically have everyone fend for themselves—but no one had ever left their respective group because of marital problems. Anyone affected by the unusual parting of such relationships was expected to tolerate it. This meant child or adult, without complaint or question. Survival before self. It was believed any exchange of words on the subject would ultimately cause the group harm, but the bickering between those involved would not. Of course, this blind, almost sniveling acceptance of rules was not for our mother. She chose not to remain with "those responsible." In a small way, I approved of her decision.

"*Ni bi ta ki ki nwa wa ma ni ta tti i tta i ye qwi.* So that you (children) will not be doing this," she said whenever she attempted to explain her plans. We were reminded of her childhood, the years she was forced to live from one family to the next as an orphan.

Long before the summer changed into autumn, the people of the tribe made sure we knew of our mother's strangeness. The children around us often made startling comments to that regard.

"Everyone is wondering why your mother is storing corn. Corn is to be eaten instead of being kept," they would voice unexpectedly.

After a barrage of questionable deeds committed by our mother, someone would timidly ask if we were going somewhere. We never had answers. The bundles of dried corn were supposed to be a secret. We knew our playmates had been instructed to say things they knew nothing about. It was simply a desire to affect the probable outcome, someone wishing adultlike talk between children could do some good. We suspected there were reasons behind the clamor, but we were too young, dependent, and afraid to do anything.

Before we realized what happened, we drifted away like a pack of breakaway clouds and disappeared in the snowy, turbulent hills and fields.

All blame—the reason why we suffered hunger and wandered over an unfamiliar landscape—belonged wholly to my father. Whether it was because of this humiliation or as a consequence of emotional breakdown—they were the same to me—our mother took us away from the central encampment in Tama County.

It is, unfortunately, this time which I will recount for you. You have made this request, for you say it will make you further aware. My memories are fresh and vivid as some of the more powerful dreams that come to me in the dark before morning. As I mature, memory doesn't fail me; instead, it grows stronger. But there is nothing more sad than reflection, *me qwi te a ka ni*. Sometimes in the comfort of my small home, I can hear those warm voices, faces, and images of the past. Often I think that the only true merriment and religious strength I underwent occurred during my youth and early manhood. All else has been a long uncomfortable adjustment to being an Indian, *E ne no te wi ya ni*, in the world of the white man.

Our grandfathers were right all along when they warned through prophecy that all earth as we presently know it would soon vanish.

We alone can determine whether life will continue or perish. It is up to us. Our failure to adhere to the *given* ceremonies will set demise into action. First, our own language and blood as they are doing now will divide us. Our words will soon be known to few and despised by many. Our elders will eventually hold the Last Ceremonies. And all because of a failure to uphold promises. There will be no reason to transfer the Principal Belief. An absence in spirituality is all that will be needed to send the portent—the Northern Lights—over the skies to the southern horizon, signaling the apocalypse, *Na i na ni ne ne na ka mi ka ki*. Through wars over flags or even natural disasters, we will have no air to breathe, no water to drink—no water for our plants.

Anymore, when I reflect on the excitement of being young again, singing the many songs, courting your grandmother, hunting and fishing, welcoming the seasons with clan feasts with my parents and grandparents, I believe death is only a profound and ecstatic recollection of the lovely past. The singing and dancing they speak of in reference to the peaceful Afterlife are not distant; we have all experienced them in our growth and maturity. They just get farther and farther as we age . . . Death, in a way, is the gracious return of all memory.

My name is Carson. You know that being my nephew. My full name is Carson Two Red Foot. In Indian I'm known as Ne bi ki be mi ba o ta, Water Runner. We descend from a legion of notable runners and messengers. All of the people, my relatives and yours from the White Crane and Principal Bear clans, that I am about to talk about are gone. Deceased. Naming them as if they were alive again will be dangerous, for the word is strong. As we speak of the dead, it is said they lapse into dreams where they are alive again. They begin to cry, and the trance cannot be broken by their kind until the naming ends.

I should not be so daring, I should not transgress our precepts, are the thoughts I feel. But who is there after me to tell these stories? No one. I am the only person left from those hard early times. This story and many others need to be recorded so generations ahead will be aware that poverty was a fact for the Two Red

Foot family, including others. Ironically, this was also a time when religion—and witchcraft—was at its highest power.

Hunger along with depression provided a gathering for this dark ugliness. The control of the supernatural. I will now take this cigarette, your Marlboro Light, and open it up. I sprinkle tobacco grains over the floor for myself and you . . .

As it was an era when crops were few and hunting sparse, we rarely had money to purchase basics like bacon, sugar, flour, coffee, and corn. The truth was, it was abnormal for us to have money. If there was any to speak of, it was rarely seen or handled, for it was quickly signed over—in the same building (post office, general store, and federal agency)—to Mr. Cox, who directed the yearly allotments from the government. The tribe was constantly in debt— to a single conniving white man. Next to the federally appointed "Chieftain," Mr. Cox was the most greedy and important person we knew. He singlehandedly determined the fate of the tribe. If he had the slightest misgivings about an individual or his or her relatives, they were severely punished by deprivation. As the mailman, fur trader, policeman, judge, grocer, and agent, he determined the value of all—food, stamps, furs, jail terms, and our dignity.

It had therefore been a good six months since the last government payout—$125 total for a family of five for the whole year of 1908. Half of which went to Cox. Although mother tried to explain we had perhaps spent a bit more money than usual, we each knew Father had taken it to make a new beginning with the One Most Afraid, a young and attractive woman.

Because of her physical beauty and precocious wit, the One Most Afraid was a frequent subject of discussion. You could say she was very popular. I had seen her on a number of occasions at the summer dances and feasts. In a way, maybe because I was closer to her in age than father—she was fourteen and I was twelve—I understood my father's attraction. Her presence was captivating: in her long ruffled red-satin dress, white collarless blouse, net shawl, and glittering earrings, she was resplendent.

There may have even been a night or two when I chanted myself asleep to her contradictory name, Ma tti qwe ta tti, Ma tti qwe ta tti, Ma tti qwe ta tti ta, until embarrassment came over me. She had men admirers by the age of ten. My father was the first to be struck. But no one ever suspected his interest would lead any further.

For three summers he took my sister and the One Most Afraid berry-picking. There was nothing wrong with this, but once when I went along to check the fish traps, I saw a game of catch and release. The scene where my father was running and laughing like a child was unnatural. Stupid me, I took part in the chase and clung like a baby raccoon on the One Most Afraid's back until we dropped. I forgot about this event until my mother asked what took place.

"In the circle of representative dolls on the ground," she said in an eerie tone and with deeply sunken eyes, "your father is the lead doll, for reasons we have yet to learn. I do know that his apparel has been cut off in peculiar areas."

The very notion of someone carving my father's face in wood and dressing his body in miniature clothes with the exact material he wore was preposterous. And to stand this caricature of him up at dusk while whispering words of undesirable intent was silly. Why all this when the One Most Afraid of the Deer Clan didn't need medicines that altered one's affection? Why my father?

While he was undoubtedly the kindest father anyone could love, I resented him. Even if he was a victim of witchcraft. There were others who I felt shared my sentiments, many others who had been deceived by his friendship and trust. Since he was next in line to be principal drummer of the White Cranes Society, no one ever expected he would leave his wife and children without word or hint, taking everything we owned: sixty dollars credit to the general store, five underfed horses, and three unfired Civil War revolvers.

Our geodesic dome lodge of reeds and bark was located in a thick wooded area between three hills on the north side of the Amanas. We were well enclosed in a valley from all directions except the south. A long meadow stretched to the banks of the Iowa River below. From the high ground where we were, a line of rock formations could be seen sticking through the ice on the river. These were fish traps left in place long ago by people unknown.

And there were springs from the hillsides that flowed to the river. Springs that became slush on the coldest days but never froze, for these were mystical doorways of the Underground Spirits, Goddesses.

To the east, about a morning's walk, was the first of our neighboring community, Gerslossen. On calm, windless days we would walk to its adjacent farms and trade beadwork, wood carvings, or wild game for bread and sausage. Sometimes we were given permission by the red-cheeked descendants of Europeans to cull their fields for potatoes or corn that had inadvertently been missed during harvest.

But it was this weekly walking distance which brought tribal emissaries to our camp. Twice. News of a breakaway, fatherless Indian family. The farmers were concerned that if we became snowbound, we would either starve or freeze to death. Many people on behalf of family and clan members came with clothes, blankets, and food in hand. They wanted Mother to change her mind before severe weather started. However, it was time, preparation, and words wasted.

"Please consider your decision carefully," the emissaries voiced. "It may subsequently take the lives of your beloved children. Think of all the disasters that could occur. Crazed criminals like the Bull Whip Man, wild wolf-dogs, and a strange place unprotected by tornadoes."

Of course, the most far-fetched disaster posed was Mother's insanity that had the possibility of killing us all. Mass murder and then suicide. Bodies gnawed and mauled beyond recognition by hungry mice and crows.

But the one question posed that bothered me the most was the aspect of food.

"How do you expect to feed your children when you can no longer pass through deep snow or when you run out of items to trade?"

To this our defiant mother didn't reply. She sat on a blanket padding with her uncombed head bowed down, her eyes glassy and red from staring at the frosted dirt floor. Her haggard, unkempt appearance indicated that her husband was dead.

Large cloth-covered pots of cooked food were brought to perhaps entice us into going back. These pots were gingerly placed on the iron grill. In anticipation the youngest children would seat themselves near the place where we usually ate. In a matter of seconds the spacious lodge interior would fill with the unbearable aroma of brown, stringy meat that had continued to cook in its juices on the day-long travel across the country. When the people left in their creaky but sturdy buggies and wagons, the warm venison and squirrel soups were quickly tossed in one dish and set outside for Me ka te i qwe, Black Face, a black-and-gray-spotted dog.

"We can't trust them," Mother would harshly whisper while scraping and washing the dishes clean. "If Black Face is dead in the morning, we'll know something was added to the broth."

Much to our regret, if only for a faint scent, the grease-stained cloths were tossed into the open fire.

"Any kind of medicine, like love medicine, *bi na i ka ni*, is witchcraft. Always remember this is how we lost your father."

That winter our mother was terribly overwrought with depression and sorrow; she went on as if she had indeed lost Father to death. She often broke into fits of tears. How we ever made it through I really don't know.

As the oldest child I was responsible for gathering firewood, checking traps and snares, and making farm visits for trade. The Creator knows I did these to the best of my abilities, but I truly felt at times we would not survive to see spring. I dreamed our frozen bodies were packed together and no one would find us until the animals had eaten away the recognizable parts. I wanted so much to hear hooves and wheels crunching over the hard snow, people to take us home. More so, when the axe dulled or chipped, when fur-animals ate their own skin and bones to escape traps, and when my "visits" dwindled to a handful of potatoes for the whole family.

On one of the coldest days when we could no longer boil and reboil the corn kernels and cobs for nourishing soup, Mother began sharpening a giant butcher knife, a meat cleaver, against the broad-axe. As soon as the blade began to gleam in the lodge, she walked out into the raging blizzard. I thought she had gone mad and nearly ran after her. I envisioned the two of us wrestling over the knife in the deep snow. So I chose to let her be.

Later, when the icy winds subsided, we heard her returning. She was talking to herself and Black Face, a lively conversation. She stopped at the entrance to the lodge, lifted the frozen blankets, and entered with a gunny sack that glistened through with blood. She threw it to the floor with a grunt. "*Ko ko tta!* Pig!" The large chunks of pork spilled out. Exhausted, she could barely grin. I secretly kicked my wet boots behind the bundle of kindling as she took off her heavy garments. We all acted surprised—and relieved.

She then proceeded to chop the pork fat into cubes and impale them on peeled willow sticks. In turn, I stuck these fat-sticks close to the roaring fire.

"It is fortunate for us that farmers cannot watch and round up all their livestock in this weather," she said with her tired eyes fixed on a single red coal.

Having followed her own footprints before they were covered, I knew what she meant. The children sat as close to the flames as possible with their knees slightly touching.

Oh, how we delighted in seeing the fat sizzle!

I can still see her behind the fence in the snowdrift with her shawl whipping in the violent gusts of wind, her arms flinging the giant knife, hacking laboriously at the protruding legs of the half-frozen and half-alive pigs.

The
Supernatural
Strobe
Light

>> «» «» «» «» «» «» «» «» «» «» «» «» «» «»

During one warm October evening in 1981, Selene Buffalo Husband and I experienced an extraordinary but true encounter with a mysterious force that took the guise of owls, fireflies, and luminescent objects of the night. For a long time afterward we shared an utmost respect for these entities, knowing they could conspire to unleash an unforgettable manifestation of supernatural power. Whether our interaction came about by accident or predetermination, we can still recount the bird, insect, strobe light, and UFO transformations shown to us by a force impervious to bullets, sacred incense, and admissions of poverty.

Although years have passed since this nightmarish occurrence, we have yet to fully understand its meaning and purpose to what was then a simple existence. While we have ultimately learned not to take our surroundings for granted, we remain wary of any unusual lights in the sky, for there was a rather long phase in our lives when each and every luminescent object came under our precautionary scrutiny at sundown.

To document what took place and to share it only means we are cognizant of invisible forces, especially the kind who have chosen to reveal themselves and interact momentarily with the unsuspecting lives of human beings.

Darkness quickly signaled a majestic end to a typical midwestern Sunday. Except for occasional groups of young, slightly injured men headed "uphill" on foot and bike after a rough afternoon of football at the pow-wow grounds, our Chevy Nova SS represented the only traffic on the community's main gravel road.

There was acknowledgment via a head nod or a hand wave from the players before a billowy cloud of dust enveloped them as we drove by. Selene and I were going home as well.

A better part of our day had been spent visiting my parents, Clotelde and Tony Bearchild, who lived in the new housing complex on the northern hilly part of the Settlement. After a week of gray skies and cold rain, the weather had been accommodating to those who wished it. Television meteorologists called the event Indian summer, which was perhaps the only positive aspect associated with Native Americans. Places where Iowans could go to literally watch the leaves change color were rolled on the screen.

Surprisingly, many urbanites took these recommendations to heart and took hundred-mile drives to gaze in profound wonder at the brilliant hues of foliage. While our homeland did not compare geographically to the picturesque bluffs of the Mississippi River valley, there were a handful of sightseers who came to the Settlement as part of their pilgrimage to "nature." To be within visual sight of the First North Americans, even if for a moment in an enclosed, air-conditioned car, lent a sense of credibility to earth's physical change.

For residents of the Settlement, it was an autumn day for whole families to sit on lawn chairs in front of their homes, observing the observers. On dry, grassy knolls above the driveways, dogs and cats sat in small clusters, basking themselves in the warmth. Everywhere on the road were dusty-skinned children on bikes and wagons, going somewhere with their dolls and toys. The legs of grease monkeys making last-minute repairs stuck out from under their cars and trucks. Elsewhere, the lonesome sound of chain saws buzzed deep in the woods.

It was also a time for veneration: a perfect, flawless day for the sending of prayers to the deities of the sky, water, and earth. All the clans—Sturgeon, Bearcap, Hummingbird, Fox-King, and Beaver—graciously assisted one another toward this endeavor.

But the sun, *ki tte swa*, which illuminated this beautiful day for all concerned—man, woman, child, beast, or Indian—was now a fiery glint on the farmland horizon.

As we passed the fairgrounds and got on the westbound lane of old Lincoln Highway 30, Selene made note of the fact that this autumn would be our third year of residence at *a ka me e ki*, distant forestland. It was hard to comprehend how three years could seem like eternity; nothing spectacular had happened in terms of our love and commitment to each other—and our work.

We still dreamed about having children, of course, but our parental instincts were not enough. (In another dimension of our minds the faces and bodies of children assembled themselves from fragmented pieces of our imagination, and they sat down across from us at the supper table. We could see them clearly; we could hear the clinking of spoons against glass dishes. Javier, the first child we lost during Selene's sixth month of pregnancy, would have been seven years old; and the other child—the one we didn't even see—would have been five. When we woke there was only silence and the occasional sound of chimes reacting to the wind.)

Since we only had ourselves to take care of, Selene and I lived in an abandoned house located on the edge of a densely wooded area near the confluence of the Swanroot and Iowa rivers. Because of its notorious history of floods, very few people occupied the riverbottoms. For us this was home. Actually, since housing was a perennial problem for the tribe, we had little choice.

The river posed serious problems, obviously, but we became accustomed to the ritual of packing and moving our belongings to high ground. We moved four to seven times a year, staying away for a week to a month until the brown water receded.

Like brazen pioneers we rationalized the inconvenience was minor compared to the privacy the secluded house offered. The truth of the matter was, after years of repeated attempts of academic study on my part, there was nothing to come back to. Living with my parents until we got situated was a definite taboo; in the past such choices had proved the cohesive family unit of the tribe was no longer applicable. My two younger sisters were highly agitated by people other than our mother and father, and my father could not eat at the table without complaining about anything. The mediator was my mother, Clotelde, but more often than not she sided with those under tension.

In the beginning the secluded floodplain seemed ideal for work and creative contemplation. Trouble was, I began to seriously wonder if I had done much of either in three years. The second Maecenas fellowship received in 1978 was helpful in terms of stockpiling supplies for a year and a half and hooking up to utility services. Were it not for my lackluster and stagnant mental condition, one could not have asked for more. Anyone else would have thrived. The covenant I had signed with the board members in Greece gathered dust and was lost in the box of poem drafts.

Slowly I was being debilitated by stress caused by the floods and tension from the volumes of poetry I had intended to compose but couldn't. Remarkably, the physical effects of stress could only be seen on a time-lapse 16mm film in weekly intervals. It was as if a carpet needle had been stuck in my ribs, deflating the vibrant self. The smile began to melt on my face, and the clothes hung on my bony body.

Selene, on the other hand, was not impaired in spirit. She stood next to me as we watched the whirring footage on the drywall, deflating at a slower pace than me but her smile and color remaining. When the supplies were depleted, she resorted to selling her beadwork—belts, harnesses, hairpieces, and other dancing regalia. The original plan was to collect enough pieces and submit slides of them to a major gallery in New Mexico. It didn't happen; she sold them at a loss. Selling them broke my heart, for I had already seen them as items I would proudly wear at my own funeral in the future.

Once we reached the Stonehouse I switched on the Nova's headlights and turned northward ninety degrees off Lincoln Highway onto another gravel road. Night usually came first to the wooded riverbottoms. In a distant field we saw the bright elevated headlights of an unsteady but effective crop-collecting mechanical monster, a combine machine, bouncing over the stumpy rows of harvested soybeans and corn. Grain dust and gas exhaust hung in the dry air. The overalled agricultural navigator was making good use of every warm minute.

For anyone to seriously consider investing one's energy and money in a garden or field at this precarious location was a bad gamble, for whatever was not a sturdy maple or cottonwood tree was susceptible to swift brown floodwaters. Yet there were many who invariably felt there was ample compensation when the harvest of cucumbers, soybeans, squash, and corn stocked the cupboards and pocketbooks all winter. The prerequisite, however, was a flood-free spring and summer.

Although we sympathized with the woes of local Indian and Caucasian farmers, our situation as inhabitants was far worse and more dangerous than the loss of crops: we stayed until debris-filled water knocked at the door. While we were oblivious to emotional and physical strain, there were occasions we chose to remain in the river. Our lights would reflect out to the half-mile circumference of land. We preferred this danger rather than face my sisters' tantrums and my father's unnecessary lectures over supper. Anything but that. They were family whose vocabulary, unfortunately, didn't include "mellow out." All we could hope for was the inurement that had previously been felt by the generations of Black Eagle Child people who lived here for the past 120 years.

My grandmother in 1915 had escaped similar floods. Her family a number of times was forced to evacuate the plains for high ground. She remembered waking one morning to the watery sounds of an unwelcome visitor rippling over the floor of the lodge. Later that day, she said, there were heroic acts by strong young swimmers who went back to the camp and recovered sacred mats and their contents from the protruding roofs of the ceremonial longhouses.

We were stunned to learn we lived in the same house where Grandmother found a bundle of glass beads and sewing utensils as a young girl. The beads provided her with a means to support herself—just like Selene. And it was on Lincoln Highway 30 where Grandmother sat with the other beadworkers and sold souvenirs to white passersby.

The gravel road from the Stonehouse stretched northward for a mile. The little-used highway was intact, but the beadworkers who once laughed, gossiped, and negotiated for prices were nearly all gone. All that remained was the glistening smoothness of the highway top.

As we drove closer to the forest's edge, Selene noticed we had neglected to leave the yardlights on when we left that morning. Before we reached the driveway by the apple tree on the east side of the yellow house, I slowed down and directed the Nova's beams in a long, sweeping motion to the water pump and behind the house to roust or spot vandals. As usual, there were none. The only items we possessed of monetary value were firearms, a Sony color television, a 16mm movie camera, and a German-built typewriter. We knew this was enough incentive for winos to break in. Any house with portable radios, cameras, jewelry, and beadwork was a target.

We were instead greeted by Curly, a black maniacal Labrador watchdog, who was chained to an anvil. From the porch, Dike, a half-Husky from Dike, Iowa, walked toward us and waited. Their red-and-silver dog-eyes tried in vain to focus into the car's interior. We looked at them and concluded everything was all right. Once I turned off the lights and the loud, rumbling engine with its headers and sidepipes, we were swallowed by the forest.

With a few beers to my body's credit the previous night, I was mildly uncomfortable. My face was warm from the aftereffects: small patches of shimmering fog traveled across the inside wall of my retina. I couldn't understand it; I had been free of a hangover all day.

We sat in the car and adjusted our eyes to the incredible blackness. When we stepped out of the car and called out to Curly and Dike, they began to bark and whine with excitement. They weren't cries of hunger or longing but something I had never heard before.

A lone screech owl called out from the southern tree line. Thinking that was the reason the dogs were jumpy, and due to a habit I had developed since childhood, I returned the owl's exact cry and hoot. It was an automatic response. For years I had blatantly disregarded my grandmother's warning about these perilous exchanges with owls. They were considered harbingers of evil, enigmatic messages which were feared by all. I was cognizant of this, yet I chose to disregard centuries of custom. Being a vocalist who sang in a similar high-pitched, falsetto style of singing, I considered my mocking returns as a form of badly needed musical practice.

The owl called out again in a stronger, challenging tone. Note for note, I returned the exact shrill. On the third call, the owl increased its vocal delivery and changed midpoint in the initial cry to a more difficult tremulous note, dropping expertly to a magnificent basslike low for the ending. I inhaled more air and mimicked the changes with the finesse of an opera singer.

Like blind persons we nimbly traced the short distance from the apple tree driveway to the house with our feet. Before reaching the concrete steps of the porch, there was a fourth exchange and then a pause.

"Jeeessuss Christ!" I sighed to Selene in a calm, nonalarming manner as she was grasping for key and padlock in front of the door. "*Ne tti wi tti mo wa na.* What a strong voice he possesses."

I should have given up then, but I couldn't dismiss the icy chill settling over my spine. Something extraordinary was pretending to be an owl. I recalled seeing a burly owl the previous night walk over the driveway in the yardlight. That same night the door began rattling when an unknown creature drew hieroglyphics upon it. Was this the picture?

"*Na wa tti ke.* Wait a moment," I said, bracing myself. My lungs and chest expanded, and an ear-piercing cry shot forth to the visitor in the tree line. Its echo traveled over the fields. I secretly hoped it was more than the owl—or whoever—could do. Unfortunately, the answer came in a fierce, terrifying shrill unlike any I had ever heard. Its supernatural wattage exploded, and we could feel its wind pushing us one step backward.

With that, I nervously instructed Selene to go inside the house without turning on the yardlights to load the .22s with hollow-point bullets.

While I waited a mild breeze brought the pleasant smell of autumn leaves. In another situation the aroma of such tranquility would have been met with welcome. Off to the south, on a road made of liquid stone, the whirring sounds of automobile and truck tires represented normalcy. In a few seconds, I prayed, this standoff with what was most likely a supernatural entity would be shattered by the loud retort of successive gunshots.

Inside the house I could hear Selene swinging out the revolver's cylinder, the systematic loading of the eight chambers. On the rationale that we face the owl in its perspective, she loaded the revolver and the rifles without roomlight. If the situation escalates, I asked myself, will I have to disrobe if all else fails?

I remembered my grandmother's words: "Night-enemies cannot see a naked human body in their realm. You can gain power over them that way because they, too, are naked. Acknowledge them with words and a drink of water set on the table or the path on your yard. Treat them as if they are guests in the day, like visitors you know. This welcome, along with your invisibility, will reverse whatever ill intentions they possess."

I started to touch the buttons of my shirt and then shook my head: I envisioned myself running stark naked in the headlights of some coonhunter's car. This thought couldn't have come at a more unsuitable time. Only if all else fails, I said to myself.

Selene stepped off the porch and walked quietly toward me. The revolver carefully changed hands. Squinting southward toward the horizon highlighted by the dim lights of Grinnell, I noticed the constellations.

When the defiant owl called out again, I cocked the hammer, aimed where I thought it sat, and fired eight quick shots. Before the ringing in my ear stopped, another owl called out shortly behind the first.

On the next loading Selene gave me a handful of bullets which I promptly stuffed into my pocket. With the cylinder full I fired another volley at the two owls, dividing the shots carefully. But the childlike wailing persisted. As I ejected the shells, a third owl joined in the macabre chorus. I reloaded and fired again.

They were less than thirty yards away, but I couldn't figure out why the gunshots weren't scaring them. My sanity began to splinter into shards of falling glass as the three demonic owls took turns breaking me to pieces. A paralysis of sorts took hold of my senses and severely readjusted their dimensions.

My breathing became fast and short, and my legs were trembling: I became the helpless green frog that in my childhood I had tossed onto the lawn mower spark plug, trembling in its last throes of life. The screams turned to electricity in my ears, and the pressure fractured the delicate bones of my legs and pelvis. I landed on the rusty hot muffler of the Briggs and Stratton and sizzled until I smelled the burned tissue of my back. I smelled the essence of the creek and the mud of my birth.

I started to unbutton my shirt. The prospect of not being seen was the only alternative; we would be on equal naked terms. After I finally convinced myself, the owls quit.

In the silence that followed, a group of fireflies flew outward from the tree line close to where the first owl was. They reminded me of bubbles headed to the clear water's surface, bumping and resting on submerged branches. Once they were out of the trees, they hovered and waited, signaling each other with intermittent body light.

The brightest firefly moved ahead to the east, and the other fireflies broke into two separate lines behind and formed a V, like migrating geese or military jets in formation.

"*Ke ne wa ki?* Do you see them?" I asked Selene.

"Yes," she replied, "you mean the jets way over there?"

"*Agwi ma i ni. Wa wa se si a ki ma i ni ki. Wi ke tti wa ba mi.* No, they are not. They are fireflies. Take a good look."

In the pandemonium we had stopped long enough to disagree on whether the small, glittery, V-shaped lights were fireflies or distant jets. At the moment Selene realized they were actually fireflies, they broke apart and disintegrated.

Next, in an old garden close to where the fireflies vanished, a sphere of soft light ascended from the ground and hovered above the tall brush. Humiliated by the owls and deceived by the fireflies, and since bullets were futile, I began speaking to the spherical light:

"*Ki na we ne i ya ne ni*, you, whoever you are, we have done nothing to deserve this, nor have we offended anyone. What is it you want when we live in poverty?"

As I recited the words to the round light (taught to me by my grandmother for such an event), my voice broke. I had never confessed this verity to anyone, much less to Selene or myself. Below me the lawn seemed to swell. To realize my own poverty and ineptness as a man—a descendant of proud people—was painful. We stood on what seemed a little earth. What had I provided for Selene? I thought of children and the days we resorted to boiling immature apples and frying bony carp—fish I had speared—for one major meal of the day. Because of this I had not stated and reaffirmed my love to Selene for . . . I don't know how long.

The round light paused as if to listen and ponder, digesting and visualizing my confession. It hovered for a second and then resumed its path toward the north. Unimpressed, the light started to encircle us as part of a greater conspiracy. Beginning with the owls in the south, the fireflies flying east and changing to jets in the southeast, the light was now east headed north.

Unaware and afraid of what transformation was forthcoming, we stepped backward, keeping an eye on the slow-moving light, and made our way to the porch and into the security of four walls. We were dumbfounded to find the utilities were out. No electricity whatsoever to distract the lights.

In a dreamlike trance we groped around in the dark and found the emergency candles and lit them in their tinfoil sconces. We spilled a box of bullets into a tin can prefilled with box elder ashes, skillet grease, and woolen lint. We insalivated roots that would combat anything unnatural and uninvited, and these we spit into the tin can. We briefly reprimanded one another for not enacting such measures earlier—from the very beginning.

As I was anointing the bullets, Selene opened the woodstove and threw in twigs and ferns of sacred incense over the red embers. We could hear the needles crackling and shooting up the stovepipe in a fiery whirl. From past unexplained occurrences we knew the chimney was capable of dispersing sacred smoke and sparks to all directions, spreading a protective shield around the house.

We reloaded the bolt action and semiautomatic rifles with these anointed bullets and went back out onto the porch. The round light was gone, but the three owls began their chorus again. With raised rifles we fired repeatedly toward them until a firefly appeared. Each time we fired the firefly's light began growing into a large, flare-colored oval mass. The transformation ascended the tree line and grew with each bullet fired. In its own spectacular light we were able to take precise aim as it flew westward over a soybean field in slow motion. On the last bullet the transformation was as large as two school buses, and it illuminated everything within half a mile.

Drifting further west over another field, the protoplasmic mass vanished. It reminded me of a Spanish galleon that once hovered on the ceiling of our house during a severe childhood sickness. The ship grew and filled the dimensions of the room, squeezing food out of my stomach and into the bucket beside the bed. Unable to jar the sensation of being in a nightmare still and steadily losing control of logic, I said, "Let's get the fuck outta here!"

We stopped to lock up the house and foolishly forgot our other ammunition. As we were walking out, Curly and Dike who had been quiet throughout the standoff began to growl toward the driveway. Before we knew it, we were blinded by a series of silent explosions of silver phosphorescent light. We straightened up and threw our arms up to protect ourselves.

From the center of the apple tree, a supernatural strobe light began to pulsate. This was the round light we had forgotten to keep track of. Its transformation, the most powerful.

"*Ki ke nay!* Hurry up!" shouted Selene, for I was momentarily overcome. I could see each individual rock and pebble on the driveway, including each delicate blade of grass.

Once we made it to the Nova and were inside with locked doors, its intensity decreased somewhat. We could look into the apple tree's emanation and not squint. The bottoms of the leaves were shadowy while the tops glittered iridescently.

After the Nova SS rumbled into operation, I backed up farther than usual hoping to align the car's front to the apple tree. In yet another feeble attempt, I turned on the high beams, but nothing happened. We spun briefly over the gravel before shooting out of the catapult.

From my peripheral vision, I was able to see the strobe light fly out from the apple tree, keeping parallel with us. Racing down the driveway, its flashes decreased and went higher over the treetops.

I asked Selene to search the glove compartment for bullets. On the last stretch to the highway, the strobe light climbed higher and jumped ahead of us so that we could see it through the windshield. It slowed to a complete halt by the Stonehouse.

At the stop sign a lone car passed by. Above us in the sky, the strobe light was now a singular light that blended with the stars. As we drove onto the highway going east, the strobe light unfroze and began moving, continuing south. Over the abandoned Milwaukee railroad tracks, the strobe light made an abrupt left turn and caught up to us in a split second. It was skimming about 150 yards away, but we were parallel again. Selene asked if it was ever going to quit.

As we approached the entrance of the fairgrounds, Selene found a single .22 bullet. When we stopped and the strobe light did the same, I shut off the engine and stepped outside with the Marlin rifle. I loaded and took aim at the light that had successfully driven us away from our residence. Even though I wished it would fly off or disappear, it remained stationary.

I curled my finger around the trigger and remembered the story of the Mischievous Twins who once tied up the Sun to keep him from completing his daily journey through the sky. Long ago hunters would aim their weapons at the sun and ask: Are you really afraid of children?

Hoping that was the last we would see of the miniature sun, I squeezed the trigger. The light shot up and became a star.

At my grandmother's we tried to compose ourselves long enough to accurately recount our harrowing experience. Grandmother, who knew all the meanings behind illogical happenings, was disconcerted. It was difficult for her to make sense of the various light transformations, the defiant owls, and the fireflies that flew in a V shape, disappearing and regrouping perhaps as a round light—the giant red oval and the strobe light in the apple tree that gave chase.

"In all the years I've been alive, I have never heard anything like this," she said. "I suggest you go back with your uncle and brother. Go look at it."

We got back in the car and drove on, feeling more frightened because an elder and healer was baffled as well.

During our wait for Al and his .30-.30 lever action, Selene spotted a movement above a forest where we used to live. O'Ryan Ridge was the tallest hill on the Settlement, and it overlooked the valley where we presently lived.

It was obvious we had been followed.

For a second I felt what we had meagerly put up as defense was the light's only link to earth. Now it was keeping its distance instead of revealing its many faces.

What if there were extraterrestrials, I questioned, tapping into our wildest dreams and fears? Wasn't this the origin of Severt's predication? My uncle, in his science fiction, maintained that 1 out of 100,000 people could withstand an extraterrestrial encounter and not suffer long-lasting psychological aftereffects. Since the extraterrestrials were faceless, they took the shapes and objects of whatever the humans were thinking. Although I didn't believe in UFOs, wasn't there something to them? And didn't one of Severt's stories detail Professor Bailey's weeding-out of victims? That Indians were best because of their psychological makeup?

With Al—the total sanity of the universe—in the car we began to wake up. We drove next to my uncle Winston's house on Whiskey Corners Road and managed to persuade him to accompany us.

On the drive back we realized how bizarre and unacceptable the whole situation was. Thank goodness our bodyguards were stone-faced and gracious enough not to ask questions. How we were ever able to explain what took place without fainting was an act of solid composure. Deep inside, with blood and muscle in conflict, we were near the point of rupture. Yet there was nowhere to run—except to the only place we knew—home.

I once envisioned my mind as a burly porcupine. Magnificent in its body armor, my mind was protected by long, fire-hardened spikes; a thousand of them covered every centimeter of my being and anatomy. What didn't make sense from the doings of others was incapable of passing through this crown of strength, this aegis. On a calm autumn night, however, my spikes bristled and shot out in all directions like majestic tracers from antiaircraft artillery. But the act of defense exposed me to the unconscious-rendering blows from supernatural hunters. They saw my light and followed it back to me. Invincible porcupine that I am . . .

So here we were, assembled like vigilantes in our yard, standing with rifles and coonlights, searching for remnants of a trickster firefly. No matter how much I wished for the psychotic wailing of a screech owl atop a cottonwood, there was absolutely nothing to assure those who had come on our behalf that a nightmare had transpired.

That night we slept at Grandmother's house. If you could call it sleep. Throughout the remainder of the night there was a nagging feeling of imbalance, an absence of equilibrium. My eyes would twitch unrelentingly when I closed them. Twice my breathing seemed to stop, and I woke up inhaling wildly.

Selene was able to drift into half-sleep, but I had to wake her when she began mumbling indiscernible words of alarm. In or out of sleep, we were still attuned to the masks of transformation.

Although we were fatigued, we drove back across the river with Grandmother the next day. She wanted to confer with the previous tenant, Alfred Pretty-Boy-in-the-Woods, our closest neighbor. She wanted to know firsthand if anything strange had ever happened during his residency near the riverbottoms. The answer was simple. No.

We couldn't believe it. Two outstanding elders in whom we had the most trust had no answers. Theories were offered, and all seemed plausible. Each lent the event more mystery and bewilderment. Something "very strong" had singled us out. We listened as the possibilities were laid out.

"Somewhere within the vicinity of the old house, there used to be a village, and your visitors were probably the spirits or ghosts of these former inhabitants. Or else they were shadows of people who were never released to the Hereafter by a Replacing Ceremony. Or it could have been a dreaded wandering disease looking for a human host. Witches are another possibility. Whatever the reason, its mission was to get rid of you from the premises by fear. This was done. But you must not accept this in defeat; you will have to go back to the house and resume what you were doing. Which is living and not bothering anyone. Don't let it weigh you down any more than it has."

She accompanied us the night we returned. I slept comfortably with her image standing by the raging flames: her arms extended against the forest and her words going up to the air with the smoke and sparks.

"Do not bother to return; do not harm and frighten my beloved grandchildren. I always pray for their well-being."

≫ ≪

Two nights after the incident, as Selene and I were walking out of my parents' home, we noticed that the night sky seemed different. After we stopped and signaled one another for confirmation, we looked skyward. Incredibly, we saw the "lights" again. Lots of them, perhaps hundreds. Some were flying over each other, or else they were trailing one another. All shapes, sizes, colors, and formations. There were also different speeds and altitudes. All the stars were moving.

We ran back into the house and told everyone to come out and observe. With the family as witnesses we felt vindicated. We stood on the driveway and watched the celestial foreground rotate.

Through a set of binoculars, Selene and I saw the phenomenal display up close. In one instance we were taken by an enormous spherical craft, which had a lower revolving section. This was the largest craft, and it was being followed by lines of dwarf lights.

On the horizon, a fiery oblong object caught everyone's attention. It was going toward the faint sunset along the western slope of O'Ryan Ridge.

The show was perfectly timed. In a matter of a few minutes they crossed over the skies of Black Eagle Child. Perhaps for fear of leaving us in emotional trauma, the transformation mask had patiently waited until our visit was over with. Upon a given signal, at the exact moment our weary eyes turned upward to see if there were any threatening movements, the motionless stars began to move.

The
Ugliest
Man in
Big Valley

In May of 1987, during the last night of contest dancing at the Weaseltail Tribal Celebration in White Swan, Washington, I spotted a tall, overweight man who could have been the identical twin of Pat "Dirty" Red Hat. Once I took note of the dark brown, rough-complexioned Yakima Indian, I couldn't help staring. The similarities were astounding, to say the least, right up to the thick sunglasses he was wearing.

We stood among the spectators near the entryway of the pavilion where the large mural of Mt. Rainier rose from the stage to the ceiling. Like everyone else, we were engrossed with the intertribal singing and dancing being performed on the congested arena. Represented at Weaseltail on Memorial Day weekend were some of the best singers and dancers of the northwestern United States and western Canada pow-wow circuit.

Immediately after seeing the twin walk to the concession stands, I turned back around and remembered previous Memorial Day celebrations Pat and I attended throughout Minnesota, Wisconsin, and South Dakota. We traveled in a monstrous green station wagon loaded with secondhand camping equipment, a Megatone 100-watt P.A. system, and a couple of "scrubs" we picked up off the road.

Since childhood Pat and I had enjoyed singing and drumming. Way before we learned the basics of the English language or "doodling" (a euphemism for killing time artistically) at Weeping Willow Elementary, we imitated the adult drum groups that gathered every Friday at the American Legion Hall.

We eventually patterned our songs from the medium and falsetto pitches of the Woodlands and Northern Plains tribes, and we called ourselves the Young Lions (after a flick about World War II). As teenagers with one summer of practices and a repertoire of five war dance songs and three pipe dance songs, we made our debut on Labor Day in 1963. Included in the group were the late Brucie "Quick Like" Maple and Dean Afraid. Later, we were joined by Tom Sparrow, Jake August, and Peter Nederland.

As the celebrations came and went, our confidence grew. We began traveling, making food and gas money. Our rewards were a pittance when contrasted with the time and energy we had invested, but such sacrifices were ingrained. Aside from entertaining our own people, we made music for the Omahas and Winnebagos of Nebraska, the Sioux of South Dakota, and the Ojibwa of Minnesota. Historically, these were neighboring tribes we had gone to war with. Unbeknownst to our hosts, we sang songs of commemoration and honor to Black Eagle Child warriors who fought against their forefathers. How times had changed! The former enemy danced and gracefully bobbed their eagle feather–plumed heads to the same songs against the backdrop of foot-long hot dogs, french fries, and cotton candy signs.

At the pinnacle of the Young Lions fame, Pat perished in a car wreck in the fall of 1976. The misfortune shook me up pretty badly, for I had been drinking with him the night before on his mother's porch. Although I deplore statistics, he was listed as the first "land claims" casualty. The "Starsky and Hutch" car he had treasured became his entombment. The evil of old treaties. To see his ghostly image reminded me of things I had forgotten.

"There is something about getting on the road and going places to sing and dance," he used to say. "It's not that we hate home and all that. For some reason, total strangers appreciate our services.

The farther away from Iowa, the better." Even in a lifeless realm he hung on to this tenet.

Hoping I was inconspicuous, I glanced at the Yakima twin while looking for Selene to return with the baked salmon. For fear of scaring the twin away, I didn't want to get caught gawking. I looked past him unsure if he could see me. It was as if he was listening more than looking—like a visually impaired person. Actually, I felt the more I watched, the better the chances of a resurrection. With a slight smirk on his face, the twin downed handfuls of the popcorn without chewing, as the fancy shawl dancers were called to the floor.

I realized quite unexpectedly that the Yakima's thick, Roy Orbison–type sunglasses were the exact kind Pat wore the morning of the accident. The county coroner, along with the tribal physician, reported the only item "not charred" were Pat's pupils, having been protected in the flashover.

In festive places like this, I postulated, where the air is infused with human energy, there's bound to be a person or two who is not real, a lonely soul who is drawn to what could have been. All Pat had to do was will himself to appear: to travel over the prairies and materialize on the Yakima Indian Reservation where no one had ever seen him, except me. Here, he could walk and mingle through the crowd, looking and listening eleven years too late.

As a frequent contributor to contemporary and traditional Native American poetry for the past eighteen years, I had the good fortune of being invited on occasion by academic institutions to read and lecture on the various poetic interpretations of my work.

"Mostly it's recognition," I recorded. "Else how could one teach about servitude? What pedagogical approach can I use to instill that the rewards of word-collecting can sometimes leave one feeling all has been for naught?" But it was for these very reasons I arrived at Eastern Washington University near Spokane as a visiting writer. Instead of preparing lectures, however, Selene and I drove through the heart of Washington state, across the Columbia River, toward White Swan.

I made it a practice to visit the closest tribes wherever I was invited to teach. Oftentimes I would ask my sponsors to coincide my visits with intertribal celebrations. On this particular visit, though, the Weaseltail pow-wow was blessed with Pat's benign apparition.

On command, somewhere in the strings and vines of a hop field, in an effort to distort facial and physical similarities he had overinflated himself with air. A few extra pounds to his gut and another "spare chin" didn't fool me. Successful visual deception was never Pat's forte. He always made the mistake of giving you too many clues. The smirk on his massive face as he pretended to watch the limber ladies dance was one; the sunglasses were another; and the most obvious was the print on the Yakima's baseball hat: "The Ugliest Man in Big Valley." Pat was the only person who had the audacity to call himself that.

If you can hear my thoughts, Pat, I mentally whispered, if you are really here, you should come up and say so. I've dreamed of this meeting before. Meeting and talking with people I met, knew, and lost.

A similar chance had passed me once in Southern California. That time a deceased relative, Hector Reveres Nothing, stood beside me in a Big Boy restaurant in Pomona. He, too, like Pat, was entombed in melted steel. Hector, with whose younger brothers I had set trotlines and hunted for pheasants, died with a machine gun welded to his hands after a Viet Cong rocket-propelled grenade brought his helicopter down. My one and only memory of him was vague, but I knew him from photographs. Although I sensed the Hispanic look-alike was Hector 100 percent, complete with metal rings on all fingers, a goatee, and golden shoulder braids on his black leather jacket, I was disabled by fear. Unable to maintain a semblance of rationality, I was bathed in my own sweat when I got to the glass door.

I can't allow this opportunity to slip with Pat, I thought. I wouldn't dismiss his antics that easily.

"Do you want a drink first?" spoke someone near my ear. As if a paramedic had just jump-started my heart, I jerked sideways and spilled Sprite on the head of a child standing next to me.

"Jesus Christ! What's the matter with you?" scolded Selene as she brushed the crushed ice from the young victim's matted hair.

"What were you thinking about? Geez, wake up! *To ki no!*" I joined in on the frenetic wiping with my handkerchief. I couldn't say anything. She would have thought I was freaking out—on an imminent resurrection in White Swan? And if it had indeed happened, did I really want to strike up a conversation with Pat? SHIT NO! Death has to be the most personal thing known to humankind.

All the same, I felt I didn't deserve this macabre trick. Instead of becoming more fearful, I became offended. I wasn't amused with a close friend playing pranks from beyond. It reminded me of the one Sunday he pointed a PPK Walther pistol to my nose, telling me a misfired round was lodged in the barrel.

"Don't be afraid, Edgar," he said assuredly. "I'll aim at your left, wider nostril and no one will know I shot you, not for days."

Growing impatient, I turned around to bravely read and confirm the print on the Yakima's baseball cap. I wasn't mistaken. The words—in reference to bachelorhood—were spoken by Pat before his accident, the year we were awarded $8,000 apiece by the government for the state of Iowa.

A study was done by two white men—one a former museum director and the other a depressed art professor—who wanted to document the positive and negative effects of money on the tribe. They were affectionately known as the "K-Y Jelly brothers, slime in suits." They were welcomed into many homes but were given lies about spending habits, whether or not we invested. The one aspect that aggravated me the most was listing Pat as the first death attributable to the sudden influx of wealth. I abhorred statistics, pretentious red dots on a chart of jagged lines. The rancid promises of the white man bearing down on Pat. A new car to relieve the guilt of 17 million acres of land stolen from our forebears. The price of frontier justice.

But why did I remember his last night of life so well?

》《

On the moonlit concrete porch of his mother's house, we were discussing bachelors, *mo tta ki a ki* or unwed men, who were hopelessly destined to be loners or hermits, living by themselves in the woods or under the social security blanket of their parents. Never to know automobiles or the wonders invented by Thomas Edison, they came out once a month from their caves, seeking a ride to town for groceries, cigarettes, and jugs. They had no use for television, radio, telephones, or women.

"When do you think it'll be too late to marry?" asked Pat. At twenty-six he was perpetually bothered by the subject of marriage, its manly necessity. He saw himself in the year 2015 as a sixty-five-year-old haggard-looking man, sitting by a cold woodstove on a rainy afternoon with his fellows, exchanging commodity surplus recipes.

"Cheap wine is the sustenance of immortality," Pat declared in a serious tone. "Drunks live long, healthy lives with it. The formaldehyde preserves their innards like frogs in science class bottles. Just look at the ones around us. Compare them to the sober but ill senior citizens; the ones most religious-minded are swatted against the floor like flies where they fossilize. It's unfair unless you employ evil against evil . . ."

What Pat said bore a certain amount of truth. There were far more elderly abusers of alcohol than those who had abstained. Along the riverbottoms there were pockets of silver-haired men who drank three to four days in a row. On weekdays they were seen on the road, cotton-mouthed, walking to the state liquor store. The next day they would be at the tribal offices, requesting and receiving court help automatically from the Alcohol and Drug Abuse Center. In exchange for signing with the program, intoxication and jail terms were suspended.

If there was anything good contributed to the tribe by the Abuse program, it came from the five full-time staff. Their combined salaries—$85,000—brought income to the community. But the patient turnover rate was deplorable. Of course, there were a handful of successes like Indianapolis Isabel, Cucumber Man, and Lorna Bearcap, the most notable, who made federal funding a reality. To convert one "chronic" every six to eight years was considered a landmark. Regrettably, it was the old chronics who proved to be the hardest, nearly irreversible cases.

"I'll be there with the red-nosed farts," continued Pat on his future, "sharing and drinking jugs of Mad Dog 20/20. Nothing to do but reminisce, weeping at the stories of people who could have been our grandchildren. That's the way I might end up, remembering the last wet kiss I had thirty years previous. I've got to find someone like myself, man. Someone who will concede ideal, employed mates are nonexistent. Otherwise, I may end up like Hoss Cartwright, the lonesome fat man in the television western 'Big Valley.'"

"It's Hoss Cartwright of 'Bonanza,'" I corrected Pat. "Not 'Big Valley.'"

"What's the fucking diff?" he replied defensively, lifting the pounder in toast to the moon and divorcées. "Either way, Edgar, I am liable to end up an ugly, unwanted man—in 'Big Valley.' Get this now, 'The Ugliest Man in Big Valley.'"

After a night of rigorous singing and drumming on a car hood, Pat had passed out that Saturday morning in the bushes behind Barry Siouxboy's mobile home. I was there among the dozens of pow-wow partygoers laughing as Pat woke and stumbled out in his baggy OshKosh overalls and dusty T-shirt. Balanced on top of his head was a pair of Mickey Mouse ears and on his feet was one Tony Lama boot.

In the orange morning, Pat was something to behold: he stood an even six foot three and weighed 290 pounds. He could deliberately block moonlight from small-framed humans, depriving them of clear summer nights. He could do the same with sunlight. His large, unsteady shadow covered the area where I waited with the other car hood musicians. My face was in the shade of one round ear. A man-made eclipse. The sun's brilliant rays rose like flames behind Pat's greasy face.

He hobbled over and demanded a beer. "Got one for Mickey, you assholes?" he joked, trying to pick from the many offers. He accepted all and stuffed them into his huge pockets. Before hobbling away like Quasimodo to search for his prized acquisition, he saluted the Mouseketeers and took one gulp from each can before crushing them like aluminum grasshoppers.

We sat on the porch comparing notes about the hazy morning. We talked about our adventures as if they took place a year ago.

Due to our geographic and cultural isolation, we were sentimental. Twenty-four hours after anything occurred, it was recollected.

"Over there was where I last saw you," I reminded Pat, pointing to Siouxboy's yard. "You were staggering to the pine trees."

"Oh yeah!" he exclaimed in a spurt. "I found my car just past the neighborhood driveway. But first I had to chase some minors out. I guess a couple of out-of-state squawhides drove my car from town. Shit, I blanked out. Anyway, the squawhides were pretty mizzed when they forked the keys over. Lucky they didn't wreck the car."

"They?" I said aloud. "But that was you driving out, right? Tires peeling and everything? People were running for cover from flying rocks."

"Yeah, that was a reckless exit. I was showing off and lost control. Smitten. We had breakfast in town and had cold beer mixed with tomato juice."

Pat suddenly stopped his narrative and looked my way.

"Ed," he stated in a somber tone. "You've got to keep this to yourself . . . OK? After breakfast, the skinny girl with oversized goggles, Belinda Carlson, asked me to ditch her chum at the campgrounds. She then proposed I take her home, to bring her here to my rugged roost. I wasn't going to do that. I convinced her to go to the woods. After stomping through the weeds and thorns, we took our clothes off underneath the water tower and began making love in broad daylight. But something catastrophic nearly happened which made me think of marriage. Here goes. I was either too drunk, overstimulated, or hungover to climax . . ."

"What do you mean?" I asked, seeking clarification.

"Are you deaf or something?" Pat returned annoyingly. "No climax! I couldn't bring the curtains down. For about one hour we kept rolling around, wrestling, and changing positions. Me, the Brahma bull, and her, the Slim Jim queen. Good erection. Fantastic visuals. Going full blast. Nothing. Theories of impotence. It was only when I applied a full-nelson headlock that things clicked. Crazy, I could have broken her chicken neck."

I was enraptured by Pat's candor and descriptions of the post-dawn encounter. He took the state heavyweight high school wrestling title in 1970, but it was extremely difficult for me to visualize applying a move on a bespectacled toothpick to achieve gratification—with Mickey Mouse ears.

» «

Pat "Dirty" Red Hat was rarely without open thoughts. The community had direct access to his nasty mind. For him, it was status. Hence, the name "Dirty" which was given him from the days at Weeping Willow Elementary.

He would tell anyone—student or teacher—what troubled or fascinated him, like sensitive skin getting caught in a zipper or strange balloons that seeped out of the sewer drains. If girls were within hearing distance he would discuss sexual-related topics without embarrassment. He was therefore the first student to receive "professional help." True, he was explicit, but people could either walk away or stay. Most, out of curiosity, listened, including the psychologist.

Coming from one of the most conservative families of the Settlement, Pat exemplified the archaic male role to the hilt. He learned the wicked craft from his father, who was known for his reverence for the female anatomy.

In 1960, at the expense of the Bureau of Indian Affairs, the Weeping Willow Elementary fourth-grade class took a field trip to Minneapolis and St. Paul. The Agent-in-Charge felt we needed to see the world outside our borders. Big city life. The haunts of Lois Lane and Clark Kent. Civilization.

Pat and I were assigned by Mrs. Weatherwax as trip partners. Before the Northern Express passed the county line, we had conspired to ambush Barbara Heart, our classmate, in the bathroom and take her clothes off.

During the five-hour train ride we didn't sleep. Instead, we walked the aisles hoping to look up Barbara's skirt as she slept beside our cautious teacher. By dawn, when the skyscrapers came into view, it became apparent Barbara wouldn't walk to the back. The entire day was spent in the tour bus catching up on sleep. Although I had a vague idea, I wasn't sure what to look for beneath Barbara's yellow skirt. In the dim lights of the cabin all I saw was the chapped whiteness of her knees.

In the hotel that night, after we had regained our energy, Pat called me and two other classmates to the bathroom. Naked, Pat looked like a giant brown walrus as he floated in the transparent soapless water. His very first bath in porcelain.

"Look at this torpedo," said Pat, lifting his wide hips above the water. His engorged penis tottered menacingly in the air before diving back down. "Next time, Barbara!" he pledged with a snort before splashing us.

If there was enlightenment about the purpose of male organs, it originated from Pat. Listening to him was more informative than the play we had watched on board a steamboat, *a sko te tti ma ni*, or the helicopter, *te te ba tti*, ride over the Twin Cities. He taught us terms like "chicken soup" and "give it a whirl." We were enthralled by stories of lovers he had observed in intimate union. Often it was his sister or unsuspecting adults who met under the bridge near his home. Like a stealthy bat, he would hang upside down from the iron beams. Lovers stood over the white sand and "whirled." For years I stoutly maintained to others that one had to stand in order to have intercourse.

By all accounts Pat was our only source of reliable information. If there was a shortage of tales, he'd find other ways to entertain. In the years we were made to take bi-weekly showers at Weeping Willow, Pat would jokingly hunch over his private parts, pull them from view from behind his closed legs, and utter gaspingly, "This is what a girl looks like, boys!" Everyone stole a look before the janitor, Mr. Matcheena, whacked Pat's fat ass with a large bristle brush.

》《

At the last intertribal song by the Chemawa School Singers of Salem, Oregon, I lost Pat's Yakima twin in the crowd. He was back out into the hop field deflating himself into nothingness. Whether or not the individual in question was who I thought he was, it was good and equally terrifying to see him.

Later, Kenneth Robe, the Weaseltail president, came and stood beside Selene and me. He eagerly pointed out the various drummers who composed their own songs, knowing it was an interest of mine. I paid attention, but Pat's apparition kept appearing in my thoughts. It was then that I began composing a memorial song for Pat D. Red Hat. There had to be an element of friendship, I noted, as well as a hint of lewdness and credulity in the song's message.

En masse, incredible rhythms with lyrics rushed through my senses. It would be one hell of a song, one that could only be sung for him in the West, heaven. "There could be no other place for it, Pat," I whispered.

Ask the
One Who
Blesses the
Roots

Mrs. Grassleggings was the third among the six
Many Nickel sisters. Like the spacing of years
between her own children, the differences
between the sisters' ages were disproportionate:
half were so much older while the other half
straggled. But the camaraderie established
from childhood by thoughtful parents went
unhindered. In fact, the sisters were closer
than most people who had lifelong troubles
with relatives. Considering the impact
modernization had upon Indian families,
it was different for the Many Nickels.
They got along. The frequent birthdays
and baby showers they held demonstrated
their tolerance. Which isn't to say strife
was absent. Mrs. Grassleggings was known
as the "uncouth sister" who brought
overgrown children to baby showers
when common sense made the others
leave theirs at home.

Baby showers were special occasions
reserved for honoring new additions
to kin. But not for sister Rose a.k.a.
Mrs. Grassleggings; she came for other
reasons. "She's got one helluva nose,"
observed the oldest sister once
when they were at a loss as to who
sent the invitation. "It isn't because
she's starving or anything like that,
I'm sure. She seems to pop up as soon
as the kettle lids are removed. She knows
we disapprove of her weight, and what
about the awful food-eating contest
she plays?" But the talking ceased
when Rose actually entered the room,
fearing a frank discussion could cause
a drinking spree. The last time they
confronted her she drowned herself
in booze the entire summer. Too
inebriated to stand, she ended up
most weekends crawling home. By sunup
she was eye-level with fierce neighborhood
dogs who mistook her for a walrus.
The youngest and least compassionate
sister once theorized Rose's obesity
served two purposes:
"(a) In winter it keeps her warm
and comfortable in below-zero winds,
and (b) she can easily conceal
the nine unwanted but inevitable
pregnancies she endured from four
different men." In a way she was right.

For the past forty years the Many Nickel
sisters never knew when Rose would go into labor.
Without risk of upsetting her, no one could
distinguish between simple indigestion

and contractions. Add to this an embarrassing,
ever-present waddle and children who shared
her gastronomical addiction, and simple things
like traveling and fishing became hazardous.
For one, there was undue stress on small-framed
bones. Secondly, if anyone twisted and broke
an ankle, the likelihood of everyone getting
injured in the act of picking up a sibling
was great. A chain reaction of brittle bones
breaking. On a hot summer day the last sight
anyone wanted was a helpless, weight-imperiled
family of walruses beached on a hazy gravel road,
roasting toward a group heat stroke.

But no one ever said anything.
Whenever her children jumped
the smorgasbord line, the sisters
would retract into their frail shells.
The gutless with thoughts aghast
could only watch goulash being slopped
onto Styrofoam plates on top of the beef
and Indian corn soup, soaking the chocolate
cake and frybread. (You wouldn't think it, but
the Grassleggings children had astute senses;
they knew whenever opinions transmuted.
Their only recourse, unfortunately,
was to gorge themselves silly
with barbecue chicken and potato salad
to assuage the guilt.)

There's a saying if a visitor frequently
arrives at or near dinner hour, he or she
is "like a Missooni." Sharing food and welcoming
people to your home with utter kindness were customary,
but there were a handful of people who deliberately
made the rounds, abusing the last vestiges
of hospitality. When Mrs. Grassleggings

herded the bloated beings behind her squaw dress
and left, this is what was said of her:
"To not bring a present for the newborn
is a misdemeanor; to line up uninvited children
first, some beyond puberty, at the smorgasbord
is a felony."

While the food-hoarding sessions duly upset
a sister or two, they relented in the end.
"She's had a rough time of it, you see,"
the sisters lamented, referring to her
distorted perception of romance. (It attracted
an unusual plethora of male companions who
repeatedly made a fool of her.)
For the miraculous attention received,
the Philistine gave presents in the form
of children. Sadly, they went ignored
and unloved. And if that wasn't enough,
events that tragically encompassed
the adolescent lives of the oldest trio
of sisters—Brook, Christina, Judith—
nearly killed her. In a way she was gone
because of her eccentricities. Consequently,
no one ever objected if sister Rose never
opened the contents of delicious-smelling
covered dishes she brought. Not even
for fried walleye with wild rice
and onions stirred in. Her specialty.
No complaints were made when she didn't
share the potent Canadian ale she kept well
stocked in the basement, drink that
was brought long distances by people
seeking her help. In time the Many Nickels—
Diane, Amanda, Sonja, Justeen, and "Chicken Neck"
Janice—became adept at forgiveness,
for each knew she would one day knock
at the door, enter without a word,
and proceed to discredit modern medicine

by curing her nieces and nephews of
fabulous diseases of the twenty-first century.

During root-induced sleep Mrs. Grassleggings
could read notes that her sisters never had
the gumption to mail. Ashamed of their Christian-
oriented beliefs, dropping to their knees and clasping
hands in a plea for help was next to faithlessness.
News of family illnesses that befell her sisters
circulated with phenomenal speed, bouncing off
the landmarks of Cutfoot Crossing, Lone Ranger,
O'Ryan Ridge, and Rolling Head valley like
a pinball. The descriptions given about
one's temperament, color, body trauma,
and eating habits were so vivid everyone
had an inkling if a familiar smile
or hospital visit was in the offing.

What wasn't dreamed by sister Rose came
by way of the NPWs—Nursing Program Workers—
who were part of the health clinic. Since
confidentiality wasn't among the rules taken
seriously, the NPWs had a knack of disseminating
freely the only true possession people had—
their health. Take for example the year
the Grassleggings girls were allegedly
victimized by their father. The NPWs swore
convincingly to the BEC Business Council
they were not responsible for "divulgence
of information pertinent to the incest case."
No one but the Head Office in Aberscene,
South Dakota, believed them—to save
federal face.

To insiders, the twelve hundred–plus populace,
it was a foregone conclusion the GED-educated
BEC employees thrived on sharing knowledge
of what ailed another. It was inconsequential

whether you were the keeper of a meteorite.
Least of all that mattered was your ideology.
You could recite the Last Daylight Words
to their departed loved ones, impart secrets
of the Transportation Packs, or teach their youth
the fundamentals of 35mm black-and-white photography—
it didn't matter. If you ogled too long at their swarthy
complexions or slurped your soup too loudly at community
potlucks, you were a target. If you made mention
of how shabby their children's dance costumes
were due to gambling addiction or questioned
why medical priority was accorded to new arrivals
who contradicted the six-month residency requirement,
you were legitimate meat. If you still rolled up
your blue jeans or drew mascara at a wrong angle,
you could expect trouble. If you had any annoying
characteristic, like proper enunciation of English
or exemplary syntax, you risked attracting their
unscrupulous attention. The NPWs grossly
personified our substandard health services.
It was clearly one facet of self-determination
the tribe would have to reconsider. There was
nothing more reprehensible than a near-illiterate
accountant, who was also the receptionist, nurse,
pharmacist, doctor's assistant, and the most
abhorrent ruse—if the office was in transition—
a doctor. Sickened by what little control
they had, the real doctors came and left
at blinding speed, and the NPWs continued
to apprise the tribe of what ailed
the Many Nickel sisters.

»«

At first the fulfillment of cures
and nonlethal "persuasion" spells came
in minute increments for Rose. Attaining

the proper skill and wherewithal to open
urinary passageways in baby males
was not done by healing compounds of peeled
red vine bark alone. Each step initiated
to ease the intestinal swelling or infection—
from the purification of the dwelling
to the preparation of strained juice
for a bath—had its own set of songs
and prayers. (This part was the hardest.
Take pity, Rose respectfully asked,
knowing full well her record was less
than ideal.) Sometimes if the illness
was more precarious than expected,
it was necessary to make the listless baby
drink the bitter tealike brew. These steps
were repeated in reverse until a warm stream
of body fluid shot out from below the bloated
bellies. The young patients would grow
into bright-eyed, zestful men bearing
expensive woolen blankets from the Amana
Colonies, canned triangles of ham,
and fine bottles of whiskey. Through
the encouragement of their grateful
parents the men rewarded her annually.
For her talented musician nephews
she hung dried stems of the blue willow
flowers upside down on their bedposts
to ward off unfriendly visitors of the night,
the kind whose bodily transformations
were accompanied by either the innocuous odor
of perfume or the putrid rot of untreated
animal hide. The dried stems stuck out
as invisible thorns and kept the sound
of beating wings and footsteps away
from the side of the house; the flowers
repelled sparks that lit in the nostril
exhale of beastly visitors; and the leaves

dropped to the floor and glowed like red
ashes around the bed.

For outdoor public festivities she made
her nephews eat the dry black pits of small
green berries that sprouted in inseparable clusters.
"So the people will have no choice but to think
highly of your new songs and fresh voices,
eat this and rub a few grounds on the drum."
Conversely, the nieces were led into tents
away from public view and told to chew
but not swallow the pits. They treated
the particles like smoke and fanned
the shoulder, arm, and leg portions
of their sequined dance regalia.
"So the people will have no choice
but to be impressed by your new outfits
and movements, address the medicine like
you would a person." The female and male
versions of clusterberry dotted the hillsides
of their home in varying shades of purple.
They were there to use as "persuasion";
yet they were also there to counteract
the wrongdoing of "another." (This part
was the most dangerous. Sorcerer's roots,
especially single-stone-throat or thorn-
in-the-instep spells, disabled those merely
seeking to improve themselves.)

She could open the doors of emaciated old men
who had hopelessly locked themselves in
the loneliness found in a coma. Through
intervention of the umbrella-shaped plants
that woke up first on the moss-covered
forest floor, the widowers would wake
with fluttering eyelids and a thirst
for water. When she cultivated the leaves,

the tone of her voice was like that
of a mother comforting a crying son.

Rose gently applied the masticated leaves
on the pale foreheads of the comatose men
before the early morning fog lifted above
the third-story room of Heijen hospital.
"To lessen the grief of losing your wife,
my son," she announced to the weeping but
unconscious men, "I bring you the strength
and effulgence of your Grandmother's forest."

She specialized in male-oriented problems.
Infertility. Lack of womanly attention.
Simple depression. Complexion breakouts.
Blood-coughing and premature balding.
Hallucinations and "mixed-up feelings."
Recurrent nightmares and feet boils.
Epilepsy and cancer. No one was turned away,
for they were there as a last resort.
Ironically, during months the tribal clinic
was run by its incompetent accountant,
her services were in demand.

In spite of her popularity as a healer,
there was a side of her few knew. To heal
was to also be familiar with what destroyed.
The yellow bird-shape series was a tantalizing
medium, provided it was used not more than
twice a summer moon. At someone's suggestion
she once instructed black, shiny flies to lead
angry wasps to the inner thighs of tribal
executives, leaving them disabled with six
welts apiece, bearing red pin-sized holes.
The mission abated further prospects
of a Settlement tour by representatives
of a chemical incineration plant

and a potbellied pig ranch. This,
she would confide to her tickled admirers,
is the power of nonlethal persuasion
upon autarchic tendencies.

She was so amazed by her gifts of persuasion
her confidence grew. It even lulled her once
to believe she was infallible. In so doing she forgot
the most important lesson imparted by her mentor,
Alice August: "That in the pinnacle of craft
all is still dependent on increments of faith
and demonstration." These were Alice's
words previous to the curing ceremony
for daughter Christina's cross-eyedness.
"Perfection is a fleeting nightwing
in the dead of a winter; it cannot be harnessed.
The slightest effort to do so will cause
suffering and loss." Becoming aware of Alice's
skills to see forward and back in the living
and the dead was to solemnly accept that Christina's
condition—fetal alcohol syndrome—stemmed
from Rose's early drinking habits and not
from the hideous acts perpetrated
by her father.

The nightmares Christina had during the nights
she was inside her drunken mother's womb
made her eyes cross. Yet they were normal
when she was born. Throughout her childhood
people complimented her eyes. As she matured,
and seeing that her mother would never defeat
alcoholism, she began developing a visual
twistedness. The Thunderbird wine in her
system aged, giving peace as a deception.

Drained by all she had done to deny
the NPWs' rumors, Rose couldn't admit
to being wrong. She still had battle scars

on her knees, and the beatings Greg took
remained on his face in the form of scar
tissue. On the "presumption" of victimization
the family had suffered immeasurably.
She wasn't quite sure how things got
to where they were.

As a child Christina did possess enchanting eyes,
but they began to lose their function the day
NPWs lied about Greg's indiscretions. Although
there shouldn't have been the slightest reason
to listen, she questioned if this was true
or not. Finally, Christina saw two of everything
except crows on the lines of utility poles.
It could have been coincidence, but Judith's
attention span succumbed to flights of fantasy
at about the same time. She would sit beside
Christina compassionately and stare into space
with her mouth wide open. Rose's suspicions grew,
as did her weight. Pressured by talk and driven
to the point of a nervous breakdown, she kicked
her husband out of the log cabin and developed
a warped sense of romance.

In a way, by having more children she wanted to make
up for the genetic flaws that came with Brook,
who had to be hidden from the public. For all
practical purposes, Brook did not exist. Not in
the tribal rolls or hospital records. People
knew there was another child, but no one knew
why she was prevented from seeing daylight
or talking to people. Which made scandal
more plausible.

It was therefore humiliation that brought
her to the doorsteps of Alice August,
a well-known healer. Under her tutelage
Rose began the slow process back to normalcy.

She regained part of what she had lost,
but not all. With the assistance of Alice,
she was instrumental in exorcising Judith's
twenty-four-hour companions, and her mouth
closed and finally smiled. Christina's eyes,
however, would never recoup a 20/20 vision
and their beauty, for she had been chosen
by the "white speckle-chested crow" to be
a constant reminder of Rose's past mistakes.
Brook was an incomprehensible "test" given
by the "orange-colored water serpent."
These became her allies in her apprenticeship
and afterward, but the cost was tremendous.
"Christina and Brook must remain as they
are as payment for our help, and your instructor
will say the same after trying unsuccessfully
to align their being," they said in her vision.
"In exchange for their suffering and yours,
we will perpetually imbue you with our power,
and it is this which will make you invaluable
to people. They will come from near and far
for your curing skills, both friends and enemies,
and young men will forever reward you with exorbitant
gifts. To boldly reject us and seek remedy elsewhere
may help your children but it will be tenuous at best.
The choice is yours. Keep in mind, though, you will
crawl the roads again and rumors will drive you insane
if you turn us down . . ."
And that is how fate came to Rose Grassleggings.
It wore a cloak made of scraps of sacred material
which could only conceal her and Judith from
the pounding hail. Her husband and their children,
Christina and Brook, stood in the ice storm
sacrificially and took punishment for all
humankind. There was simply no more room
in the cloak. Long before any of them knew what
was happening, all had been predetermined.

From whatever good we can glean from the plight
and triumph of this meager earthly existence,
it is never enough. So that a few of us
will celebrate and walk the full course
of this gift called life, many will suffer.

Sister Rose made a choice on our behalf—
and it was one she never regretted . . .

Junior Pipestar: The Destiny Factor

»《»《»《»《»《»《»《»《»《»《»《»《»《»《»《»《»

Junior:

After the disastrous summer of 1968, I packed
my suitcase and stuck my thumb out for a ride
north on Highway 63. When the semitruck drivers
asked if I was headed for Waterloo, New Hampton,
Rochester, or Red Wing, I said, "Way farther than
that, man." It was a quest for identity,
a longing for origins, a desire to pry
myself from the stump on the road,
propelling myself northward on skinned
knuckles toward the acquisition of beautiful
language. (And I don't mean Her Majesty's.)
That was the premise of my departure,
the excuse I made. Not being enough
of myself, I told people with questions,
I yearn to speak and sing in the language
of my nonexistent people.

Leaving the Claer township family farm
was the best decision I've ever made.

Considering I was still haunted
by the vengeful beacon and using
"Lauren Bacall" as an example, I lifted
my roots from the sidewalk and left.
Culturally afflicted and stigmatized
with hobbleleg and root-rot, no good-byes
were exchanged with my aunts and uncles.
No promises to be back were made.
No hugs or tears. I made my exit Indian-
style before the trees changed color,
long before the season of introspection
began. Who could blame me?

I learned several things about life from
frequent visits made to Black Eagle Child.
In part they were solid reasons not
to ever go back. There are nomads
who appear and vanish throughout
our lifetimes. Their faces are forgotten,
but their feats are recited in circles
where people reminisce. I have been one
of them, a sallow face on the whizzing
train of clowns. Although I wish I could
blame a duplicate of myself, a twin,
an insensitive opposite, it was one
person alone who drove into Why Cheer
and asked where the Indians lived.
It was me. A case where the curious
observer became a county celebrity.
Since little else happens there, stories
are told and retold with uncanny regularity.
The community thrives on bits of tragedy
and humor it experiences. For example,
you could never tire of hearing Jordan
Rattlelot talk about graduation night,
1956. The night would be painstakingly
recounted, and there'd be descriptions

like the night's scent and the words
spoken, their intimate inflections—
and even the items of clothing worn.
Or should that be clothes not worn?
In my case, anyway. I'd be a fool to think
I could ever shake the "Circus Acrobat Meets
Half-Woman" story. (The sharp turns I have
taken in this vehicle called my body are not
mine; I see them being taken but the sensation
is one of physical detachment. As such, there
have been situations when disaster was the best
thing that could have happened.
Do you believe in that possibility? That odd
twist? Making disaster into inspiration?
Well, it happened that summer.
It was as if there were ghostly trespassers
swirling around me, making the people
I met assume disguises of people they
were not. Brook . . . Brook Grassleggings,
the antishadow, was pivotal in that regard.)
It was a macabre punishment I assure you,
but I came away believing there's a reason
behind everything. Although I suspect Brook
was an unsuspecting accomplice for the crutch-
wielding phantasm, I secretly thank her/him
the end of every summer for the winds
of humiliation that swept me to New Province,
Canada. Pinelodge Lake, where we were from.
In the same breath I acknowledge Facepaint
and Bearchild. Without their pugnacity for piranhas,
the award-winning photograph "A Buck Buck-Naked"
would not have been.

It took a total of six days to hitchhike across
Minnesota—the largest stretch. In spite of fatigue
and surges of homesickness, I was revived by the first
steps made on Canadian soil. I found myself

on the perimeters of a wilderness with a tattered,
pencil-drawn map of directions to my grandfather's
former village. Unafraid, I set forth through
the endless thickets, swamps, and woodland
jungle. On the tenth day when my rations ran
out, I met an elderly gentleman from Ketchi
Nepisi, Great Water, village, who spent
his summers in the historic but foreboding
lakeside ruins, meditating with the heavens
and harvesting wild herbs and medicines.

Jack Frost was preparing to take leave
of Pinelodge Lake the day I stumbled
into his camp: in his bright-red star-
quilt blanket wrap, black mirrored leggings,
and floral-designed breechcloth, he stood up
and adjusted the two eagle feathers on his
otter turban. He was more annoyed than
the pet eagle who announced my presence
by screeching and talon-slapping its stand.
Mesmerized by his lustrous ceremonial attire,
I was speechless. Except for a couple of accessories,
the old man could have stepped out from an 1839
time period. There were glistening shells
for earrings attached to long white bones
tipped by serrated and arrowtail-shaped red-
and-white ribbons that reached below the shoulders;
a white collarless shirt embroidered with flowers
outlined his jutting chest; and over the rib line
were vertical stripes of red Czech cutbeads.
Gathered on and below his throat were five
necklaces made of dentalium shells, glass pony
beads, turquoise, and antique commemorative
medallions of silver that were once peace offerings
from distant kings and queens; over the breast
portion of his shirt were elaborate beaded designs
of lavender buffalo skulls. He balanced his body

and wardrobe on moosehide moccasins and two
crooked arms.

There were no lips I could see. No expression
except a wrinkled scowl that collected in the middle
of his forehead and a beady, hate-filled stare.
The summer-long reflection of the lake water
had doubled the sun's glare, for he had an even,
brownish stain. The age lines on his face were more
defined when contrasted with the fluorescent pastel
colors of the Air Canada traveling bag strapped
over his back. "Where did you disappear from?"
he asked in the deafening din of the flustered
watchbird's squawks. "Iowa, sir," I returned,
keeping a wary ear on the crazed eagle
who swung in circles like an expert gymnast—
only this one was feathered, possessed razor-
sharp talons, and was trained to attack intruders
if the notched tether snapped.
"Now where in the hell may that be?"
he demanded, placing a pair of sunglasses
on the bridge of his wide, twitching nose.
"The United States," I said, pointing
to the south. It was then that the enormity
of the trek began to dawn upon me.
"I wonder what could bring you
to this place," said the old man
after he gave me a sandwich of frybread
and sausage. "You're sure far from home,
wherever that may be." Before I could respond
he brought his hand up swiftly beside his stern
face like an officer saluting. He motioned me
to keep still. "Do you hear them?" he whispered
with palm trembling. "The singers; the drumming."
Over the crashing waves, there rose a choir
of barely audible voices. For less than
a second I heard music before the wind
carried it away. "That's the clearest

I've ever heard them, these spirits who
perform ceremonies in daylight hours
far below the lake."

And so that was how my interest in the music
of my ancestors began. It could have been
children beating the hell out of a junk car
miles upshore—for all I know—but Jack Frost
was insistent they were spirits in the midst
of a celebration or feast somewhere beneath
the lake. "Even the gods, they too
gather to eat, pray, and sing. Simply
because they were ritual-presenters doesn't
mean they don't do the same themselves.
Belief and its practices are ongoing.
Today, for instance, we are hearing
the ghosts of your great-great-grandparents,
for they are there, taking part. They rejoice
in your arrival." But the only emotion I could
detect came from the excited, twirling eagle.
Whether the songs were the garbled attempts
of children pounding away on the rusted
hood of a distant truck or whether
the wind-drowned music indeed originated
from underwater divinities, I would never know.
I slung Frost's belongings over my shoulder
and became his apprentice right there and then.
No questions asked. With failing eyesight
he needed help collecting the remaining plants,
tying and drying them on the roof rafters,
meticulously identifying and sorting
the plumed ones from the bristles,
the sweet ones from the bitter, the male
from the female, the healer from the destroyer,
or vice versa.

Aside from learning the medicinal benefits
of a Canadian forest and prairie, I coaxed

Frost into teaching me the forgotten dialect
of Pinelodge Lake. Few, however, dared
to remember it for fear of conjuring
the Blue Decree. Who could blame them?
There were nights when an eerie light
skimmed over the lake. When word spread
along the expansive lakeside of my return,
many felt I was a doomed soul. Among
the baptized my association with a credible
healer and clairvoyant was not taken well.
There was trepidation. For years few wandered
into our isolated region. "Are you lonesome?"
Frost would often ask in midsentence
during one of his discourses on ethnobotany.
"Me no give stinkin' shit," I would say,
impersonating Luke Warmwater's renowned saying.
The truth was, the bold words of a forest
transient and a weak heart didn't mix.
I was lonesome for the most irrelevant things—
a bottle of Coke and cheeseburgers, the "on"
switch of a television, and the svelte, tanned
bodies of white girls at the city swimming pool.
There were no cars to hop into and cruise
the streets. As for alcohol, the destiny factor,
whatever was brought to the old man by patients
was consumed for relatives who drank it long
before us and had gone on to the Hereafter.
We drank for the specific purpose of being
blessed with their divine intervention.

The Frost domain was rugged and punctuated
with a frightful quietness. We handwashed
our belongings, grew food annually from
the gardens, trapped fur animals
for supplemental income, and hunted moose
and deer for our sustenance during fall and winter.
Before and during icemelt we fished for northern
pike with lures we handcarved from wood

and inlaid with pieces of cheap metal jewelry.
I will admit on occasion I longed for
the indolent countryside, the geometric
landscape of fields, livestock, farms,
and the people I befriended in the stark
neighborhoods of the Claer township.
Boastful critter I ain't, believe me,
but the Frost indoctrination soon made
the past expendable. In the face of adversity
I sought only to cure the root-rot and hobbleleg
syndrome. If it meant abandoning Charlotte
and the aunts, then it had to be. I cared
for them. These were the only women I ever
truly loved.

The songs of the Lake People I eventually heard
one afternoon, calling out desperately
in forgotten Pinelodge words: the sounds
of rain on the pines, the snow collecting,
murmuring, and growing heavy on branches.
The Thunder-Visitor spoke in voices
of the prairie and bush, through
the whistles and calls of the birds
and animals. Don't forget, grandson,
the Lake People urged. Stay clear
of the light that encircles the rocky
beach and pine saplings. No rite can prevent
the Blue Decree from punishing spiderwebbed
figments of memory. Remember this as you travel,
for your place is not here.

In his best regalia, which included beaded cuffs
with mittens and moccasins with beaded soles
I had crafted and given as gifts, I buried Jack Frost
in the "garden of our purpose" fifteen years ago.
Because of the distrust bred by those baptized,
the pet eagle and I were the sole mourners.
Even the eccentric Luke Warmwater didn't show.

We then set out westward on foot as Frost
had instructed into Saskatchewan and Alberta,
settling on the outskirts of Indian communities
and helping a few establish the initial cleansing
through sweat lodges, songs, and medicines.
I took "Pipestar" from an eight-year-old Saskatoon
girl who was my first patient. Perhaps I was hers
as well, for she looked into my past and saw
sadness. "You never used to be like this,"
she said in a pinpoint assessment. "You come
from a lonely place, and you're in another life.
Behind your arm, near your shoulder, there's
a design, a scar which is a drawing. It shows
a pipe and a star. The pipe stands with you
and the star has protected you all along."
She was correct about the scars. In my youth
a bicycle handle had been used as the drawing
medium via an accident. And Jack Frost
had transferred the ownership and care
of a feather-fringed pipe that stood
beside me as I slept, requiring only
the smoking of tobacco in its bowl every
four moons in the light of the morning star.
I made a promise to the little girl to transfer
the Standing Pipe rights to her one day.
"I knew that," she said nonchalantly
as she unwrapped the foil on a stick of gum.
"Just as your benevolent teacher knew you'd
carry his teachings, I knew I was next.
He took your grandfather's place. In his
plans he left you slowly so that you would
not be devastated when the day came.
He deliberately prolonged his death
so that all he knew would be yours,
so that all you know and own
will be mine."

Black
Eagle
Child
Quarterly

The fall 1965 issue of the *Black Eagle Child Quarterly*
contained the sad news that the state legislature had reneged
on its long-held promises of twenty new houses
with indoor plumbing. The prominent headline read:
"Youthman Throws Cantaloupes at State Officials."
The caption and text below the photograph
of the splattered cantaloupes read:

"All Hope of Flushing Toilets Down the Drain
for Twenty BEC Households:
Claude Youthman, 35, of Cutfoot Crossing,
walked out the courtroom on August 14,
Tuesday, under the assumption he was acquitted
of charges of deadly assault with a 'round-shaped
projectile' levied against him by the state.
When the prosecuting attorney proclaimed,
'Your Honor, we submit,' in reference
to the visual evidence of the weapon,
Youthman misinterpreted 'we submit'
to mean the attorney had given up.
He was subsequently apprehended

for serious assault and terrorism
before he stepped off the courthouse
lawn.

"During Farmers Market in downtown Why Cheer
a month previous, Youthman contended 'a mean group'
of white men 'in good, clean clothes were listening
when theys weren't suppose ta' when his wife Henrietta
was accosted by a farmer with lewd suggestions.
'She knows little language. The white man's. Yours,'
he said to Judge Manez. 'When farmer say "put it in,"
she ran away and told me. I get mad and go ask farmer
why talk dirty? To get soap and wash mouth.
But they laugh, the farmer and men in the long
black car. I not know he (farmer) mean a sack
to put cantaloupe in.'

"Representing the state was the county attorney,
Tom Katz, who based the case on a series
of photographs taken at the scene.
One photograph of split cantaloupes
was enlarged to the size of a blackboard,
and another showed the open-mouths of a crowd
in dismay. 'This is a mockery of the good
relations we have with our Indians,'
testified the mayor, who later said
he wasn't anywhere near Farmers Market
where the event transpired. 'Whether I was
there or not is irrelevant. I came to tell
the folks at the capital we are genuinely
sorry for what happened. We vow to take better
care of our natives. We'll drive them home,
if necessary, when we detect telltale breath.'
When Judge Manez asked the mayor if he felt
the subject was under the influence at the time,
he said, 'When are they not? He probably was.
They are no different than children who need
strict supervision. The sad part is, they're

full-grown A-dults who oughta know better than
to act out their frustrations in a public forum.
That's why they're overly dependent on us.
They need to be more appreciative of what
they acquired from us thus far and not be
a burden to us good, tax-paying folks.'
The jury and courtroom audience applauded
the mayor's words of wisdom . . ."

Getting arrested proved to be the most audacious
thing that ever happened to Claude Youthman.
But he had this queer, nagging feeling
a monumental change was taking place.
Where it would take him and when
and how he would unboard he did not know.
All his life he had taken precautions
to maintain a mile's distance from
the type of inhumanity represented
in the county. In his wildest fears
Youthman never anticipated becoming
an innocent passenger aboard a train
of outcasts. Being away for five years
was, therefore, an unnerving experience.
He now knew where the two railroad tracks
that diagonally crisscrossed the Settlement
went. He was enlightened. The trains were
capable of stealing breath from those
he knew and dearly loved, but the rails
also led to federal prisons.

Abandoned as a child—the stories of his origins
were purposely kept vague—he grew up under
the care and attention of his grandfather,
Jim Percy, a kind-hearted leader
of the Star-Medicine Society.
Never quite understanding his
purpose, Youthman became hermitlike
after dropping out from Weeping Willow

Elementary in the fifth grade. He could
not stand the prospect of one day being
questioned about his mother and father.
They were unknown; he knew of none.
This blank spot had a frightening
effect on his psyche.

If there were doings sponsored
by his grandfather, he would lock himself
in the attic with his magazines of sensational
crime and jubilant Hollywood personalities—
Audie Murphy, the war hero, and the exquisite
Elizabeth Taylor. Those who came up the hill
to participate in ceremonies never sought
him out of curiosity, for all were aware
the darting figure or a creaking tree branch
was indication he was nearby. If by chance
someone accidentally caught him around
a corner or in a closet, he would look
down, stumble out sideways, and not look up
until he maneuvered his way to the staircase.
In spite of his introvertedness, the visitors
found him pleasing in appearance. He had oily,
jet-black hair that graced his classic slanted
eyes and high cheekbones, and he wore brown
summer shirts and gray baggy denims.
What did bother people was the fact
they only saw a profile. Even though
Youthman would tense up around strangers,
he remained photogenic. The people glanced
at his visage and then politely looked away.
Hunching his bony back over his tightly folded
arms, he brought his jaw to one of the shoulders
and kept it there. When addressed directly
the young man would pucker his large lips
and speak in a deep voice. He was his own
ventriloquist and wooden dummy. Ed Sullivan.
He made speech without facial gestures

an art form. A renowned spearfisherman once
equated the "young hermit's" lips to the lips
of a walleye in its last throes of life
over the frozen river. "As the walleye dies
from the puncture wounds of the barbed tines
and the subzero weather, it stiffens
and every fiber and nerve can be seen on
its lips. This is the way I see Claude when
he talks. He grits his parched mouth so much
the only movement you see is his quivering
lip muscles. Why does he do that anyway?"
The grandfather of the recluse usually
had no explanations.

Enclosed in the subhuman surroundings
of a Kansas prison, Youthman completely
reversed his outlook and philosophy.
By scooping up triangular edges
of his facial skin with a jagged piece
of glass he sewed himself with carpet
thread and curved needle to the iron bars.
Satisfied the exterior mask would peel
cleanly at the end of a backward run,
he severed himself from the hunchbacked
figure—and was born. From the musty
compartments of his paranoia the black-
and-yellow wings broke out, extended,
and dried out in the red prairie wind.

He took advantage of the prison's exemplary
reeducation program to acquire an art history
degree with an emphasis in Postimpressionism.
The numbness that came with incarceration,
a condition he felt was as close to death
as anything, prompted his obsession
with school and eventual survival
in prison. More important, he pledged
to forever understand the English language,

to avoid finding himself in dire circumstances
again. The world would not be right without
a walleye-lipped, oily-haired hunchback
who kept a shriveled image of his aboriginal
self in a Kinney's shoebox. In the dark before
dawn, he would unravel the tanned, glossy face
and suspend it on a wire hanger. Growing tired
of holding it at arm's length, he would hang
the mask on the gray wall and stare at it.
By so doing he was able to train the wings
to flex from their shoulder harnesses.
At first light the butterfly's hold on
the ceiling weakened, and Claude Youthman,
who long concerned himself with aspects
of aerodynamics, flew.

By the fourth year he was writing editorials
for the *Wichita Times-Republican*, the exclusive
Sunday issues. He penned treatises on the redundancy
of corporal punishment of American Indians.
"It is noteworthy to keep in mind," wrote one editor
as part of a series introduction, "that while Youthman
is a convicted felon, his arguments on federal law
vs. state law vs. tribal sovereignty issues deserve
consideration. What is especially startling
is the fact he is one person who benefited
from the penal system. Without the ridiculous
'cantaloupe' crime for which he was unjustly indicted
Youthman was destined to merely live out his life
as a woodsman and illiterate dreamer."
(July 6, 1970)

Throughout internment Youthman balanced
social concerns with neck-deep studies
in cathedral structures and ancient marble
sculptures. In those years in Grandfather's attic,
listening to Perry Como and the McGuire Sisters,
he chipped and gouged his way with a sharpened

spoon and rusty penknife, producing thornwood
statues of "Audie" and "National Velvet."

It was then that a Father Jeff Caster heard
of his skills and gave him an art history book
and a set of expensive oils and brushes.
Of the art that Youthman could duplicate
on canvas and thumbtack to the attic wall,
it was the works of Toulouse-Lautrec and Seurat.
Youthman's late interest had complications.
The *A tta i ka na ni*, Sioux tipis, he did
in pointillism resembled cone-shaped bubblegum
vending machines. He longed for exact reproduction,
images you could almost touch, like Christ's crown
of thorns he made for Grandfather or the duplicates
of Elizabeth's horse, but there he remained,
right on through college, with a painting
technique he was comfortable with and stuck with.

Taken by postcard renditions one day of what
an incarcerated Indian sees in a glance,
he initiated the "Gray Indian Series."
The act itself was controversial.
Using large canvases made of layered
newspaper and flour paste, he depicted
365 days of the color of imprisoned light.
On each of the twelve canvases
he divided the days as geometric shapes—
octagons, diamonds, circles, rectangles,
and stripes. Into each shape was filled
an intense or subtle degree of gray.
That was all. There wasn't any kind
of humanness. Just a different shape
of gray he saw each day. The Goslin Art
Institute of Omaha, Nebraska, upon seeing
photographs that accompanied the editorials,
sponsored the first exhibition. *LIFE* magazine
followed with an interview with the celebrated

"American Indian Artist and Self-proclaimed
Revolutionary: From Cantaloupes to Cathedral
Buttresses." The Honorable Governor was obligated
to attend, and he sat at the reception table
with Youthman. "Then what does the 'Gray Series'
have to do with Postimpressionism?" opened Youthman
rhetorically upon his introduction, shaking
the silver chains and the wrist of a federal
marshal he was shackled to in protest.
"This is what I was asked by the warden
when the Goslin Institute first proposed
the exhibit. The warden's no dummy,
I told myself, but I'd be a darn fool
to believe he came up with the question.
He was coached, and all in an effort
to stifle my notoriety. He knows I will
speak of deplorable conditions, maggot-
infested food, and the urinal stench
of my living quarters. Simply posing
an 'art' question carries little weight.
Studying Postimpressionism was the best choice,
and it is a tranquil place from where
abstract visions are shaped—today."

National celebrities are made daily,
and their reigns end just as quickly.
The world is full of actors who weep
at footage of old but famous movies.
It pains them to remember the short-lived
glory. For artists and revolutionaries nothing
remains but laminated clippings and embossed
invitations with signatures of dignitaries
who later became unknown themselves.
And so it was for Claude.
The good people of Kansas wrote a total
of four replies to his editorials
from a circulation of four million.
From the publicity of *LIFE* he received

$10,000 for the paintings
and invitations to sit on several prominent
boards in the East. He also obtained permission
to purchase art supplies for prisoner-artists,
but a few found ways to inhale the paints,
thinners, and aerosols, killing the project.
Upon hearing this, museums and galleries
ceased communication. The public television
crew from WITC who had stated categorically
they'd be there to film his prison release
and drive him back to Iowa never showed.
It was only after he had been waiting four hours
that an apologetic telephone message arrived:
"Mr. Youthman: We are sorry but WITC has changed
priorities midstream and has opted to do
a piece on Molly Dolly, chosen this year
as the loveliest artist by People of America.
We are sending a taxi instead and will be
glad to pay for the first twenty miles
to the interstate." Claude Youthman took
the taxi ride, got off at an overpass,
and hitchhiked the rest of the way
to Black Eagle Child.

》《

Henrietta, Mrs. Youthman, the ingenuous one
whose honor Claude was defending on that day
of infamy at Farmers Market, cried at the sight
of her husband as he limped up the hill
past the water tower. She dropped the plate
of beads and rushed out to the porch. She stood
and waited while the miniature souvenirs
of moccasins and canoes (what would have been
Claude's bus fare) dangled from her blouse.

Claude's homecoming was largely uneventful.
Except for the brief hugs and touches

he received from his wife and grown children,
nothing had changed: the front door still
had one hinge missing; the same greasy curtains
were there, held by a stone-smooth yarn string;
and the tribe was still without indoor plumbing.
While impermanence was not a reality they knew,
he became embittered. When his family made
the first physical contact with him ever,
he openly wept. Indians never needed to touch
each other to demonstrate love and affection.
More so if you were once a recluse like Claude.
You could touch or kiss someone in the family
all your life—or you could not. In the end,
when someone's presence was no longer,
the pain of their loss or absence
was the same. He planned to rest
before venturing back to society
to pick up where he left off—
or would he?

He had learned to fight the establishment
from behind the prison walls, to correct
injustice. He hoped he could do the same
for his home. "To make this a better place
to live" as the billboard on Highway 63 read.
At first, he was welcomed with a community dance,
and the BEC Business Council congratulated him
with pithy sentences. The tribe knew about his
exploits, for Henrietta had submitted his editorials
to the *BEC Quarterly*. The neighbors were amazed
how "an illiterate woodsman" was able to circumvent
disaster. After that, getting rides into Why Cheer
for groceries and typing paper was easy.
The people were glad to chat with a notable.
But they couldn't fathom his intellect.
Instead of listening and responding
to what he planned to do with health,

education, and socioeconomics, they spoke
about family spats and burned food.

Claude Youthman had taken five years off
from social or family responsibility.
The small benign things began to take
precedent. He wanted to savor lost moments
with Henrietta and their grown children.
From afar, however, he began to jot notes why
the tribe could not prosper economically.
Later, he read them aloud to himself,
Henrietta, and admirers who visited:

"Politics here are comparable to a birthday party
attended by a dozen robust children on a hot summer
afternoon. There is excitement, as well as apprehension. The fun and honor of it is simply being
invited to the affair; the reality is that only
one birthday occurs per child per year. Picture
this, if you will. After the party has swiftly
gone past the food, dessert, and the unwrapping
of presents, the children sit back, digest,
and exchange idle chitchat. Soon, even before
the parents are finished cleaning and clearing
the tables, some children demand the games
commence. The parents smile kindly before
wiping their sweaty brows. The children
giggle uncontrollably as balloons are inflated
and attached to their ankles with string.
They are then herded to the center
of the room where everyone can see them.
One concerned parent leans down and gives
last-second instructions. The object,
of course, is to bust as many balloons
as possible while keeping yours intact.
Those who cannot stand the thought
of losing 'jump the gun' by stomping

on the balloons of unsuspecting participants
before the countdown is given. The game stalls
and new balloons are inflated. When the game
finally starts there is chaos. In the same
vein, the tribe will cooperate to a certain
degree. Food and pleasantries will be shared
and exchanged. The trouble starts when a novel
proposal is submitted for consideration.
Someone will become outraged for not
having thought of it before. And that person
will instigate the first trampling, and others
(relatives and loyal band members) will follow
suit. Without evaluating if the novelty could
benefit the tribe, the balloon-busters begin
jumping up and down without really knowing
why. How does this tribe function then?
People are not apprised of anything that
may affect them. All is done without
their knowledge and approval by false
leaders. That means you, Lardass . . ."

As the years progressed, the rebellious
vigor he acquired in prison began to diminish.
Stirring changes he once shared with people on
rides to town were next to zero. He began
to realize why no one ever paid attention:
few possessed the voracity to follow through
with their own ideas.

By the time he secured a part-time position
as "tribal arts instructor" at Weeping Willow
Elementary in 1988—a program which had been
written by a former teacher, Lorna Bearcap,
(another success story)—he had a master's
in art history. He should have been content
with published articles on the "Post-Gray
Indian Series," but insights as to why

234

the tribe was an inept, bureaucratic
monstrosity were formulated. He concluded
the people who were running the tribe
were the real "illiterate dreamers."
The BEC Business Council allowed its
welfare, health, education, and commerce
committees to promote a greed or help thy-
self system. This is what Lorna Bearcap
had desperately tried to convey shortly
before she was dismissed from Weeping Willow.
As the only BEC college-educated teacher,
she had been instrumental in developing
programs whereby students were taken beyond
the barbed-wire fence. But her feats drew
the ire of the retarded advisory board.
After she had obtained grants in excess
of half a million dollars, she was accused
of "exploiting the school's singers and dancers."
The funds were then embezzled or shifted
to baseball diamond restoration (located
on a known floodplain), intertribal basketball
tournament trips (party time), or (rigged)
dance competitions. Nepotism brought about
a school principal with a degree in mechanical
drafting and welding. There were embarrassing
audits that made the lead-ins on television news.

Lorna Bearcap's last memo to the advisory
board chairman (who was reportedly caught
lollipopping one of the Hyena brothers) read:
"When a true genius appears in the world,
you may know [her] by this sign, that the dunces
are all in confederacy against [her].—Jonathan Swift."
Thus ended the extraordinary efforts of a person
who crawled out from the brewery ditches
and made a drastic change for herself—
and for students whom she deeply cared about.

Like Claude, Lorna took the highway sign
seriously. Because her employers could not,
she was viewed as an obstructionist.

"The school has been relegated for years
with a monumental task of being the last carrier
and bastion of identity. To this end a unique
bilingual/bicultural curriculum has been
written and adopted. Unfortunately,
it is a disgrace. The school tries
in vain to convey the most rudimentary
skills, yes, but the students' retentive
abilities—to think, speak, and write
in our language and to recall precepts,
myths, and rules to live by—are far
from exemplary . . .

"We perceive the antiquated institution
as a gleaming aircraft whose defective
nuts and bolts are about to pop in flight
eight miles above. With all due respect
to our alma mater, unless the craft
can be completely 'overhauled,'
administration and direction-wise,
it faces further structural and academic
deterioration. There is something deeply
disturbing about a child who cannot begin
a conversation in our mother tongue,
and even more if a proper sentence
cannot be composed in English . . ."

The tribe patched itself back up by shinnying
up a tree, licking its wounds, and forgetting
anyone ever took the thousands of dollars.
Disguises were poor: new trucks were driven
and satellite dishes installed, but the children
of the suspects wore ragged clothes. Unfortunately,
the state and federal agencies chose not to file

charges, which gave a green light for repetition.
The commodity surplus cheese and flour supplies
were depleted by various committees for Indian
taco sales; clothing items that had been donated
and trucked in by wealthy Boston people
were resold to the tribe; gas and clothing
assistance through the welfare department
were distributed among the working people
at the BEC tribal center; Social Security
checks and ADC checks were channeled,
skimmed, and reissued; monetary or land
donations were kept a secret and divided
by the Business Council. The list
of improprieties grew, and Bingo
Extravaganza was just around the corner.

Claude Youthman forgot about enlightening
the "Outside World." He set aside his paints
and brushes, and he sat down to write a letter
of complaint to a reputable Republican.
He detailed the despicable goings-on
in the *BEC Quarterly*. "Before we can
even begin to focus on the future we
must dispose of our own pretentious scum."
Before the Weeping Willow advisory board
had a chance to fire him, he resigned
under the lights of a press conference.
Lorna Bearcap was there also. Here they were,
the only people who had miraculously educated
themselves and remained. Now they were being
ostracized for revealing ugly truths.

But the infighting was far from over. In fact,
it had just begun. The common BEC man or woman
had no right to define and dictate policy.
They sought the advice of hereditary leaders
in absentia, and they grew more determined
than ever that all problems were attributable

to the lack of divine leadership.
In their opinion elections were over with.
With divine leadership, the Black Eagle Child
Nation would grow strong again.

Even though the blood which coursed
through the veins of the true Chieftains
coursed through theirs vicariously,
Claude Youthman and Lorna Bearcat sat
together at the kitchen table and penned
the first of their diatribes,
the WEEPING WILLOW MANIFESTO.
There was no other resolution.
There had to be an immediate
return to the Old Ways
beginning from the bottom
up.

The
Man Squirrel
Shall Not
Wake

Winter 1989

We've never had it easy,
thought Ted Facepaint as he lay still
in the cold sheets of a rigid bed.
If we Indians don't kill each other off,
the whites certainly will. What kind
of statistic would that make me
in the annals of "Patient Abuse"?
How would it read? Point one thousand
of one percent of all minorities in the state
die while under medical care? Would they attribute
my death to a boa constrictor made of plaster?

His eyes remained sealed and motionless
as they stagnated in their thick, gel-like
sockets; yet he could distinctly smell and hear
all that was going on around him.
But mostly there were dialogues
within his body. And the only speaking
voice was his. Being both the speaker
and listener, he smiled in his mind
as he equated his mute condition with

the mythological wolf character
whose eyes had been shit upon
by the raccoon as he slept,
putting a permanent end to the hunt.
The sight-impaired wolf eventually
drowned after being directed to a river
by talking trees. A bloody conspiracy.
His thoughts shifted . . .

I am an animist to begin with, but I know
more now how the belief is applied.
Those outside this fabric of tissue
implicitly believe a life exists here—
within me. But how does one bring a tree,
a crusty-eyed wolf, or a concrete-fractured
statue to communicate? There isn't a shred
of ethereality in a sculpture of my image
with corroded wire supports protruding
throughout. Right?

Everywhere was the smell of alcohol
and sickness. Sterile nausea.
Several machines were gurgling.
Life-support systems? Unknown people,
alive and dead, would alternate visiting him;
they let their presence be known by handshakes
or the wiping of his brow with the backs
or palms of their hands, and sometimes
they spoke in indiscernible voices. Once
there was even a woman who kindly massaged
his bare chest with a cool washcloth;
her touch was soothing until bright blue
lightning shot out from the washcloth
and penetrated his numb heart. His spine
arced upward involuntarily. There's no
response, she said in panic. The shadows
braced themselves and stood back. "Clear!"

The lightning came down sideways and struck
the octagon drum of his heart. The long
fingers of the explosion reached outward
but found no horizon. No rain. Nor the Red-
hatted Grandfather. The chest-washing
was repeated four times. Just when he
reached the rapids and was about to swim
into the fury, a treble snag hook on a leader
caught his tail fin and forced him to shore.
He would not reach the destination upriver.
Now there was a vast emptiness, an ever-present
state of dream. He was not lost or afraid
he may not wake up, speak—or move.
At least he retained the ability to think.
He thanked the kind woman and her washcloth
for that. In the dead space phosphorescent
balls of lightning floated down and cooled,
creating their own microcosms of life.
If the four "watching" Swanroot salamanders
represented living ones who can regenerate
severed limbs and other body parts,
would the Fourth Star take pity
on his hopeless condition by bringing
back daylight? He begged: I am beholden
to your presence; I patiently await
your voice. At any moment, Ted thought,
sparks will be emitted by the star-boulder . . .

Only four days previously he had driven
himself to the Heijen Medical Center
after being badly beaten by three Indians
in ludicrous disguises. He was still mizzed
as he lay on one of the examining tables
of the emergency room. And it was three
and a half hours before a Dr. Heijen and a nurse
began cleaning the puncture wounds a sharpened
screwdriver had made in his ribs. To prevent

air from entering or blood leaving,
Ted had taped himself in a measlelike
fashion with gray duct tape. The arm
with multiple fractures dangled
in the delicate hands of the doctor.

"What did you do to get yourself
here?" asked the doctor. Ted began detailing
events which brought him to emergency.
Besides, Gita, the Danish nurse, was curious.
She rolled up the duct tape in her palms
and made free throws to the trash can,
looking over to Ted to check if he was watching.
"Thanks to George Bush," spoke Ted with swollen
eyes fixed on the shapely ultra-white uniform,
"I got pummeled and stabbed for refusing
laced grass from three Indians wearing
Halloween masks: one wore an Aunt Jemima
type of mask complete with bandana
and oversized dress; another who spoke
in a stuttering fashion looked like Mr. Hyde
with the cape and top hat, only this one
wore a white tennis skirt; and the third mask
depicted a face of a teenager with a case
of acne gone wild. The latter was wretched;
the slime so real. A red face on a red man
is hardly a disguise! A classic case where
Retin-A has only intensified the problem.
Major Zittsville, mon. And the Aunt Jemima
perpetrator's breath had the putrid odor
of chewing tobacco. That much I know, Doc.
So I know who they are. Three depressed
cross-dressers. 'The horror of it all,'
to quote Brando. But had I known this
would have occurred, I would have given
the Puzzy Bros. a green light—
by all means give me a hit!"

242

The nurse giggled before apologizing
in a cheap Zsa Zsa Gabor accent,
"Oh, pleez forgive meh, Indin,
for asking. I'm horrendezly nosey."
The doctor followed up by saying,
"Didn't George Bush come to Iowa
yesterday?" The boisterous nurse and
the giddy patient reflected.
"Yes, he was here," said the doctor,
answering his own question. "Bush did
a radio program for our farmers
and gave a brief fund-raiser speech
for Dan Frazier." Listening, Ted squirmed
in agony as the fiberglass cast was applied
on his fractured elbow. He couldn't understand
why an educated man could be so gullible.
"After the Malta summit, Doc," spoke Ted,
"do you really believe the President
of the United States would give us
150 minutes?"

The doctor stopped the winding motion
of the fiberglass wrap and looked down
the crooked arm of the inebriated Indian.
He wasn't sure what came over him,
but he was beginning to despise
the vile creature. On a roll
with the European angel, Ted continued
to recite his trickster theories, unaware
the backhoe had ruptured a political nerve.
"In jest I tell kids that rock concerts
are megabuck rip-offs. The only bands
who play Iowa are imposters—and damn
good ones! Rolling Stones in Ames,
shit, is a poor man's fantasy!
McCartney's next—right? After Buddy
Holly and Ritchie Valens lost it

in Clear Lake, would you tease fate?
Whoever came as Bush was first-rate."

Dr. Heijen attempted to defend George,
but his comments were muffled by his assistant's
squeals. As the patient and nurse laughed
together, the doctor chose to deliberately
tighten the cast on Ted's inside elbow
and wrist, including points where the bone
snapped. He could barely control his anger
as he advised Ted to expect swelling,
purple fingers, and numbness. There
were pills for that, but there'd be no
follow-up to determine if the cast was set
right. The screwdriver wounds were not serious,
he diagnosed, they just looked like they were.
"Yeah, like bullet holes on a squirrel
with its insides and muscles glistening
high atop a tree," countered Ted sarcastically.
"The squirrel, although half-dead, knows
enough to go home and die."
Before leaving the room for another patient,
the doctor leaned over the table, stared
downward at Ted for the last time, and spoke:
"Well, go home then, Man Squirrel."
From Ted's upside-down perspective, the doctor's
mouth was where the eyes should be and the eyes
were his mouth, the nose a grotesque growth
with small openings directed to the sky,
and behind his balding well-rounded jaw
a lightbulb was suspended in a silver
stainless steel bowl, giving off an eerie
radiance reminiscent of the halo around Jesus
Christ's head in the painting done by his brother,
Christopher, at Circles-Back house. The halo
was the nicest thing; the wearer, the Bush
defender, was not: frothy saliva
collected and trickled up from the corner

of the gaping, talking eye of Dr. Contradiction.
The evil secretions of Satan, was how Bearchild
would have put it. He remembered the analogy
from the night he first took Edgar
to Well-Off Man. The dual personality
of your belief, he had aptly prognosticated,
is an unequal balance of life and death.
One knows not which is on the outside—
the halo or the horns, for they have shown
historically they are one and the same.
The Star-Medicine changed Bearchild's
twisted perceptions, but they had somehow
remained with Ted over the years.
The doctor, for example, did not bother
to claim the destroyer or the healer status
when queried. But it soon became evident.
The eyes of the doctor's mouth wordlessly
expressed a seething hatred for the inferiority
Facepaint exemplified. Dr. Heijen bore no
compassion whatsoever for the wasted mortal.
Within him, the kindling of a racist fire
was set ablaze, and the kettle of blood
boiled and surged like a great sea
until the huge waves blinded what
little guidance the pilot once had.

In his spiderwebbed mind Ted could vaguely make
out a tainted photograph, in which the subjects—
Edgar Bearchild, Junior Pipestar, Brook Grassleggings,
and himself—were superimposed over one another.
He squinted and was able to make out the images
and their personal history: in a measure taken
once to counterattack night-enemies in the form
of owls, Bearchild said he had contemplated
equaling their nakedness by stripping his clothes;
Junior was driven to the brink of insanity
and eventual redemption by an imaginary light;
Grassleggings shed her amorphous snakeskin

and shocked those who saw; and Ted,
with the history of the desert sprawling
behind him, was now bare and unconscious
at the Heijen hospital.

He had vastly underestimated the female hyenas
and the fact they became even more fierce
during a night hunt. After the obscure landscape
had shaped itself against the concave clouds
for twenty-one years, they had successfully
planned their impassioned revenge.
He should have known the marble-sized
reflections dashing in front of the headlights
of his car came from the skulls of African predators.

Ted thought solemnly about the cast
of characters he met on that fateful 1968 night:
Mathylde, the "snake tongue" matriarch,
was now famous for excitedly yelling "Blinglo!"
when she won at the American Legion Hall bingo
games. Her daughter, Matty Jr., was also
renowned as the incompetent Needy Services
worker. (There were also unsubstantiated
reports she sold "fondling" rights to her
handicapped or ill relatives in order to pay
for new cars and VCRs by preying on their
monthly checks.) And two of the "Three Stooges,"
Curly and Moe, resorted to wearing dresses
and pasting cosmetics on their cinder-embedded
faces when they could no longer bear to look
at their hideousness. The youngest of the trio,
Larry, the one with real complexion problems,
faithfully followed his brothers. They got on
the area rosters of packing plants as undependable
employees who always managed to weasel back
to herding pigs when the plants had suffered
more injuries than usual or exhausted their supply
of good workers. The unusual Hi-na lot were halfway

reliable for a month "as either or" before
the stench of pig shit got to them,
nauseating them enough to vomit.
Frustrated, the mother once was said
to have ordered roasted pig heads from
a butcher, wrapping them in cellophane
and curled ribbons as presents for her boys.
It backfired. They wore the heads as masks
until they could no longer wear them.

Ted speculated the month must have ended when
he bumped into their sparsely fleshed snouts.
With their last paychecks, they must have
purchased new dresses and masks for the Mardi
Gras. What a time to celebrate!
The screwdriver stabbing stopped when
he agreed to stop kicking their oysters.
And when he made each confess who
they were, gender-wise, they whimpered
and trotted away in horror toward the woods
as the truth slammed against their eardrums.
Following behind were "Blinglo" and "Matty J,"
turning around thrice to bark and growl.
Although the mother and daughter had no
reason to limp, the others did.
Ted became amused again at the aftermath
until the exposed nerves in his ribs began
pulsating a mysterious telegraphic message,
the Morse code of an imminent celestial
revelation.

The last frantic prayer he made years
ago nearly baked him alive on the Nevada
desert. The protective light he longed
for came as requested but in the form
of a flaming sun. The Fourth Star
was strangely absent. He assumed
it was retribution for the Pepsi

bottle clubbing. Didn't the swirling
sentinels permit any life-saving measures?
Would they take into account that he
was an accomplice and not the perpetrator?
That the depressed white man planned
his own murder and not him?
At the point when the Nevada Highway
Patrol peeled his body off the desert
and brushed away the sand and flies
he regained consciousness.
Ted was agitated for receiving
what he did not ask for.
"What matters in the end, buddy,"
the perspiring patrolman lectured,
"is that you're breathing. Whichever holy
star you thought we were is unquestionably
the least of your nihilistic problems."
They drove him to a convenience store
where he bought a pair of cutoffs, thongs,
a Hawaiian shirt, and a bus ticket to Why Cheer
with the folded bills in his sock.
Since then there had been an overpowering
sense of being directionless; since then
he had been immensely alone in the tainted photo.

The anaconda fiberglass cast Dr. Contradiction had set on his fractured arm
squeezed the natural flow of blood
so tightly it gelled up, reacting
like diesel fuel in subzero wind chills.
Ted's arteries clotted, sending destructive
razor-edged pieces tumbling through his body.
Damming up, cutting through. Embolism?
Apoplexy? Is that what the shapes
said it was? He could recall
the biggest shards as they traveled
noisily and in slow motion through
his heart and brain like a dozen axes

being dropped down an abandoned elevator
shaft. From the bottom the ringing
of metal on metal rose up and delicately
snipped the spiderwebs until the word
P-O-G-R-O-M was spelled. Yes, the slaughter
of self was well organized, Ted whispered
in the deepest recesses of his moldy mind.
The spider's flag quivered.

Somewhere beneath the Salamander Effigy
in one of the log-lined, elongated cubicles
Ted gripped the vine-wrapped staff. Beside him
the kettle drum began to resonate to the unseen
drummer's playing. He then proceeded to sing
the songs of the Black Stone, the Fourth Star.
Stirred into being by the euphony,
the four "watching" figurines crawled
toward him over the frosted dirt floor,
reciting a familiar story in rhythm
with Ted's excrescent music:
"There were once two young men
who wanted so desperately 'to do something'
they unwisely chose to visit us for their needs.
In spite of the words offered by their grandfather
they ate and drank the Star-Medicine together
and laughed at our expense. In looking back
we see the carelessness you have exhibited
toward your faith." Following the admonition
from the foursome, a spotted fawn cautiously
emerged from the doorway, came in, and bit
his hand. The tin rattle Ted was holding
dropped as he attempted to resist, stopping
the song. Shaking its head, the mischievous
fawn wouldn't let go. Ted's arm gave way
and separated from the elbow joint.
No blood spewed forth, for the fiberglass
serpent had it cauterized. The immobile arm
was then dragged to the center of the room

where a cooking fire and an iron grill
suddenly appeared beneath it. With the arm
burning, thin wisps of smoke were lifted
by a draft to the ceiling where a series
of multicolored fireflies began to blink
through the cracks of the peeled logs.
They came through and made a star formation
in the air, the Three-Stars-in-a-Row.
The little earth swelled beneath
and the Deer Man, having ridden
to the surface in bubbles from
an underground waterway, maneuvered
his way up the peak on his pointed hooves
in one continuous sliding motion. The stars
were removed from the purple night sky
like clusterberries and brought down
to his dinner tray by a miniature
thundercloud. The dark, circling cloud
rumbled in low, murmuring tones as Ted
chewed the coallike substance.

The first physical sensation came from
someone massaging his feet. He moved them
in response and the hands tightened.
Facepaint gasped from his dry mouth.
"Take it easy," spoke a kind-voiced woman.
Opening his eyes, the very first person
Ted saw was the opulent Mrs. Grassleggings.
In a steady vertical motion she
was lightly brushing his face with an eagle-
wing fan. From the rich, fragrant scent
of cedar being emitted from the snow-white
plumage, he knew the fan had been blessed
with the Ancient Fire of his Grandfathers.
There would be tranquillity. He drifted
back to sleep in the breeze, knowing
he would wake again.

With his talons wrapped firmly around
the knotted limb of a tall cottonwood,
he began to sew and mend the injured wing
with his beak. Toward the west, the fiery
rays of the sun broke through a row of clouds
and lit the earth below in brilliant reds
and yellows. As the brittle leaves fluttered
on either side of him, Facepaint took this
as a signal to begin navigating his way home.
He peered out past the smoky hills before
unfolding and stretching his wingtips
upward to test them. Confident the sutures
would hold, he ruffled his speckled chest,
leaned forward, and took flight,
keeping altitude at treetop level.

Afterword

In the spring of 1970, during a smoggy, oily-aired evening in Southern California, I jotted down what was perhaps the first outline of this book. It was a simple one and in some respects no different from the drafts to poems I later published. The one aspect, however, which made this outline stand out for many years was the intriguing set of chapter titles and synopses.

Today this outline and the accompanying notes are held permanently between the cold pages of a spiral-backed tablet in storage. They have always been a few feet away, but their sensitive memories have kept me at arm's length—until today. To have gently lifted these words from the light green pages by breathing a heart's pulse into them is a startling juxtaposition to the computer monitor which now records these final entries.

The poetic journey in the making of *Black Eagle Child* has been a most comprehensive project in terms of message, content, and stylistic approach. There has also been divergence. Considering that the poetic forms I have adopted and adapted (from English, a second language) have little significance in the tribal realm, word-collecting was met early on with varying degrees of apprehension. Whenever I entertained the prospect of sitting down at the desk,

Wa wa to se, Ada K. Old Bear's grandfather.
State Historical Society of Iowa.

getting beyond serious, and holding these thoughts long enough to boldly arrange their sequences in order, I discovered forthright our shadows change imperceptibly in accordance with the sun's ascension and descension. As a result, there was work which never materialized. Because of the differences of the bilingual/bicultural worlds I live in, it sometimes seems as if what is actually published turns out to be a minute and insignificant fraction of one's perpetual metamorphosis.

Putting stories to page has been a task and a half, for the characters and their situations are taken from both autobiographical experiences and imagination. In the delicate ritual of weighing what can and cannot be shared, a greater portion of my work is not based on spontaneity. And a large segment of what is presented for public dissemination is not so much an act of revealing elements that are close to me as it is an exercise in creative detachment. The most interesting facet in all of this has been the artistic interlacing of ethereality, past and present. As such there are considerations of visions, traditional healing, supernaturalism, and hallucinogen-based sacraments interposed with centuries-old philosophies and customs. Since these verities are still a prevalent part of modern tribal society, the divisions between dream and myth are never clear-cut.

The creation of *Black Eagle Child* was equivalent to a collage done over a lifetime via the tedious layering upon layering of images by an artist who didn't believe in endings, for the sweeping visions he wanted to capture were constant and forever changing. It was therefore essential to depict these visuals in increments, to keep these enigmatic stories afloat in the dark until dust-filled veils of light inadvertently revealed their luminescent shapes.

My literary perspectives were often subject to bouts of over-concern and grave underestimation of self. Given the number of season-long debates that were held to determine whether the material presented was unnecessary or sacrilegious, there's no doubt an entire book could have been written. One winter, with space becoming more precious, I was forced to incinerate boxes of reasons—pro and con. While I remained enamored with writing and the meticulous rituals one goes through in bringing thought to page, the relationship of the creator and the created worked best behind the iron borders of this word-collector consciousness.

In most tightly knit societies, one must be keenly aware of social responsibility. For the Mesquakie—People of the Red Earth—it is no different. Circumspection is the paradigm of harmony. But as with everything modern and "civilized," there are often casualties among the ignorant, deprived, and unknowing. I, for one among many, plead guilty to the preceding statement. In extreme cases, one's forgetfulness and insincerity are not effronteries; they are irreversible, unending truths which began in 1492.

Long ago when I first started to publish my work locally, I was apprised by my grandmother to not ever be "dissuaded by anyone" and to continue with only good intentions in mind. While she obviously realized I was too young and naive to know of Importance, she nevertheless taught there were things I could not write about. For years I truly thought I possessed valuable knowledge. The fact was, I didn't know anything. Yes, I may have heard, seen, and experienced firsthand extraordinary occurrences of reality "gone astray," of steps taken into transmutable dimensions, but they could only be seen and understood from one angle: in retrospect.

Reviewing my work with scrutiny and keeping distant from

transgression of certain codes and precepts have become inherent parts of the storywriting regimen, the premise being that words have an innate sense of power. With early word-collectors (or informants) and their personal disasters as examples, my grandmother also forewarned commentary was destructive when untethered, for it had the capacity to either inflict or self-inflict harm. As much as has been permissible, I have attempted to hold on to this tenet.

Remarkably, now that my destination is within sight, whatever energy I am able to conjure can only be a semblance of elation. For that I am grateful. There was a time when it could have been worse: I once read of an ancestor who was so exhausted from a military-sponsored interview that he lay still for hours in his parents' lodge. For a person whose world had been mystically laid down by a Creator with a fundamental set of understandings and spiritual teachings, I imagine there had never been a structured and compartmentalized perception of Mesquakie ideology as that shown by the white-skinned people, *wa be ski na me ska tti ki.*

Whether or not the account is authentic, I can commiserate with this exhausted character, for there have been occasions when I thought the best recourse was to reconsider direction, questioning what purpose the narratives served—until the state of vexation passed.

The philosophy that espouses cosmic insignificance, a belief that humans are but a minute part of world order, has shaped my words. My expectations are simply to express myself as only an accomplished instrumentalist can, to arrange in melodic and tragic tones the common chords of one's abraded existence. Yet there exists a ceaseless feeling that more needs to be said than what was offered in the space and time given.

》《

The Black Eagle Child Settlement is a fictitious counterpart of the central Iowa sanctuary where I am an enrolled, lifelong resident. The character Edgar Bearchild mirrors in part my own laborious Journey of Words. He finds himself in a unique but precarious "little earth" where writing becomes the sole means of salvation.

Ma kwi ba tti to, my great-grandfather.
State Historical Society of Iowa.

Encouraged early on by close relatives, Bearchild accepts the medium but he is somewhat late in doing so. As a result, he wants to unfold the mysteries that transported him to the pinnacle of poetry writing. In the process he discovers concrete answers, like windfish, are elusive. Bearchild merely intends to finish out the whizzing star's cataclysmic course, to be (as Paddy McAloon of Prefab Sprout of England writes and sings) the "Fred Astaire of words."

Ko ta to, my grandmother, on my father's side.
State Historical Society of Iowa.

Ted Facepaint, on the other hand, is a composite of a dozen people met, known, and lost in the last forty years. He's a jigsaw puzzle, an imbrication of humanity, whose pieces belong to everyone. Despite Facepaint's gallant efforts to rid the future of physical and social impediments, there is never a guarantee the passage will go unhindered. His spiritual beliefs and convictions surpass most, but he alone does not think so, for he comes from an unfamiliar place where radiant people freely give away the gift of introspec-

Tama street scene. From the author's collection.

tion. Meeting him along the way toward his sky-answering quest, people held out their cupped hands and saw vividly the cascading plainness of their lives. It frightened those who lacked the maturity to grasp the bitter world, while those experienced saw past the technological clutter, seeking signs of validation.

Facepaint is a rare personality who is intrinsically attuned to the night sky, and he keeps an ever-present watch for any change, any subtle repositioning of the Orion constellation.

Like nomads who surface and resurface in our lifetimes, there are unassuming and effusive characters like Rose and Brook Grassleggings, Claude Youthman, Patty Jo and her "Hyenai," Junior Pipestar, and Pat "D." Red Hat who themselves are composites of other people. They would almost have to be, for the comic and tragic situations they experience border extraordinary and "non-ordinary" reality. There is, however, a deliberate intent to portray their situations as being no different from those faced by anyone else caught up in this diverse but prismatic sea of humanity. There are bound to be successes in the storm of adversity, just as there are disconcertion, loss, and resolve. And permeated throughout are experiences endemic in tribal society. While a few possess an uncanny ability to detect watery voices rising from the lakes and rivers, the rest of us are convinced the sound is the garbled music of inexperienced vocalists pounding on a rusted truck hood upshore. While these few will always appear despondent and unpredictable, it is frequently their doting powers of healing that work and come through when modern medicines fail.

Throughout the twenty years I have been involved with writing, I have attempted to maintain a delicate equilibrium with my tribal homeland's history and geographic surroundings and the world that changes its face along the borders. Represented in the whirlwind of mystical themes and modern symbols, of characters normal or bizarre and their eventual resolve, the word-collecting process is an admixture of time present and past, of direction found and then lost, of actuality and dream.

Having had the good fortune to study, teach, and contribute to contemporary American Indian literature, I have taken this long-awaited opportunity to capture personal and historical fragments of a midwestern tribal community called Black Eagle Child. The geographically and culturally isolated society consists of progressives and conservatives who revolve around the hierarchy of clan names. Historically, there was equality in the First-Named systems, but materialism and greed spawned novel methods by which to manipulate others. The day divine leadership was deemed unimportant was when the sacred myths began to crumble under the wheels of suzerainty.

In the ancient bloodways there obviously remains what is perhaps a disjointed facet of the Mesquakie storytelling tradition, which has inevitably been infused with dynamic trends. Surprisingly, these voices and personas have been at odds more than they have been synchronous. Both, however, resound wholly with imagery, thought, and profound messages for humanity.

This type of rendering has been an artistic process for me, the creative emulation of thought through extraordinary, tragic, and comedic stories of an imagined midwestern tribal existence. It has never sought to be more than that.

ALSO BY RAY A. YOUNG BEAR

The Invisible Musician

Winter of the Salamander